The Hurried Child

David Elkind

··········

The Hurried Child

Growing Up Too Fast Too Soon

··········

Third Edition

DA CAPO PRESS

A Member of the Perseus Books Group

Set in 10.5-point New Baskerville by Bookcomp, Inc.

Cataloging-in-Publication data for this book is available from the Library of Congress.

ISBN-13: 978-0-7382-1082-7
ISBN-10: 0-7382-1082-X

Published by Da Capo Press
A Member of the Perseus Books Group
http://www.dacapopress.com

Da Capo Press books are available at special discounts for bulk purchases in the U.S. by corporations, institutions, and other organizations. For more information, please contact the Special Markets Department at the Perseus Books Group, 11 Cambridge Center, Cambridge, MA 02142, or call (800) 255-1514 or (617) 252-5298, or e-mail special.markets@perseusbooks.com.

10 9 8 7 6

To the beloved memory
of my sister Ruth

Contents

Preface to the Twenty-fifth Anniversary Edition

••••••••••

In the introductory prefaces to the two earlier editions of this book, I addressed changes in the hurrying behavior of parents, schools, and the media that occurred over the intervening time intervals. In this introduction to the twenty-fifth anniversary edition of the book, however, I take a broader social perspective in order to document what might, without exaggeration, be described as the reinvention of childhood. This reinvention is the result, in part at least, of the ways in which electronic media have come to permeate our lives over the last quarter of a century.

From a historical perspective, a quarter of a century is only a brief moment in time. Nonetheless, there are some moments in time that are major turning points in social evolution. The past twenty-five years may well be regarded as such a turning point, having witnessed extraordinary technological advances that have revolutionized the ways in which we live and work. The magnitude of this transformation is what led literary scholar and media maven Marshall McCluhan[1] to argue that electronic media are bringing about a new era as powerful, if not more so, than the one ushered in by the introduction of print in the fourteenth century. Print elevated us from a preliterate, oral culture to one based on the printed word. McCluhan contends that electronic technology has ushered in a new media culture that is as far removed from the culture of print, as the culture of print was from the preliterate, oral culture that preceded it.

It remains to be seen whether McCluhan's observation is correct, in whole or in part. What is not in doubt is the fact that advances in information technology over the past quarter of a century have metamorphosed not only society in general, but child and family life in particular. When I wrote *The Hurried Child* in 1981, I had no inkling of the technological revolution that was to come. Indeed, I wrote the manuscript in pencil on lined, yellow pads, typed it up on an electric typewriter, and sent the manuscript to the editor via parcel post. This new introduction, written in 2006, was typed on a computer and sent to the editor as an attachment to an e-mail over the Internet. My concerns for children in 1981 were equally bound up in the culture of that era. I was concerned about schooling and sport programs for children that were age inappropriate and stressful, about the effects of sex and violence on television, and about the influence of rock and roll music.

In the time that has elapsed since that initial publication, those concerns already seem quite dated, if not naive. In the interim we have become a screen culture. Television, computer, and cell phone screens are now permanent fixtures in our homes, our businesses, our restaurants and bars, and our airports. We do much of our work, shopping, banking, and game playing online. Wireless laptops, cell phones, and Blackberries keep us in touch even when we are on vacation. Our hurried and hurrying society, which I wrote about in the first edition, has become even more so with the pervasiveness of electronic media. In response to user demands, computers are faster than ever before and have grown exponentially in memory. We chafe if we have to go online via a phone line, which is so much slower than a cable or wireless Internet connection. To make e-mail as immediate as a phone call, instant messaging (IM) was introduced and now competes with the phone as a regular means of communication.

The electronic media have simply reinforced our need to hurry and our ability to get things done quickly. Much of this spills over into our child rearing and education. Indeed, the revolutionary nature of the last quarter of a century is reflected in at least five new innovations in the lives of children. These new features of child life have grown more powerful across these last decades and continue to do so. In many ways, our new technologies have radically transformed childhood, and not always for the better.

Infant Education

From a child development point of view, perhaps the most significant transformation in child life has to do with the new attention to stimulating infants and young children. Infancy and early childhood are now the focus of hurrying. Over the past twenty-five years there has been an explosion of programs aimed at stimulating and educating infants and young children, not to mention the fetus in the womb. As to the latter, there is now on the market a fabric pouch made by BabyPlus, which is meant to be strapped to a pregnant woman's stomach and gives off, according to the company ad, "scientifically designed rhythmic sounds that resemble a mother's heartbeat. The rhythm of the sounds increases incrementally and sequentially as the pregnancy progresses. The . . . sound patterns introduce your baby to a sequential learning process, built upon the natural rhythms of their own environment."[2]

Although there is little or no research in support of any of these programs or materials, this has not prevented advertisers from making rather extravagant claims regarding their benefits. For example, the ad copy for this pouch goes on to say, "Babies and children enriched with BabyPlus are more relaxed at birth, with eyes and hands open, crying little." It also claims that "they reach their milestones earlier" and "have longer attention spans."

In a similar vein, but for babies, not fetuses, the athleticBaby video ads are equally upbeat. The ad for *athleticBaby All-Star* claims that it "shares a lively array of sports related imagery, puppets and young children engaged in active play. The entertaining presentation offers babies and toddlers an inspirational introduction to physical activity and a variety of sports, including basketball, soccer, tennis, baseball and golf."[3] What infants and toddlers can gain from watching basketball, soccer, and tennis leaves me baffled.

These programs are just the tip of the iceberg. There is also a whole series of Baby Einstein DVDs, a vast array of animated LeapFrog learning products, and computer programs for infants and toddlers—the so-called lapware. These products are called lapware because an infant is supposed to sit on his parent's lap while punching a large mushroom-shaped mouse that makes things happen on the screen. The advertised claims for these programs are as dubious as those for BabyPlus and athleticBaby.

Nonetheless, the infancy and early childhood education/stimulation market is booming. Today, DVDs, videos, computer programs, exercise, swimming, and even sport classes for the very youngest children have grown into a giant industry. From 2002–2004 alone, sales of Baby Einstein's *Number Nursery* and Brainy Baby Company's *Left Brain* have tripled to $100 million. And "kidvids," marketed to children from six months to five years old, are hot sellers. Taking account of the fact that 4 million babies are born in the United States each year, executive editor Stephanie Prange of *Video Store Magazine* says, "You can mine this market forever."[4]

The popularity of these materials is directly related to the introduction of computers, VCRs, and DVD players into the home. These technologies now take up far more of the infant's and young child's time than did the record players available when my sons were growing up. Videos and DVDs are much more invasive, as they provide visuals as well as sound, and unlike records, they can play for hours at a time. In addition, the array of programs available through these media is enormous—a vast repertoire of past films and TV programs is now available for home use.

The profusion of these products and programs for infants and young children poses a real problem for parents. On the one hand, an infant or young child quietly watching a video or DVD can provide his or her parent the time to do needed chores around the house. On the other hand, we do not really know what impact such programs have on infants and young children, and whether they are actually impairing the child's immature visual and auditory systems. There is also the risk that watching television can induce habits of passivity that work against later active learning and playing.

While a limited amount of television watching will probably do no harm, it should never be a substitute for active involvement with a child. That is the real risk of all these programs—parents may get the idea that the programs are more important than what the child gains from being talked to, sung to, or played with by a caring adult. That is simply not the case. The greatest gift a parent can give to an infant or young child is to actively engage them in meaningful exchanges. That kind of interaction is particularly important considering the second, closely related, new trend.

Out-of-Home Care for Young Children

While related to the changed nature of infant education, a development of the past twenty-five years has to be considered separately. In 1971, Congress enacted the Comprehensive Child Development Act (CCDA), a bill that would have mandated attendance to federally run centers for almost every preschool child in the United States. It was vetoed by President Nixon, who noted in his veto message that the measure would have the effect of pledging "the vast moral authority of the federal government to the side of communal approaches to childrearing as against a family centered approach."[5] His argument was that taking young children out of the home and putting them in day care facilities would "destroy the American family." Much has changed since then, and our negative attitudes regarding out-of-home care by nonparental and familial caregivers have all but disappeared. Today, 12.5 million children, 63 percent of the nation's children under five, are in some type of child care each week. On average, children under five of working mothers spend 36 hours a week in child care.[6]

Out-of-home care for infants and young children is a mixed benefit for children because the effects of out-of-home care depend so much upon the quality of the care provided. When the facility is clean and well looked after, when the teachers are adequately trained and the child to caregiver ratio is low, children can thrive. For those child care facilities that fall below these standards, the effects can be less salutary. This new, accepting attitude with regard to out-of-home care for young children presents a pressing social issue that should command powerful attention from our legislatures. As a society, one of our greatest priorities must be to provide affordable, quality, and accessible child care for all those parents who need it. Other countries, which are overtaking us in all domains, are doing a much better job of providing for young children than we are. As the next innovation makes clear, we also need to do a much better job of regulating what is being sold to children.

The Child As Consumer

Closely related to this avalanche of materials for fetuses, infants, and toddlers and to the prevalence of out-of-home care for this age group, is a third equally powerful innovation aimed at older children. It is based on a new conception of the child that emerged over this same time period. During the Puritan era, the child was viewed as born with original sin, and in need of salvation. The Darwinian revolution ushered in the humanitarian perception of the child as a young organism. Like the young of other species, the child was regarded as innately innocent, playful, and in need of protection. With the social revolutions of the 1960s, the child came to be seen as competent, ready, and able to deal with all of life's vicissitudes. These included divorce, extended day care, two parents working, media bombardment, and more.

Over the past several decades, at least in the purviews of those who merchandise to the young, a new perception of the child has been promoted. This is the idea of the child as consumer. Viewing the child in this way reflects a tectonic value shift. The perceptions—misguided or not—of the child as sinful, innocent, or competent all arose from a genuine concern for the health and welfare of the child. In contrast, viewing the child as a consumer does not stem from any concern for the well-being of the young. Rather, this perception is driven by the profit motives of those who merchandise to children.

The commercialization of childhood, as it has come to be called, is the topic of a number of recent scholarly and popular books. In *Kids' Stuff: Toys and the Changing World of American Childhood*, sociologist Gary Cross shows how toy manufacturers now look to children's desires, rather than to parental values, for guidance in creating their playthings. In her book *Branded*, journalist Alissa Quart documents the many ways in which teenagers are induced and seduced into acquiring brand loyalties. More recently, in her book *Consuming Kids: The Hostile Takeover of Childhood*, psychologist Susan Linn reveals many of the unscrupulous tactics merchandisers use to sell their products to the young. Psychologist Juliet B. Schor's book, *Born to Buy*, is particularly powerful in showing how deeply and broadly the commercialization of childhood has penetrated our society. Even the Girl Scouts have been co-opted and now take camping trips to the mall. This suggests another equally ominous trend, the fact that children are becoming more sedentary.

Childhood Moves Indoors

Still a fourth innovation, related to both technology and the commercialization of childhood, is the increase in video games and television networks for children. In the 1960s there were only twenty-seven hours of programming per week for children, and most of this was on Saturday mornings.[7] Today, there are fourteen networks that regard children as their main audience twenty-four hours a day. According to a recent Kaiser Family Foundation study, preschoolers are likely to spend as much time in front of the television or computer screen as they are playing outside, and this is three times longer than the time spent reading. Another Kaiser Family Foundation report suggests that older children, between ages 8 and 18, average six hours a day using electronic media, and because they often attend to more than one medium at a time (multitasking), the exposure to media is closer to eight hours a day.[8] In contrast, the time children spend riding bikes and doing other active, outdoor activities is down significantly from even a few short decades ago. Children are becoming increasingly sedentary, and obesity and type 2 diabetes are now serious health threats to children.

When I first wrote this book, I was most concerned about the stress our culture placed on children and the mental health consequences of continued emotional upset. Today, however, the sedentary lifestyle introduced by our new technologies makes child physical health an equally important concern. Although the popular perception is that many schools have eliminated recess and have increased the amount of homework children are being assigned, neither of these is entirely correct. Between 83 and 86 percent of school children have up to a half hour of recess per day.[9] In addition, according to Tom Loveless of the Brookings Institution (an independent, nonprofit research and policy organization), the great majority of children at all age levels spend less than one hour studying on a typical day—an amount that has not changed substantially in the last twenty years.[10] So apparently children have as much free time as they did in the past. The issue is how that free time, whether on the school playground or at home, is spent. The answer is fairly clear. According to a University of Michigan survey, over the past twenty years the number of minutes children devote to passive spectator leisure, not counting television but including watching sports, has increased fivefold, from thirty minutes to over three hours. [11]

The Technologically Empowered Student

The fifth and final innovation of the last quarter of a century is one that I believe is positive and offers the most hope for the future of children in our society: the increasing penetration of computer technologies and programming into our schools. Reforms in education can be brought about by ideas or by technology. In the recent past, ideas have not been successful. Some forty educational reforms (like the curriculum reform movement of the 1960s, the "back to basics" movement of the 1970s, or even the more recent cooperative learning model of the 1980s and 1990s) have been introduced over the last few decades, but none have had more than a short shelf life or been broadly implemented.[12] Computer technology is different and has the potential to produce a real and lasting transformation of our educational system.

I believe this is true because computers are changing the way we think about education. First of all, computers are making education a level playing field, at least for schools where the technology is broadly and effectively implemented. Consider the teacher/child relationship—children now equal or surpass some of their teachers in computer and information technology skills. In addition, thanks to the Internet, children have access to vast amounts of information with which to build upon and augment what they are learning in school. Secondly, some of the computer technologies, like simulation, can transform the way subjects are taught. For instance, now students can visually recreate the Civil War, the Gold Rush, and even the San Francisco earthquake of 1906 in their history classes. When subject matter is brought to life in this way, it is more exciting than reading about it in a text. Thirdly, many of the gaming techniques of discovery and problem solving can be combined with curriculum to make learning more interactive and fun. Finally, computer programs can be designed to accommodate different patterns of abilities and learning styles, and thus speak to individual differences in ways that textbooks never could. The coming revolution in education will, I believe, blunt some of the excesses engendered by the commercialization of childhood. To be sure, there are risks associated with the new technologies, and they can be a curse as well as a benefit. I believe that when, thanks to technology, we allow young people to actively participate in their own education, this will minimize the risks and increase the benefits of the coming revolution in education.

Always Changing, Always the Same

While emphasizing the changes that have come about since the first edition of this book, I would be remiss if I did not also remark on what has remained the same. It still takes a mother nine months to carry a baby to term. The ages at which children learn to walk, talk, and learn the three Rs have not changed, even with all the efforts to introduce them earlier. Parents are still the major influence on children's overall development, and children still need our love, our support, and our limit-setting. And what I appreciate now, much more than when I first sat down to write this book, is the importance of free, self-initiated, and spontaneous play to the child's healthy, mental, emotional, and social development. This kind of play is increasingly silenced by the innovations described above. At the close of the first edition of this book I wrote, "In the end, a childhood is the most basic right of children." With the changes that have come about since that first writing, I realize I must amend that phrase to read, "In the end, a playful childhood is most basic right of children."

··········
Preface to the Third Edition

··········

As I began to work on the third revision of *The Hurried Child*, a call from a reporter reinforced my decision to update the book. The reporter wanted to know my opinion regarding a debate between the mothers of two six-year-old girls that reflects a broader debate among parents of young girls. One mother let her daughter wear makeup and dress in rather seductive clothing. The other mother believed this was unnecessary and would not let her daughter wear makeup or clothing that was not suited to her age level. The mother who allowed her daughter to wear makeup justified it on the basis that she was just having fun and that she would not allow her to do this as she got older.

My response was predictable. I can see no good reason to allow a six-year-old to wear makeup and to dress in this way. If the little girl wants to play grown-up, she can smear on her mommy's lipstick and stumble around in her high heels. On the other hand, letting her daughter use real makeup and wear seductive clothing is asking for trouble. First of all, this might alienate the girl from her peers. Second, once she has been given permission to use makeup and to wear such clothing, she will not be easily convinced to give it up as she grows older. Third, there are a lot of unsavory people out there who might be attracted to a girl outfitted in this way. I see many negatives and no positives in letting a young girl be made-up and dress in an adult fashion.

The Continuation of Old Pressures

This example suggests that, as we enter the new millennium, past pressures on children to grow up fast have continued unabated.

Many of the problems that I described in the preface to the second edition have only gotten worse. The concept of child competence, which drove much of the hurrying of childhood in the previous decades, is very much alive today. Parents are under more pressure than ever to overschedule their children and have them engage in organized sports and other activities that may be age-inappropriate. Unhappily, the overtesting of children in public schools has become more extensive than it was even a decade ago. In some communities even kindergarteners are given standardized tests. Media pressures to turn children into consumers have also grown exponentially. A letter to presidential candidates Al Gore and George W. Bush, signed by a wide range of professionals, says, among other things:

> *At a time when childhood obesity has become a major health problem, purveyors of food high in fat, sugar, and calories are the biggest television advertisers during children's peak viewing time. Studies show that obesity is linked to television viewing and that obese children appear to be more susceptible to "feel good" messages embedded in food advertising.*

The combination of ubiquitous media and virtually unrestricted marketing practices make obsolete the conventional wisdom— promoted by the industry—that parents can protect their children from commercial culture. Unless families retreat to the woods, it's inescapable. To some extent, parents can mitigate the effects of marketing, but even if advertising is limited at home, children are exposed at friends' houses, on the street, the playground, in super-markets and even in school.

The marketing of violence to children and youth has also increased since the last edition. This trend was recently attacked in a report by the Federal Trade Commission, released in September 2000. The report detailed how:

The entertainment industry deliberately disregards its own ratings system and markets violent music, movies and video games directly to underage children. The report revealed internal corporate plans to use Girl Scouts, Boy Scouts, 4-H Clubs, comic books, and even school newspapers to sell products that the industry itself has deemed inappropriate for children under age 17.

The report found that 80 percent of R-rated movies were targeted to underage children. But that wasn't all. Nearly 30 percent of music recordings with explicit content labels expressly identified teenagers as part of the target audience and 70 percent of "mature" video games were pitched to younger teens. In one instance, an R-rated movie was actually test-marketed on focus groups of ten- to twelve-year-olds.[1]

Given the continued pressures on children to grow up fast, it seems important to update the sections on the hurrying engaged in by parents, the schools, and the media. With respect to parents, I am adding a section in the parenting chapter on peer-group parent pressure. After talking with parents all over the country, I have found that many are really trying very hard not to hurry their children, but feel forced into it because of what other parents are doing, namely, enrolling their children in organized sports and other programs. This problem is particularly pernicious for the parents of young children. If parents do not enroll their children in these programs, their children are left without playmates. I want to talk about the risks of these programs and some of the options parents have who don't want to make use of them.

The hurrying pressures at school continue unabated. The problems of testing that I described in the second edition have only grown worse. Testing has become more pervasive and is now used in some communities as the criteria for promotion and graduation. The pressure for academics has even led some school systems to eliminate recess so that children will have more time for the basics. On the other hand, there have been some positive innovations. Block scheduling, having secondary students take only four classes of an hour and a half each, makes good sense and improves performance. It gives young people more time on task, and reduces time in the halls, where most of the mischief takes place.

Unfortunately, a similar informed innovation has not been introduced at the early primary level. In fact, there is a crisis in kindergarten and the first grade. This crisis justifies adding a new section to Chapter 3. In this section I review the kindergarten/first grade promotion-retention dilemma that is causing problems in school systems across the country.

With respect to the media, the prevalence of inappropriate material for children has grown worse. Every week, it seems, a new obscenity is permitted on the television screen. Increasingly, nudity and salacious behavior are broadcast in the early evening hours. Moreover, at a time when the number of programs for children has declined, programs that depict adolescents has proliferated. So, in this chapter, I will not introduce a new section, but I will update the examples of television programs, films, books, magazines, and music that do no support healthy growth and development.

In Chapter 4 it is a pleasure to highlight one of the few bright lights on the media horizon, namely, the Harry Potter books. The success of these books reinforces my arguments about the need for age-appropriate story material for children. Unlike many television and computer games, Harry Potter challenges children's imagination and speaks to children's unique ways of thinking and feeling. The success of these books bears witness to the fact that, despite the ever more extraordinary technologies that surround them, children still are enthralled by the magic of a good story.

New Pressures

If these past pressures on children and adolescents were not enough, the omnipresence of computers, the evidence from new brain research, and the explosive use of the Internet have added to the demands that children feel, think, and behave as more competently and mature than their age would warrant. Although technological innovations have many positive benefits, they have often been misused to sell parents programs and practices that are not in the best interests of children. Accordingly, I am adding a new chapter to the section on the Dynamics of Hurrying, on Computers, Brain Research and the Internet. In this chapter I will detail how these new technologies are being used to pressure parents into engaging their children in activities that put them at risk for no purpose.

These new technologies, and the many other wonders of the modern world, make it an extraordinary time to be alive. We can experience the entire world, even the moon, in ways that no other generation could. Nonetheless, new technologies and opportunities also present new challenges to both parents and children. We simply need to appreciate that common sense is never out of date. Good judgment tells us that children need to be introduced to this exciting new world at their own time and pace and in keeping with their developing abilities and interests. If children are acquainted with the world of technology in this developmentally appropriate way, they will be able to enjoy its use and reap its benefits.

In closing, I have decided to include the preface to the second edition. Written a decade ago, it provides an index of how things have changed and how they have remained the same with respect to hurrying children to grow up fast.

··········
Preface to the
Revised Edition

··········

When I wrote *The Hurried Child,*
now almost a decade ago, I was trying to describe something new
on the American scene—a transformation in our treatment of children that was as momentous and as far-reaching as the changes in
our behavior toward women and minorities. Yet because there was
no explicit movement associated with a changing view of childhood
and children, the transformation was in place even before we were
aware that it had happened.

In my subsequent books, *All Grown Up and No Place to Go* and *Mis-
education: Preschoolers at Risk,* I attempted to further document how
our changed treatment of adolescents and of young children was
making life harder rather than easier for them. We have been
"unplacing" teenagers by progressively removing the markers that
set the limits and boundaries of age-appropriate thought and
action, I wrote. And we are "miseducating" young children by teaching them the wrong things at the wrong time for no purpose. In
these books, as in *The Hurried Child,* my aim was not only to document the transformation in our treatment of young people but also
to make clear that children have had to pay the bill for many of the
social revolutions that occurred in our society since the 1960s.

In *The Hurried Child* I wrote that the once-prevalent conceptions of children, summaried in metaphors of the child as a blank
slate and as a growing plant, were already dated in the postindustrial United States. I wrote that a new conception of children was
in the making, and that it had to be the underlying explanation
for our contemporary hurrying of children and youth. Although
I did not know then what that conception was, I know now. Our

new conception of children and youth is epitomized in the metaphor of the Superkid. Like Superman, Superkid has spectacular powers and precocious competence even as an infant. This allows us to think that we can hurry the little powerhouse with impunity.

Our changed treatment of women and minorities has also been fueled in part by new conceptions of their competence. The new conceptions of women's and minorities' competence came about because earlier images of them did them harm or disadvantaged them. But this is not the case of our new conception of child competence. On the contrary, our previous conception of children as growing persons in need of adult care and guidance created a social environment conducive to healthy childrearing and education. It led to child-labor and compulsory-education laws, to universal immunization programs, to the Aid to Dependent Children legislation, and to the WIC program, which provided nutrition to indigent pregnant women. By the 1950s our children were healthier, more protected, and better educated than at any other time in our history.

To be sure there was discrimination, and there were inequalities of schooling and unequal opportunities. But these were part of broader patterns of discrimination against minorities in general and women and were not targeted to children as children. Accordingly, our new conception of children and youth as ready to deal with all of life's offerings did not emerge to correct an intolerable situation, particularly for middle-class children. Rather, the conception of child competence, and the hurrying of them to grow up fast that it entailed, was first and foremost an accommodation to changes in adult society.

Divorce, single parenting, two-parent working families, and blended families had become the middle-class norm, and the conception of children as growing and in need of adult nurture, protection, and guidance became a fountainhead of parental anxiety and guilt. For today's parents, childrearing may often be in conflict with career, with finding a new mate, with loyalties to children from previous marriages, and with retaining even a modest standard of living. Our new family styles make it next to impossible for the majority of parents to provide the kind of childrearing that goes along with the image of children as in need of parental nurture.

Nonetheless, many parents who are living the new lifestyles still remain invested in the more traditional values of parental nurturing. Those values asserted that one parent needed to be home with the children when they were young if the children were to realize their full intellectual, personal, and social potential. Thus, many contemporary parents feel residual guilt about placing their children in the care of others during the early years. The conception of children as competent to deal with, and indeed as benefiting from, everything and anything that life has to offer was an effective rationalization for parents who continue to love their children but who have neither the time, nor the energy, for childhood.

Our contemporary conception of Superkid, then, competent to deal with all of life's vicissitudes, must be seen as a social invention to alleviate parental anxiety and guilt. Far from correcting injustices visited upon our children, the conception of child competence has, in fact, had just the opposite effect. The truth is that children in contemporary America, including advantaged children, are less well off today than they were a couple of decades ago.

Just a few statistics help tell the tale. Infant mortality is up after more than a century of decline. More children are living in poverty today than two decades ago. There has been a fifty percent increase in obesity in children and adolescents over the last twenty years. Our teenage pregnancy rates are the highest for any Western society—twice those of England, which has the next highest rates. Suicide and homicide rates for teenagers are triple what they were twenty years ago. Educationally, SAT scores have plummeted, and at the other end, some fifteen to twenty percent of young children are "flunking" kindergarten. And perhaps most frightening of all, in the United States today, millions of children are being medicated to make them more tractable at school and at home. This is a several-hundred-fold increase over the last five years. Clearly, the Superkid conception has not been a boon to children.

All this is much clearer to me today than it was when I wrote *The Hurried Child*. At that time I was most concerned with making the point that children no less than adults were experiencing stress. I wanted to alert parents, educators, and health professionals to this fact and to have stress regarded as a basic dynamic in all learning and emotional problems. I hoped too—naïvely—that I might help move us toward a conception of child and youth competence more in keeping with our substantial knowledge about human growth and development.

I realize now, after years lecturing, writing, and doing talk shows and print media interviews, that such efforts will not change the prevailing conception of child competence. The conception of child competence is much too functional for it to be given up just because the research, clinical experience, and expert opinion concur that it is both incorrect and unhealthy. We are going through one of those periods in history, such as the early decades of the Industrial Revolution, when children are the unwilling victims of societal upheaval and change.

At such times, our critical judgment is suspended, and supporting evidence, however questionable in favor of the invention, is quickly accepted, whereas evidence to the contrary, however strong, is readily dismissed. A good example of this seemingly unconscious rejection of evidence that is not in keeping with a favored conception is a recent *New York Times Magazine* article on early reading. The article began with a review of studies by investigators who were doing some of the most important work on brain function and reading. The consensus of these researchers was that reading is an extraordinarily complex process and that a certain level of brain development is required before the comprehension of symbols is possible. The solid research evidence was thus against early instruction. The article gave greater coverage, however, to the erroneous pontifications on early brain growth and learning by physiotherapist and self-anointed educator of infants and young children Glen Doman. We are listening, even through such usually reliable sources as *The New York Times,* to those who tell us what we want to hear rather than to the less palatable scientific facts.

Even the facts are being distorted so that they will be in keeping with our new enthusiasm for the notion of child competence. Some researchers recently reported that measures of fetal heart-rate activity give evidence that a fetus can differentiate between the mother's voice and other voices. Extrapolating from this finding, some workers created a whole educational program and a "Prenatal University" that instructs parents to read Shakespeare and to play Mozart for the fetus in the womb. Presumably this stimulation enhances the child's IQ and gives him or her a "leg up" on the competition. In case the parent's voice is low, a "Pregaphone" was invented—a large plastic plunger attached by a plastic hose to a smaller plunger—by which the parents can amplify their voices when talking to the genius in the making!

When we look at the United States at large and at the materialistic values that dominate our thinking in the 1980s, it is easy to understand why the conception of child competence has been reinforced on every side. For parents, child competence spelled the reduction of guilt and anxiety. And for American business, child competence spelled money. Superkid pulled back the drapes to reveal a whole new vista of opportunity for all those entrepreneurs ready and eager to exploit parental guilts and anxieties. And for the education system, its feckless efforts at reform could be justified; downward extension of the curriculum, longer school days and years, and more homework became efforts to get young people to use their idle Superkid competence.

In short, child competence has become part of our way of thinking because it serves many different functions in contemporary American society. None of them benefit children, and many of them unduly stress young people.

Unfortunately, children do not organize, have no access to the media, and do not vote. They are relatively powerless to improve their own condition. Children need adults who will advocate for them, as I have tried to do in this book. Unfortunately, the need for child advocacy is even greater today than it was when *The Hurried Child* was first published.

What is most troubling about our embrace of the notion of child competence is that it reflects our tendency to accept the increasing and unrelenting stresses on today's young people as "normal" and our willingness to rationalize them as actually beneficial for children! Although this is an understandable human tendency, it adds to the burden of stress children are already experiencing.

From this perspective, my first aim in this revised edition is to update some chapters and the examples and the statistics in others to provide evidence that, as we move into the 1990s, children are just as hurried and stressed as they were in the late 1970s and the 1980s. My second aim is to illustrate some of the ways I have seen our society try to avoid recognizing that these stresses exist. We can't turn back the clock and do away with many of the pressures on today's children and youth. My goal in this revision is to get us to acknowledge that such pressures exist, and to help young people deal with them as effectively as possible.

Avoiding the Issue of Child Stress

Long ago, Sigmund Freud described some of the many ways that we deceive ourselves in order to avoid anxiety and guilt. One way we do this is to *transform things into their opposite*. One can see a glass as either half full or half empty. If we flip from one perspective to another, we have transformed something into its opposite. Another way we deal with unpleasant feelings and emotions is to *displace* them from their real object onto some other, perhaps less dangerous object. After work, for example, we may displace our anger at the boss by chopping wood. A third mechanism is *projection*, whereby we attribute our feelings and motives to others. The liar and thief trusts no one. All these defenses can be usefully adaptive at times, but when we use them to gloss over the stresses suffered by children, they are not adaptive.

Transformation into the Opposite

In the 1980s, the rapid growth of women in the workforce and the lack of parallel growth in affordable, quality child care has led to a dramatic increase in the number of "latchkey" children. Although it is difficult to determine the exact number of children who are at home alone on a regular basis for extended periods of time, the number has to be in the millions. If parents need to work and support the family and if child care is not available or is out of reach financially, they may have few options other than to leave the children alone.

Nonetheless, most professionals agree that children below the age of eight should not be left home alone on a regular basis. For this age group, parents should make some kind of provision for child care. After the age of eight the situation is a little more ambiguous, and this is where the turning-into-the-opposite comes in. Being home alone is a stressful experience for children. This is particularly true if the neighborhood is not a safe one. Children are likely to turn on the lights and the television, and they may hide in the closet.

It is troubling, therefore, to read in some women's magazines as we do today that the latchkey experience is "good" for children! It supposedly teaches them responsibility and self-reliance, and it gives them quiet time in which to do their homework. A necessity is thus neatly turned into a virtue! Please understand, I am not saying that parents should never leave children alone. What I am saying is that we have to accept the fact that it is a stressful experience for young people. If we accept that fact, we can give them strategies for dealing with potential dangers such as someone coming to the door, fire, accidents, and so on. Giving children the telephone number of neighbors and instructing them in the use of a small fire extinguisher and first-aid kit are ways of preparing them for the eventualities of being home alone. Such simple preparation can help to reduce the stress of the latchkey experience.

Displacement

Divorce has become commonplace in the 1980s. Although the divorce rate is no longer on the increase, the proportions of couples seeking divorce will, according to projections, remain at the high rate they attained in the last decade. Divorce is painful for everyone involved, but it is particularly so for children. In the first edition of this book, I was concerned that parents, caught up in their own neediness, feelings of inadequacy, and anger tended to ignore the feelings of rejection and loss that their children experience. Although this self-centeredness at a time of stress was understandable, it was necessary to help parents decenter a bit and to help the child cope as well.

Now, however, in some parts of the country I see a somewhat different problem emerging. The sentiment seems to be growing that every child whose parents divorce should automatically go into therapy! This was certainly *not* what I had in mind, nor is it in keeping with most professional opinion. What we wanted divorcing parents to do was to talk with their children about their fears and anxieties. At such times children need to be reassured that both parents will continue to love them, that they will not be deserted, and that they will continue to be looked after.

Unfortunately, automatically putting a child in therapy may give the child just the opposite message. In fact, it is a kind of displacement on the part of the parent. The child, not the divorce, is now what the parent should be concerned about. But what does putting a child into treatment by himself or herself alone say to the child? Even in this day and age, many adults still have a great deal of trouble with the idea of going to a psychologist or psychiatrist for help. To such an adult, therapy and counseling are an indication of weakness and of an inability to solve one's own problems. Many children feel the same way.

Accordingly, when children are singled out for treatment, they are likely to feel that something is wrong with them and not with the family. In effect, the child rather than the family becomes the patient. This happens, by the way, not only in divorcing families. In my small private practice, I have yet to see a case of spontaneous emotional disturbance. Children just don't develop emotional problems the way they get the measles or the mumps. The emotional problems of children always reflect emotional problems within the family. In my practice, I now insist on seeing the whole family or I will not take the case.

When a family is going through separation and divorce, placing the child in treatment can add to the child's stress. In such an instance, the parents have recognized that the stress exists, but they have taken the wrong measures to alleviate it. And they do this because they have displaced the problem onto the child rather than kept it on the breakdown of their family. We have to recognize that these situations are a family problem, not a child problem. Therapy may be a good idea, but at least one parent should accompany the child, and the treatment should be for both of them, not just for one of them.

Projection

At one of my lectures to parents, a father raised his hand and asked the following question: "I have an eight-year-old son, and his grand-mother—my mother—recently committed suicide. I believe it is important to tell my son the truth about how she died before he hears it from someone else. But my wife thinks I should just let it alone. What do you think?" My response was that I could understand his pain and anguish about the manner of his mother's death, but I did not see how telling his eight-year-old son would help matters. It was unlikely that someone would mention it to him, and he would probably not understand even if they did. Perhaps when the boy is a teenager, I suggested, he might be told about it. But for now it seemed best just to let him mourn his grandmother's death.

This anecdote illustrates the parental mechanism of projection. The father had a strong need to talk about his mother's suicide, but this got projected onto the child and became "the child's need to know." It was not the child's need that was in question but the parent's need. Projection is another way in which parents ignore many of the stresses their children are actually experiencing and impose new and unnecessary stresses upon them. I believe that many of those who would teach young children about AIDS, nuclear war, and child abuse are really dealing with their own anxieties and fears by projecting them upon children.

Studies have shown, for example, that young children really can't distinguish between "good touching" and "bad touching." Nor can young children comprehend the threat of nuclear war, which entails a level of comprehension and understanding that they will not attain for many years. This does not mean that we should neglect to teach young children, in age-appropriate ways, about the dangers of the world. It does mean that we should be more honest in separating out our own concerns, and more care-ful not to impose further stress by projecting those concerns onto our children.

These are but a few of the ways in which our acceptance of child competence leads us to engage in defenses that add to, rather than subtract from, the stresses they are experiencing. We may be stuck with the conception of child competence for the foreseeable future. But we should not add to the stresses it produces by treating its consequences as virtues rather than as unpleasant necessities.

Part I

**Our
Hurried
Children**

I
Our Hurried Children

The concept of childhood, so vital to the traditional American way of life, is threatened with extinction in the society we have created. Today's child has become the unwilling, unintended victim of overwhelming stress—the stress borne of rapid, bewildering social change and constantly rising expectations. The contemporary parent dwells in a pressure-cooker of competing demands, transitions, role changes, personal and professional uncertainties, over which he or she exerts slight direction. We seek release from stress whenever we can, and usually the one sure ambit of our control is the home. Here, if nowhere else, we enjoy the fact (or illusion) of playing a determining role. If child-rearing necessarily entails stress, then by hurrying children to grow up, or by treating them as adults, we hope to remove a portion of our burden of worry and anxiety and to enlist our children's aid in carrying life's load. We do not mean our children harm in acting thus—on the contrary, as a society we have come to imagine that it is good for young people to mature rapidly. Yet we do our children harm when we hurry them through childhood.

The principal architect of our modern notion of childhood was the French philosopher Jean-Jacques Rousseau. It was he who first criticized the educational methods for presenting materials from a uniquely adult perspective, reflecting adult values and interests. Classical *paideia*—that is, the value of transmitting a cultural-social heritage—was a good thing, said Rousseau, but the learning process must take the child's perceptions and stage of development into account. In his classic work *Emile,* Rousseau wrote, "Childhood has its own way of seeing, thinking, and feeling, and nothing is more foolish than to try to substitute ours for theirs." More specifically, he observed that children mature in four stages, and just as each stage has its own characteristics, it should also have a corresponding set of appropriate educational objectives.[1]

This idea of childhood as a distinct phase preceding adult life became inextricably interwoven with the modern concepts of universal education and the small, nuclear family (mother, father, children—not the extended family of earlier eras) in the late eighteenth and early nineteenth centuries, the heyday of the original Industrial Revolution. The transition is well explained by futurologist Alvin Toffler: "As work shifted out of the fields and the home, children had to be prepared for factory life. If young people could be prefitted in the industrial system, it would vastly ease the problems of industrial discipline later on. The result was another central structure of all [modern] societies: mass education."[2]

In addition to free, universal, public education, the emergent society tended to create smaller family units. Toffler writes, "To free workers for factory labor, key functions of the family were parcelled out to new specialized institutions. Education of the child was turned over to schools. Care of the aged was turned over to the poor houses or old-age homes or nursing homes. Above all, the new society required mobility. It needed workers who would follow jobs from place to place. Torn apart by migration to the cities, battered by economic storms, families stripped themselves of unwanted relatives, grew smaller, more mobile, more suited to the needs of the [workplace]."[3]

While industrialization proceeded apace, the cultural recognition of childhood as a discrete life phase was given strong social reinforcement in the late nineteenth century with the establishment of child psychology as a scientific discipline. Work in this field began with the so-called baby biographies—minutely detailed accounts by observant parents of their infants' behavior. Bronson Alcott, father of Louisa May, contributed one such study, as did Milicent Shinn.[4] Jean Piaget, the celebrated Swiss psychologist, carried on the tradition when he took time off from his collective studies of children to observe at close range (and write about) his own three offspring.[5]

Around the turn of the century, G. Stanley Hall, generally regarded as the founder of the laboratory study of children, initiated the ill-fated "Child Study Movement." The extensive questionnaires he designed that parents and teachers administered to children by the thousands proved to be terribly error-prone and inexact. However, Hall had more success in founding Clark University, and the school's department of child psychology, carefully cultivated by Hall, led the nation in research and training in the new field, producing scientists of the eminence of Arnold Gesell and Lewis Terman.

After the Second World War, child psychology entered its boom period. Whereas before the war there were only two scientific journals reporting research in child development, today there are more than a dozen. All university departments of psychology include psychologists who are studying topics as varied as adolescence, learning in infants, socialization, peer interaction, sexual development, attachment and loss, the measurement of intelligence, learning disabilities, language acquisition, and so on. In short, we have accumulated a large library of data and knowledge about the period of life we call childhood. It is indeed no small irony that at the very time the stress of social life and change is threatening the existence of childhood, we know far more about childhood than we have ever known in the past.

What is even more curious is the degree to which this scientific knowledge is available to and consumed by the general public, for the research explosion in child study has been matched by a corresponding blaze of popular books about children. Often, well-known child psychologists undertake to "translate" scientific findings into useful applications. As early as 1894, the renowned psychologist T. Emmet Holt informed readers of his book *Care and Feeding of Children* how to prevent chafing: "First, not too much or too strong soap should be used; secondly, careful rinsing of the body, thirdly, not too vigorous rubbing, either during or after the bath; fourthly, the very free use of dusting powder in all the folds of the skin. This is of the utmost importance in very fat infants."[6] Holt was merely the first in a seemingly endless line of distinguished (and not so distinguished) "translators" of scientific child psychology into a popular idiom. Perhaps the two best-known are Arnold Gesell's *The Child from Birth to Five* and the incomparably influential *Infant and Child Care* by Dr. Benjamin Spock.[7] Each year an awesome number of books, some very well written and others less so, appear with titles such as *Working and Caring, The Good Enough Parent, Ourselves and Our Children, How to Raise Your Child to be a Winner, Know Your Child, Growing With Your Child,* and *Teenagers.*[8] Workshops and courses are available in every community in the country to guide and assist adults involved with the rearing of young people. If we hurry children to grow up too fast today, then, it is surely not done out of ignorance.

Miniature Adults

Today's pressures on middle-class children to grow up fast begin in early childhood. Chief among them is the pressure for early intellectual attainment, deriving from a changed perception of precocity. Several decades ago precocity was looked upon with great suspicion. The child prodigy, it was thought, turned out to be a neurotic adult; thus the phrase "early ripe, early rot!" Trying to accelerate children's acquisition of academic skills was seen as evidence of bad parenting.

A good example of this type of attitude is provided by the case of William James Sidis, the son of a psychiatrist. Sidis was born at the turn of the century and became a celebrated child prodigy who entered Harvard College at the age of eleven. His papers on higher mathematics gave the impression that he would make major contributions in this area. Sidis soon attracted the attention of the media, who celebrated his feats as a child. But Sidis never went further and seemed to move aimlessly from one job to another. In 1930 James Thurber wrote a profile of Sidis in the *New Yorker* magazine entitled "Where Are They Now?"; he described Sidis's lonely and pitiful existence in which his major preoccupation was collecting streetcar transfers from all over the world.

Such attitudes, however, changed markedly during the 1960s, when parents were bombarded with professional and semiprofessional dicta on the importance of learning in the early years. If you did not start teaching children when they were young, parents were told, a golden opportunity for learning would be lost. Today, there are tax-supported kindergartens in every state, and some twenty-three states are considering programs for four-year-olds. In too many schools kindergartens have now become "one-size-smaller" first grades, and children are tested, taught with workbooks, given homework, and take home a report card. The result of this educational hurrying is that from 10 to 20 percent of kindergarten children are being "retained" or put in "transition" classes to prepare them for the academic rigors of first grade!

How did this radical turnabout in attitudes happen? There are probably many reasons, but a major one was the attack on "progressive" education that occurred in the 1950s and that found much education material dated. The Russian launching of the Sputnik in 1957 drove Americans into a frenzy of self-criticism about education and promoted the massive curriculum movement of the 1960s that brought academics from major universities into curriculum writing. Unfortunately, many academics knew their discipline but didn't know children and were unduly optimistic about how fast and how much children could learn. This optimism was epitomized in Jerome Bruner's famous phrase, "Any subject can be taught effectively in some intellectually honest form to any child at any stage of development."[8] What a shift from "early ripe, early rot"!

The trend toward early academic pressure was further supported by the civil rights movement, which highlighted the poor performance of disadvantaged children in our schools. Teachers were under attack by avant-garde educators such as John Holt,[9] Jonathan Kozol,[10] and Herbert Kohl,[11] and they were forced to defend their lack of success by shifting the blame. Their children did not do well because they came inadequately prepared. It was not what was going on in the classroom but what had not gone on at home that was the root of academic failure among the disadvantaged; hence Head Start, hence busing, which by integrating students would equalize background differences.

One consequence of all this concern for the early years was the demise of the "readiness" concept. The concept of readiness had been extolled by developmental psychologists such as Arnold Gesell, who argued for the biological limitations on learning.[12] Gesell believed that children were not biologically ready for learning to read until they had attained a Mental Age (a test score in which children are credited with a certain number of months for each correct answer) of six and one-half years. But the emphasis on early intervention and early intellectual stimulation (even of infants) made the concept of readiness appear dated and old-fashioned. In professional educational circles readiness, once an honored educational concept, was in disrepute. In the late 1980s, however, readiness is coming back into vogue, as an increasing number of children are being retained or put in transition classes because they are not "ready" for the demands of first grade.

The pressure for early academic achievement is but one of many contemporary pressures on children to grow up fast. Children's dress is another. Three or four decades ago, prepubescent boys wore short pants and knickers until they began to shave; getting a pair of long pants was a true rite of passage. Girls were not permitted to wear makeup or sheer stockings until they were in their teens. For both sexes, clothing set children apart. It signaled to adults that these people were to be treated differently, perhaps indulgently; it made it easier for children to act as children. Today even preschool children wear miniature versions of adult clothing. From overalls to LaCoste shirts to scaled-down designer fashions, a whole range of adult costumes is available to children. (Along with them is a wide choice of corresponding postures such as those of young teenagers modeling designer jeans.) Below is an illustration from a recent article by Tim Appelo, suggesting that whatever the latest trend in adult fashions, the kiddie version is sure to follow:

> If the folks run around in Reeboks, their juniors toddle in Weeboks. Executive parents schedule meetings with a Filofax Day Runner; their kids count on a Filofax Play Runner to keep track of birthday parties and other boffo networking opportunities. Sony recently launched an immense $2 million campaign for My First Sony, the first major manufacturer's line of sophisticated electronics equipment designed specifically for knee-high audiophiles. ("Why should tiny ears have to listen to tinny sounds?") One perfumery is hawk-

*ing Whiffy Wear Cologne for Kids ($10); another perfume ad fea-
tures a 4-year-old in Miami Vice whites leaning rakishly against a
scaled-down Mercedes, along with the copy: "Gregory's pourjeune
homme created especially for young gentlemen with discriminating
taste."[13]*

When children dress like adults they are more likely to behave
as adults do, to imitate adult actions. It is hard to walk like an adult
male wearing corduroy knickers that make an awful noise. But boys
in long pants can walk like men, and little girls in tight jeans can
walk like women. It is more difficult today to recognize that children are children and not miniature adults, because children dress
and move like adults.

Another evidence of the pressure to grow up fast is the change
in the programs of summer camps for children. Although there are
still many summer camps that offer swimming, sailing, horseback
riding, archery, and camp fires—activities we remember from our
own childhood—an increasing number of summer camps offer
specialized training in many different areas, including foreign lan-
guages, tennis, baseball, dance, music, and even computers.

Among such camps the most popular seem to be those that specialize in competitive sports: softball, weight training, tennis, golf,
football, basketball, hockey, soccer, lacrosse, gymnastics, wrestling,
judo, figure skating, surfing. "Whatever the sport there's a camp (or
ten or a hundred of them) dedicated to teaching the finer points.
Often these camps are under the direction, actual or nominal, of a
big name in a particular sport, and many have professional athletes
on their staffs. The daily routine is rigorous, with individual and/or
group lessons, practice sessions and tournaments, complete with
trophies. And, to cheer the athletes on with more pep and polish,
cheerleaders and song girls can also attend."[14]

The change in the programs of summer camps reflects the new
attitude that the years of childhood are not to be frittered away by
engaging in activities merely for fun. Rather, the years are to be
used to perfect skills and abilities that are the same as those of
adults. Children are early initiated into the rigors of adult competition. At the Dollars & Cents Camp in Florida, campers as young
as eleven years old attend lectures on mutual funds and learn how

to read *The Wall Street Journal*. Competition at camp and at home is one of the most obvious pressures on contemporary children to grow up fast.

There are many other pressures as well. Many children today travel across the country, and indeed across the world, alone. The so-called unaccompanied minor has become so commonplace that airlines have instituted special rules and regulations for them. The phenomenon is a direct result of the increase in middle-class divorces and the fact that one or the other parent moves to another part of the country or world. Consequently, the child travels to visit one parent or the other. Children also fly alone to see grandparents or to go to special camps or training facilities.

Aviation officials estimate that 500,000 children, some as young as five years old, fly alone each year. In response, some airlines have made special arrangements for their young customers. Continental Airlines has "club" rooms for children at its major terminals in Denver, Houston, and Newark. Transtar Airlines even has a frequent-flier program for children. While such accommodations help, young fliers still present unique problems.

Gwen Souza, a United Airlines flight attendant, remembers comforting a young girl who was devastated when she got her first period in midair. No one had ever really explained menstruation to her. "So I did," says Souza. "I think I made her laugh a lot about the experience."

PSA flight attendant James Reilly recalls a six-year-old who wouldn't let go of him when the plane made an unexpected late-night stop in Arizona. "It was a hundred degrees out there and around midnight," recalls Reilly. "The kid was scared and was clinging to me."

Reilly says he often feels sorry for some of his young charges, especially those who bounce between divorced parents and have trouble adjusting to the constant change. "They often tell us about the divorce, the visitation rights, their parents, and their parents' dating patterns," he says. "Some of them are really upset."[15]

Although, as these examples illustrate, airline personnel take good care of unaccompanied children, traveling alone can be stressful. And the usual stresses of traveling can be accentuated by a child's personal concerns. Young children in particular may feel that they are abandoning their parent or are being abandoned. Being in an airplane with strange people and going to a different living arrangement requires young children to make adaptations that are more appropriate to older children and adults.

Other facets of society also press children to grow up fast. Lawyers, for example, are encouraging children to sue their parents for a variety of grievances. In California, four-and-one-half-year-old Kimberely Ann Alpin, who was born out of wedlock, is suing her father for the right to visit with him. The father, who provides support payments, does not want to see Kimberely. Whatever the decision, or the merits of the case, it illustrates the tendency of child-advocates to accord adult legal rights to children. In West Hartford, Connecticut, David Burn, age sixteen, legally "divorced" his parents under a new state law in 1980. While such rights may have some benefits, they also put children in a difficult and often stressful position vis-à-vis their parents.

The media too, including music, books, films, and television, increasingly portray young people as precocious and present them in more or less explicit sexual or manipulative situations. Such portrayals force children to think they should act grown up before they are ready. In the movie *American Beauty*, a teenage girl, who presents herself as sexually active, attracts her girlfriend's father who is going through his mid-life crisis, and who almost takes her to bed. Similarly, teenagers put songs such as Christina Aquilera's "Come on Over," suggesting that the boy will be rewarded with sexual favors if he does so, high on their chart of favorites. Television also offers many examples of sexually active teens in programs such as *Dawson's Creek* and in reruns of *Married with Children*. Shows like *Baywatch* are like TV versions of *Playboy* and *Penthouse*.

The media promote not only teenage sexuality but also the wearing of adult clothes and the use of adult behaviors, language, and interpersonal strategies. Sexual promotion occurs in the context of other suggestions and models for growing up fast. A Jordache jean commercial from a few years back depicted a young girl piggyback on a young boy and highlighted clothing and implicit sexuality as well as adult expressions and hairstyles.

But can young people be hurried into growing up fast emotionally as well? Psychologists and psychiatrists recognize that emotions and feelings are the most complex and intricate part of development. Feelings and emotions have their own timing and rhythm and cannot be hurried. Young teenagers may look and behave like adults, but they usually don't feel like adults. (Watch a group of teenagers in a children's playground as they swing on the swings and teeter on the teeter-totters.) Children can grow up fast in some ways but not in others. Growing up emotionally is complicated and difficult under any circumstances but may be especially so when children's behavior and appearance speak "adult" while their feelings cry "child."

The Child Inside

Some of the more negative consequences of hurrying usually become evident in adolescence, when the pressures to grow up fast collide with institutional prohibitions. Children pushed to grow up fast suddenly find that many adult prerogatives—which they assumed would be their prerogatives—such as smoking, drinking, driving, and so on, are denied them until they reach a certain age. Many adolescents feel betrayed by a society that tells them to grow up fast but also to remain a child. Not surprisingly, the stresses of growing up fast often result in troubled and troublesome behavior during adolescence.

The findings of a 1985 study reflect a rush to experiment that is certainly one consequence of growing up fast.

> *In the largest drug-use survey ever undertaken, over 200,000*
> *6th- through 12th-grade children admitted to behavior that would*
> *horrify their parents if they knew. Our children are using drugs*
> *in ever-increasing numbers—and at younger and younger ages.*
> *They're popping pills and smoking pot on the school bus, getting*
> *drunk in their cars and at their friends' houses and even snorting*
> *cocaine in their own homes.*[16]

The rush to experiment is perhaps most noticeable in teenage sexual behavior. Although survey data are not always as reliable as one might wish, all the studies point to a dramatic increase in the sexual activity of teenagers since the 1960s. In the early 1960s about

10 percent of teenage girls and some 25 percent of teenage boys were sexually active. As we enter the twenty-first century, the number of sexually active teenagers is more than 50 percent, and the percent of sexually active teenage girls is now slightly higher than the number of sexually active teenage boys. "Things that supported remaining a virgin in the past—the fear of getting pregnant, being labeled the 'town pump,' and disgracing the family—have disappeared," observed Melvin Zelnick, professor of Public Health at John's Hopkins University.

Young people themselves are very much aware of this trend. "I'd say that half the girls in my graduating class are virgins," says an eighteen-year-old high-school senior from Iberia, Louisiana. "But you wouldn't believe those freshman and sophomores. By the time they graduate, there are not going to be any virgins left."

There are a number of troubling consequences of this sexual liberation. Currently, 1 million teenage girls become pregnant each year. This is the highest teenage pregnancy rate in developed countries. In any given year, about 50 percent of pregnant teenage girls give birth, 40 percent are aborted and another 10 percent miscarry. It is estimated that of girls who are fourteen years old today, 25 percent will be pregnant at least once before leaving the teen years.

The good news is that the teen birthrate has been steadily declining. In 1995, the rate of childbearing among women between the ages of 15-19 was 90 births per 1000 women. In 2001, it is about 50 births per 1000 women. The bad news is that this decline is much more an index of the increased availability of abortion than it is of a decline in teenager pregnancies. Although the rate of teenage pregnancies has really not changed that much over the last hundred years, the number of teenagers who give birth out of wedlock has increased over this time period. Currently, about 50 percent of teenage births are to unmarried teens with about 5 percent of these given up for adoption.

Although the threat of AIDS appears to have altered adult sexual behavior, this does not seem to be the case for adolescents. Teenagers account for a significant portion of all cases of venereal disease reported each year, and their share seems to be increasing.

The causes of this enhanced sexual activity among young people today are many and varied. The age of first menstruation, for example, has dropped from age seventeen about a century ago to age twelve and a half today. Fortunately this seems to be the lower limit, made possible by good health care and nutrition. However, this age of first menstruation has remained stable over the past two decades, so it cannot account for the increased sexual activity of young women during this period. Other contributing factors include rapid changes in social values, women's liberation, the exploding divorce rate, the decline of parental and institutional authority, and the fatalistic sense, not often verbalized, that we are all going to die in a nuclear holocaust anyway, so "what the hell, have a good time."

Although the media are quick to pick up these sexual trends and exploit them for commercial purposes (for example, the cosmetics for girls four to nine years old currently being marketed by toy manufacturers), the immediate adult model is perhaps the most powerful and the most pervasive. Married couples are generally discreet about their sexuality in front of their offspring—in part because of a natural tendency to avoid exposing children to what they might not understand, but also because by the time the children are born, much of the romantic phase of the relationship for many couples is in the past.

But single parents who are dating provide a very different model for children. Quite aside from the many complexities that arise when a single parent has a friend stay the night, single parents are likely to be much more overtly sexual than married couples. With single parents, children may witness the romantic phase of courtship—the hand holding, the eye gazing, the constant touching and fondling. This heightened sexuality, with all the positive affection it demonstrates, may encourage young people to look for something similar.

It is also true, as Professor Mavis Hetherington of the University of Virginia has found in her research, that daughters of divorced women tend to be more sexually oriented, more flirtatious with men, than daughters of widowed mothers or daughters from two-parent homes.[17] Because there are more teenage daughters from single-parent homes today than ever before, this too could contribute to enhanced sexual activity of contemporary teenage girls.

While it is true that some young people in past generations have engaged in sex at an early age, have become pregnant, contracted

- More than 7 percent of students were threatened or injured with a weapon on school property during the previous school year with male students significantly more likely than female students to have experienced threats and injuries.

Violence and the threat of school violence are powerful stressors and have significant effects upon students, teachers, administrative staff and the very process of education itself. Stress impairs children's ability to learn and teacher's ability to teach.

A National Educational Goals Panel survey conducted in 1993[20] gives evidence of how stress affects schooling. More than 22 percent of children in grades 3-12 were less eager to attend school than they had been because of the threat of violence. In addition, 16 percent of the students said they were less willing to talk in class for fear of recrimination by other students. At least 25 percent of all the students from grades 3-12 said that the level of violence they had experienced or witnessed had a detrimental effect upon their education. The survey also reported that 7 percent of eighth grade students stayed home from school the previous month out of fear of violence at school. The Centers for Disease Control and Prevention survey mentioned earlier (1995) found that across the country 4.4 percent of students missed at least one day of school during the preceding six months because they felt unsafe either at school or on the way to or from school. African American and Hispanic male and female students were significantly more likely than white male and female students to miss school because they felt threatened.

The most disturbing finding in recent surveys of youth is the increase in the frequency with which weapons are brought to schools. Although the rate of increase varies among different states and communities, the fact of increase is common to all. Between 1987 and 1994, for example, gun carrying increased 138 % in central Texas.

In this study[21], those who carried guns, compared with those who did not, were more likely to have been victimized themselves, to be more risk seeking, to have used crack cocaine, to have fewer strategies for avoiding fighting and to feel a greater need to fight under a variety of circumstances. In survey of teachers the researchers reported that students carrying a gun were three times more likely to earn poor grades than students who did not carry guns.[22]

Although the fatal school violence episodes are fortunately rare, their effect is powerfully magnified by the attention paid to them be the media. The following are a few examples of more extreme cases of school violence:

In 1989 in Portland, Connecticut, a junior high school student was suspended for refusing to remove his hat. He subsequently returned to school with an assault rifle, killed the janitor and seriously wounded the principal and secretary.

In 1996, 14 year-old honor student in Moses Lake Washington, walked into a math class armed with a high-powered rifle and two handguns. He opened fire and killed two students and a teacher and critically wounded another student.

In 1996, a teenager in Lynville, Tennessee, angry about a traffic incident, carried a rifle into a crowded school hallway and opened fire. A teacher and a student were killed

In 1998, two students aged 13 and 11, set off the fire alarm at Westside Middle School in Jonesboro, Arkansas, and then ran to the trees near the school. As students and teachers filed out of the building, they opened fire killing a teacher and four students. Eleven other students were wounded.[23]

The more recent Columbine high school shooting is but another, even more terrible, example of the phenomenon of school violence. There are no easy answers to school violence and the examples given above are probably unique and almost impossible to predict. While in fact, there has actually been a decrease in overall school violence during the last years of the twentieth century, young people's fear of school violence continues to grow.

School violence is often linked to the amount of violence children see on television. But that link is weak at best. On the other hand, it may well be that television contributes to young people's fear of violence. A recent survey[24] of a large representative sample of over 3,000 programs aired between 6:00 AM and 11:00 PM looked at the amount and type of violence portrayed. The investigators found that violence occurred in a majority of the programs, and often consisted of aggressive acts that went unpunished and that were imbedded in a humorous episode. Only rarely did the programs indicate that there might be long-term consequences of violence or present it in a context that might suggest an anti-violence theme. So much attention has been paid to the effects of TV violence on children's aggressive behavior, that an even more potent effect may have been ignored: the widespread fear of violence among young people, even in places that were once considered safe, namely, the schools.

The last hurrying-related teenage phenomenon I want to discuss is teenage suicide. In general the suicide rate increases across the whole life span. Although there are few instances in childhood, the number of suicides jumps up sharply in adolescence. As of 2001, suicide is the third most common cause of death among teenagers after motor vehicle accidents and homicides. (Some motor vehicle accidents are suicidal in intent).[25] The rate of suicide has tripled over the last thirty years. The contributors to teenage suicide are multiple and complex, but it does not seem unreasonable to suppose that some of the contemporary hurrying stresses on teenagers, from the competition for high grades and getting into good colleges, to the pressures to use drugs and become sexually active, contribute to the increase in the number of young people who take their own lives.

Among teenagers, suicide often appears in clusters that strike more often in affluent suburbs. In the 1970s, Chicago's northside lakefront "Gold Coast" communities saw a 250-percent increase in suicides. And this occurred despite vigorous community efforts at suicide prevention. In this community (as in others described below), the combination of affluence, high pressure, marital discord, drugs, and school failure becomes lethal for some young people.

A nineteen-year-old from Glencoe, Illinois, says, "We have an outrageous number of suicides for a community our size." One of this teenager's friends cut her wrist and two others drove their cars into trees. "Growing up here, you are handed everything on a platter, but something else is missing. The one thing parents don't give is love, understanding, and acceptance of you as a person." And Isadora Sherman, of Highland Park's Jewish Family and Community Service, says, "People give their kids a lot materially, but expect a lot in return. No one sees his kids as average, and those who don't perform are made to feel like failures."[26]

In the 1980s outbreaks of cluster suicides have occurred in other affluent suburbs, from Plano, Texas, to Westchester, New York. Not atypical was the pattern of cluster suicides that occurred in suburban Bergenfield, New Jersey. In early March 1987, four Bergenfield teenagers drove their brown Camaro into an unused garage, closed the door, left the motor running, and waited. This deliberate suicide followed the suspicious deaths of four Bergenfield teenagers over the preceding nine months. Shortly afterward, another Bergenfield teenager also died from car fumes in a closed garage. The day after the Bergenfield accident, two teenage girls in Alsip, Illinois, were found dead in similar circumstances.

Chicago psychiatrist Harold Visotsky succinctly states how pressure to achieve at an early age, to grow up and be successful fast, can contribute to teenage suicide: "People on the lower end of the social scale expect less than these people. Whatever anger the poor experience is acted out in antisocial ways—vandalism, homicide, riots—and the sense of shared misery in the lower income groups prevents people from feeling so isolated. With well-to-do kids, *the rattle goes in the mouth and the foot goes on the social ladder.* The competition ethic takes over, making a child feel even more alone. He's more likely to take it out on himself than society."[27]

Adolescents are very audience conscious. Failure is a public event, and the adolescent senses the audience's disapproval. It is the sense that "everyone knows" that is so painful and that can lead to attempted and successful suicides in adolescents who are otherwise so disposed. Hurrying our children has, I believe, contributed to the extraordinary rise in suicide rates among young people over the past decade.

All Grown Up and No Place to Go

Sigmund Freud was once asked to describe the characteristics of maturity, and he replied: *lieben und arbeiten* ("loving and working"). The mature adult is one who can love and allow himself or herself to be loved and who can work productively, meaningfully, and with satisfaction. Yet most adolescents, and certainly all children, are really not able to work or to love in the mature way that Freud had in mind. Children love their parents in a far different way from how they will love a real or potential mate. And many, probably most, young people will not find their life work until they are well into young adulthood.

When children are expected to dress, act, and think as adults, they are really being asked to playact, because all of the trappings of adulthood do not in any way make them adults in the true sense of *lieben und arbeiten*. It is ironic that the very parents who won't allow their children to believe in Santa Claus or the Easter Bunny (because they are fantasy and therefore dishonest) allow their children to dress and behave as adults without any sense of the tremendous dishonesty involved in allowing children to present themselves in this grown-up way.

It is even more ironic that practices once considered the province of low income citizens now have the allure of middle income chic. Divorce, single parenting, dual-career couples, and unmarried couples living together were common among lower income families decades ago. Such arrangements were prompted more often than not by economic need, and the children of low-income families were thus pressured to grow up fast out of necessity. They were pitied and looked down upon by upper- and middle-income parents, who helped provide shelters like the Home for Little Wanderers in Boston.

Today middle income parents have made divorce their status symbol. And single parenting and living together without being married are increasingly commonplace. Yet middle-income children have not kept pace with the adjustments these adult changes require. In years past a child in a low-income family could appreciate the need to take on adult responsibilities early; families needed the income a child's farm or factory labor would bring, and chores and child-rearing tasks had to be allocated to even younger members of the family. But for the middle-income child today, it is hard to see the necessity of being relegated to a baby sitter or sent to a nursery school or a day care center when he or she has a perfectly nice playroom and yard at home. It isn't the fact of parents' being divorced that is so distressing to middle-class children, but rather that often it seems so unnecessary, so clearly a reflection of parent and not child need. As we shall see, it is the feeling of being used, of being exploited by parents, of losing the identity and uniqueness of childhood without just cause that constitutes the major stress of hurrying and that accounts for so much unhappiness among affluent young people today.

It is certainly true that the trend toward obscuring the divisions between children and adults is part of a broad egalitarian movement in this country that seeks to overcome the barriers separating the sexes, ethnic and racial groups, and the handicapped. We see these trends in unisex clothing and hairstyles, in the call for equal pay for equal work, in the demands for affirmative action, and in the appeals and legislation that provide the handicapped with equal opportunities for education and meaningful jobs.

From this perspective, the contemporary pressure for children to grow up fast is only one symptom of a much larger social phenomenon in this country—a movement toward true equality, toward the ideal expressed in our Declaration of Independence. While one can only applaud this movement with respect to the sexes, ethnic and racial groups, and the handicapped, its unthinking extension to children is unfortunate.

Children need time to grow, to learn, and to develop. To treat them differently from adults is not to discriminate against them but rather to recognize their special estate. Similarly, when we provide bilingual programs for Hispanic children, we are not discriminating against them but are responding to the special needs they have, which, if not attended to, would prevent them from attaining a successful education and true equality. In the same way, building ramps for handicapped students is a means to their attaining equal opportunity. Recognizing special needs is not discriminatory; on the contrary, it is the only way that true equality can be attained.

All children have, vis-à-vis adults, special needs—intellectual, social, and emotional. Children do not learn, think, or feel in the same way as adults. To ignore these differences, to treat children as adults, is really not democratic or egalitarian. If we ignore the special needs of children, we are behaving just as if we denied Hispanic or Indian children bilingual programs, or denied the handicapped their ramps and guideposts. In truth, the recognition of a group's special needs and accommodation to those needs are the only true ways to insure equality and true equal opportunity.

2

•••••••••

The Dynamics of
Hurrying: Parents

•••••••••

Americans have traditionally employed two contrasting metaphors for childhood. The first of these, perhaps originating in our nation's agricultural-rural past, describes the child as a growing plant that needs to be nourished and looked after but that nevertheless may be trusted to unfold according to its own inner dynamic of growth. In this metaphor the child absorbs the surrounding world and takes it into himself or herself. Walt Whitman captured this "imbibing" process consummately in *Leaves of Grass*:

> *The schooners, the waves, the clouds,*
> *the flying sea crow, the fragrance*
> *of saltmarsh and mud, the horizon's edge.*
> *These became part of that child who went forth everyday*
> *And who now goes and will always go forth everyday.*[1]

The best formulated scientific version of the plant metaphor is that offered by the late Jean Piaget, who saw the child's intellectual development as part of the ongoing larger process of biological adaptation. For Piaget, human intelligence is thus best understood as an extension of this adaptation. Thinking, like digestion, transforms incoming information in a way that is useful to the individual. But thinking, like vision, also adapts to the constraints of the surrounding world. Like a plant or an organism, thinking both changes and is changed by the environment.[2]

Another metaphor—equally old and intellectually honorable—construes the child in physicalist rather than biological terms. The sixteenth-century English philosopher John Locke gave this view its classic formulation when he spoke of the child as a *tabula rasa,* or blank slate (tablet), upon which life experience is written.[3] Our modern industrial age has given a slightly different twist to the Lockean formulation; we see the child as a kind of "raw material" to be molded and shaped by parents, education, and social institutions. John Watson, the psychologist credited with founding the school of behaviorism, epitomized this approach in his boast, "Give me a dozen healthy infants and I'll guarantee to take any one at random and train him to become a doctor, a lawyer, artist, merchant, beggarman, thief."[4] A similar boast echoes through the pages of B. F. Skinner's bestseller of the 1950s, *Walden Two,* a book that introduced the concept of "engineering" the behavior of children (and indeed of all human beings in a society) along "adaptive" and "healthy" lines.[5]

The two metaphors, then—the child as growing organism with its own emergent identity and the child as malleable material awaiting society's imprinting—abide with us, representative perhaps of the two discrete social economies, agricultural and industrial, of our past and present. In contemporary America, those who work regularly with children—teachers, counselors, caretakers—tend to adopt the metaphor of the growing organism. They envision the school, thus, as a farm where living things grow freely, each according to his or her own rhythm and season. On the other hand, it is not surprising that the denizens of government (administrators, law-enforcement officials, juvenile authorities, and so forth) prefer the view of children as malleable entities awaiting the imposition of form from without. From their perspective, schools are less farms than factories, and the child in question is less a tree than an assembly-line product, predictably fashioned and quantitatively measured.

And yet perhaps both metaphors are already dated, for even as we pause to observe and describe our society, it is changing around us. We have, for example, already developed an economy where both farm and factory employ a far smaller percentage of the work force than formerly. The number of people employed in the vast service sector of our economy now exceeds in size the old industrial proletariat of the early twentieth century. Robots, automation, miniaturization, and computerization render the traditional labor-intensive factory (and factory worker) obsolete, much as enormous tractors, combines, sprayers, and reapers have radically and permanently altered the agricultural landscape. High technology, genetic engineering, and information processing utilize different talents, strategies, and facilities from those of the traditional factory or farm.

Such developments cannot fail to affect our views of self and family. As we move into the postindustrial era, we will certainly fashion appropriate metaphors to conceive childhood. And it is very much within this context of a changing society, economy, and family and value structure that we must view our new-found propensity for hurrying children to grow up fast. As yet we lack a metaphor to describe this hurried view of child-rearing, but unfortunately we have the thing itself. One possibility, of course, is that in a time of straitened economic circumstances, we are reappropriating the medieval view of seeing children only as miniature adults ready to enter the work force. The increase in child abuse and exploitation today (also characteristic of the middle ages) would tend to support this hypothesis, as would the increase of adult crimes (theft, robbery, murder) committed by children. On the other hand, despite its apparent relevancy, such a view neglects the profound truth that we are not innocent about children—as our medieval forebears perhaps were—nor are our economy and society primitive. Disingenuous in some degree, we are not innocent. To be sure, we harass our children with some of the emotional-intellectual-social demands of adulthood yet at the same time we treat them—often ostentatiously—as mere children. Sometimes we go so far as to infantilize them (even adolescents) by permitting them to have messy rooms, to leave things lying about, to get up at odd hours, and to eat junk food. We thus recognize children's special estate at the very same time that we hurry them to grow up fast.

What are the ways parents hurry children? And what powerful motivations and distractions cause us to disregard the mountain of knowledge we have about childhood and child development, about the special needs and identity of young people?

The beginning of an answer lies in the theme that was touched upon earlier: rapid change. The bewildering rapidity and pro-found extent of ongoing social change are the unique hallmarks of our era, setting us apart from every previous society. For us, in the foreseeable future, nothing is permanent. Stress is an organism's reaction to this change, this impermanence. We live, therefore, in a time of wide-spread, deep-seated stress; it is a companion that is so constant, we may easily forget how completely stress pervades our lives.

While we shall later examine the concept of stress in greater detail, I will here point to three particular sources of stress for parents as adults that have flourished dramatically in recent years. First, we are more afraid: the threat of violence, theft, and intimidation is now a permanent possibility in life in urban America. Every inhabitant of a major city (and many suburban and exurbanites as well) knows someone who has experienced, or has personally experienced, physical attack in some form.

We are more alone: separation and divorce statistics have reached new highs; and while some people choose to live alone and feel most comfortable in solitude, there are more people today who live alone because they are unable to find a suitable partner.

We are more professionally insecure: the threats of restructuring technological unemployment, inflation, recession, rising prices, and so on are also prevalent.

People who are stressed, like those in ill health, are absorbed with themselves—the demands on them, their reactions and feelings, their hydra-headed anxieties. They are, in a word, egocentric, though not necessarily conceited or prideful. They have little opportunity to consider the needs and interests of others. This state of affairs has not gone unnoticed—far from it. Social critic Tom Wolfe minted the apt phrase "me decade" to describe the absorption with "personal potential" that characterized the 1960s and early 1970s.[6] Historian Christopher Lasch has labelled our society "the culture of narcissism"—and narcissism, in psychoanalytic theory, is the attachment of the self to the self as to a primary love object.[7] It is likely that the much-noted self-centeredness of the 1980s epitomized in the term "Yuppie" is, in large part, a response to the stress of living in a society where inconstancy is the only constant and where the needed roots and abiding familiarities of life—private and public—are easily eradicated or never develop in the first place.

The prevalence of self-centeredness puts us squarely in a dilemma in regard to raising children. If it is to be done well, child-rearing requires, more than most activities of life, a good deal of decentering from one's own needs and perspectives. Such decentering is relatively easy when a society is stable and when there is an extended, supportive structure that the parent can depend upon. Until recently the traditional cultures of Japan and China offered fine examples: a well-defined, stable social structure freed parents from the stress of adapting to constant social change and instead permitted them to focus their adaptive powers on the growing and changing children in their midst.

But consider the adult male in the contemporary United States. In an economy distorted by inflation, infiltrated by computerization, miniaturization, and automation, pressed grimly by foreign imports, he may well fear for his job. If he is employed in a metropolis of the old industrial Midwest, he now wonders whether he will have to learn a new occupation or skill and relocate to a new city or state, leaving behind the security and network of friends and family. Many of his friends are divorced, separated, or having affairs, and he wonders whether his life won't follow in suit. His church may be giving him conflicting messages—if he is Catholic, for example, his local priest may be saying one thing about birth control and sex, and the Vatican may be saying another. Whom to believe? What to cleave to? He never stops hearing about crime, the deficit, and the growing danger of nuclear proliferation and the possibility of world war or environmental disaster. He worries about the negative health effects of food additives, coffee, saccharine, cholesterol, red meat, and any one of a hundred common consumer items.

Or consider the single mother who is trying to raise three children with little or no financial support from a former husband. (Half of the children in the current generation are likely to live in households headed by single parents.) Such women are concerned not only about finances and the welfare of their children but also about being alone when the children are grown. Add to this the fact that working women are still paid less than men, are too often sexually harassed on the job, and have trouble getting financial credit on their own.

Such a man, such a woman—their numbers are increasing in our society—may expend so much effort coping with the daily stress of living that there is little strength or enthusiasm left over for parenting. They—we—are unable to put our knowledge about children into practice. We hurry children because stress induces us to put our own needs ahead of their needs.

Parents may justify their actions by reverting to the metaphor of the "infinitely malleable" child. Caught up in our own coping struggle, inundated with the multifarious demands of life, we prefer to think of our children as endlessly flexible and resilient materials. As such, they may therefore be expected to adapt easily to our (adult) needs, schedules, interests, perspectives. We expect them to adapt more to adult life programs than we adapt to their child life programs. Yet the opposed metaphor of the child as growing plant also has dangers. It may lead to a romantic conception of childhood as a time free of conflict, fear, struggle, or demand. This, in its own way, is just as dangerous a notion as the contrasting one of infinite malleability, and it has led to the overpermissiveness that is nearly as much the hallmark of our era as hurrying.

Specifically, then, how do parental stress and the metaphor of child as raw material become transmuted into hurrying? We have seen how adults under stress become self-centered and therefore have considerably more trouble in seeing other people in all the complexity of their individual personalities. People under stress tend to see other people in the shorthand of symbols, not the often hard-to-decipher longhand of personhood. Under stress, we see others as certain obvious, easily grasped stereotypes and abstractions. When we are ill, other people often symbolize health; when we are fearful, others appear intrepid and courageous; when we are depressed, life seems to present us with nothing but the happy-go-lucky. While we (or they) may imagine that we react to them as John, Mary, and Fred, we are in fact treating them as simplistic stereotypes, and this is because we are too wrapped up in our own illness, fear, or depression. Thus with our children; it is as objects or symbols—not as full subjects—that we hurry them.

Why do people under stress have recourse to symbols? To what end do they use them? Basically, people under stress are not only self-centered, they also lack energy for dealing with issues apart from themselves. Symbols, oversimplifications really, are energy-conserving. Parents under stress see their children as symbols because it is the least demanding way to deal with them. A student, a skater, a tennis player, a confidant are clear-cut symbols, easy guides for what to think, to see, and how to behave. Symbols thus free the parent from the energy-consuming task of knowing the child as a totality, a whole person. Symbols also conserve energy in another way. They are ready-at-hand targets for projecting unfulfilled needs, feelings, and emotions. Thus, by treating children as symbols, parents conserve the energy needed for coping with stress and have ready-made screens for projecting some of the consequences of stress, fear, anxiety, and frustration. Such energy conservation, however, is really not "cost-beneficial," for in treating our children as symbols—in hurrying them—we harm them and, ultimately, ourselves.

The Child as Surrogate Self

Parents who go to work—which is to say, almost all fathers and many mothers—are under more stress today than at any time since the Great Depression. In many businesses, human beings are being displaced by machines. (For example, with computer printing, the honorable profession of linotype operator has been all but eliminated.) Many blue-collar workers must confront the reality that they will have to learn a new trade. Their counterparts in the white-collar professions encounter harrowing job insecurity as companies' fortunes rise and fall with inflation, lowered productivity, undependable government contracts, and restructuring. The anxiety created by such circumstances is an obvious form of stress.

Moreover, the joy and team spirit of work relations in many industries have disappeared. Professor Lester Thurow of the Massachusetts Institute of Technology attributes the competitive edge that Japan and Germany have over the United States to the flourishing spirit of cooperation and *esprit de corps* in these countries. He points out that "many workers in Japan receive a third income from bonuses based on company profits, a form of compensation U.S.

labor has been loath to accept."[8] And Akio Morita, chairman and co-founder of Sony, says, "Teamwork historically is, I think, the American way. But your managers soon forgot that. They got greedy; they viewed the worker as a tool. That has not been good for the American products or American companies, and it has hurt your competitive stature in the world."[9] It is also not good for worker satisfaction. The dog-eat-dog atmosphere in the U.S. workplace is oppressive and conducive to general dissatisfaction among employees.

Similar problems occur among white-collar workers. I recently met with a number of school administrators from an affluent north-eastern suburb. Their story echoed that of others I had heard from such groups across the United States and Canada. These men and women were in their thirties and early forties and were good at what they did, but they saw little chance for advancement and, in any case, received no recognition for their work from the superintendent. Raises seemed to be apportioned on an arbitrary or uniform basis, without reference to the quality of work of the individual. In short, for any number of reasons, the greater part of the meaningfulness and satisfaction of their work had disappeared for these people.

Yet this same group waxed enthusiastic when they talked about their children and, more especially, their children's participation in team and individual sports. Although I have no statistics to back up such a generalization, I would venture that there is a strong tie between job dissatisfaction, on the one hand, and a disproportionate concern with offspring's success in sports, on the other. Children thus became the symbols or carriers of their parents' frustrated competitiveness in the workplace. The parent can take pride in the child's success or blame the coach for his or her failure. In any case, the parent soon vicariously invests more of a commitment in the child's athletic life than in his or her own work life. And as job dissatisfaction now arises earlier in professional careers, compensatory interest in children's participation in sports often arises when the children are very young.

Not surprisingly, however, the intensity of the parents' interest, and the "freighted" or vicarious nature of it, weighs on the child and robs the sporting activity of its playfulness and pleasure. The well-known sports writer John Underwood recently produced a telling indictment of the Little Leagues—the worst destroyers of the playfulness of sport.

> *The sine qua non of sport is enjoyment. When you take that away, it's no longer sport. Perhaps the worst creators of specialists are the Little Leagues in all sports. Although some observers believe there's much value in them, the Leagues have their own ethics. "Abolish the Little Leagues," says philosopher Robert Weiss. "Forbid'em," says sociologist David Riesman.*
>
> *Sports psychologist Bruce Ogelvie laments the sickening arrogance of Little League coaches, too many of whom are unqualified. Some coaches, says another psychologist, Thomas Tatlio, even "think sports is war." They make eight year olds sit on the bench while others play, learning nothing beyond the elitism of win-at-all-costs sport. Token participation—an inning in right field, a couple of minutes in the fourth quarter—can be equally demoralizing.*
>
> *To visit on small heads the pressure to win, the pressure to be "just like mean Joe Green" is indecent. To dress children up like pros in costly out-fits is ridiculous. In so doing, we take away many of the qualities that competitive sports are designed to give to the growing process.[10]*

During the last ten years, parents have been under new pressures to place their young children in organized sports. The spectacular success of golfer Tiger Woods has many parents wondering whether they should start giving their young children sports training. Tiger Woods is being described as perhaps the greatest golfer in history and he started playing at age three. It seems reasonable to infer, then, that the earlier you start a child on a sport, the better he or she will be. However reasonable that inference might seem, it happens to be wrongheaded. Consider Mozart: An aspiring composer approached Mozart and asked the musical genius to teach him how to write a symphony. Mozart replied that perhaps he might start with something a little less ambitious, like an etude. The questioner took umbrage at this reply and said, "But you wrote a symphony when you were eight years old." Without hesitation, Mozart responded, "Yes, that is true, but it is also true that I didn't have to ask how." The point of this story, of course, is that you cannot take the exception as the rule. Tiger Woods, arguably the Mozart of golf, shouldn't be taken as the model for creating gifted golfers. You just cannot learn to be gifted.

There are many reasons why contemporary parents are tempted to place their children in organized sports at an early age. Certainly the idea that the earlier you start, the better chance you have of great success is one of the reasons given. Another is parental peer pressure. When most of the parents in the community have their children on a soccer team, in Little League, or ballet, there are no playmates left for the child who does not participate. Unless the child is enrolled in comparable programs, there is no one in the neighborhood to pal around with. Another reason to enroll young children in organized sports stems from fear. Many parents today are afraid to tell their children to go out and play. They feel much more comfortable if their child is in a program where there are lots of children and adult supervision. Finally, many parents believe that participation in sports will help to foster their child's self-esteem and feelings of competence as well as to learn cooperation and competition. Each of these excuses is an unfortunate example of the power of parental peer pressure.

Earlier Is Better

Wrongheaded ideas have the nasty habit of catching on more quickly than correct ideas. The belief that earlier is better in relation to early childhood is one such wrong idea that seems to have caught on, and it is difficult to combat. With respect to sports, there is no reliable evidence that starting children early in an individual or team sport gives them a lasting advantage or edge.

On the other hand, any sport in which the whole family can get involved—like skiing—can be a wonderful family activity. Parents themselves are knowledgeable participants and as long as a child is involved in age-appropriate ways and with age-appropriate equipment, the experience can be positive. It is quite a different matter, however, when parents who are not involved in the sport engage their child in such an activity. Too often, parents put a child on a soccer or baseball team, or give him or her tennis or skating lessons, not because it is a sport they want to enjoy as a family, but rather in the unfounded hope that this will ensure his or her becoming an Olympic athlete.

Such an expectation is entirely misguided. First of all, a young child's body is differently configured than an adult's body. A three- or four-year-old child has a head about one-fourth the size or his or her body, the equivalent of an adult with a beach ball–size head. A young child's bones are not fully calcified and his or her muscles have not attained full volume. What this means is that playing adult sports may put undue stress on young bodies. In fact, there is now a subspeciality of pediatrics, pediatrics sports medicine—created exclusively to deal with sports injuries to children. We now know, for example, that Little League pitchers should not throw curve-balls because of the stress it places on young arms. There is no evidence that starting a preschooler in any organized team sport gives him or her a lasting advantage. On the other hand, there is abundant evidence that to engage in adult sports at an early age can put children at risk for long-lasting injuries.

The Neighbors' Kids

When we hear the term "peer pressure" we think of young teenagers who are often influenced by their friends. Equally, if not more powerful, however, is parental peer pressure. Such pressure can be both direct and indirect. When every other parent is buying their child Nike shoes or the latest fad toy, we find it hard to say "No" to our own child. We don't want our child to feel different from the other children or to be excluded from their talk or play.

A less direct form of parental peer pressure occurs when other parents put their children in organized sports programs so that there are no longer any children in the neighborhood who are available for free play or just hanging out. If you believe strongly that to put young children in organized sports puts them at risk, then you should not enroll him or her in such programs. There are a number of options. One option is to find other parents who feel as you do and arrange for your children to play together. Alternatively, you can use the lack of playmates as an opportunity for your children to learn to be comfortable on their own, to discover their inner resources of imagination and creativity.

The Dangers Outside

In the not-too-distant past, parents felt free to tell their children to go outside and play. Cars were neither as numerous nor as powerful as they are today. There were also many more open fields, even in urban areas, than there are today. There was also much less concern about children being abducted or meeting up with violence.

It is certainly true that contemporary neighborhoods, both urban and suburban, are more congested and that traffic is much heavier than even a few decades ago. There are fewer open spaces and playgrounds, though the number of children is greater than ever before. We just haven't kept up with our population growth. I am troubled and saddened to see our public play areas so overcrowded. It is not equally true, however, that children playing in the neighborhood are that much more at risk than in the past. The real difference is that now, thanks to television, we learn about every violent or obscene crime against children in alarming and graphic detail. As a result, it often seems that such incidents are more prevalent than they really are. On the other hand, the dangers from traffic are real enough.

Finding places that are safe from vehicular traffic and that have facilities for children to play is a real challenge in today's world. Of course, enrolling a child in an organized sport is one way to ensure that he or she gets a supervised play experience in a safe play area. But that is only one among several parental options. A good, developmentally appropriate early childhood program, for example, will provide young children with all of the exercise and social interaction they require for healthy development. Such programs almost always have attached play areas with paths for tricycles, sandpiles, climbing apparatuses, and much more.

Another option is for parents to organize play groups in your house or backyard or at a local park. Children are quite creative when given the chance to play on their own. Given a safe area, adult supervision, and a few props such as balls, sand pails, old clothing, and the like, children have a great time engaging in play of their own invention. It may take a little time, but certainly no more than driving children to and from sports venues. So, yes, young children do need adult assistance in finding acceptable, safe play areas. Providing adult supervision after having found such a place is a good idea. But all of this can be accomplished without enrolling the child in any individual, or group, adult sport. At the preschool age children will gain much more from their own spontaneous play than they will from any organized sport.

Learning Self-Confidence, Self-Esteem, Cooperation, and Competition.

Parents who advocate engaging children in organized team or individual sports often stress that through them, children who participate in these activities learn self-confidence and self-esteem as well as cooperation and competition. In response to this claim, the first thing that needs to be said is that there are any number of ways in which young children can learn self-confidence, self-esteem, cooperation, and competition. Children learn self-confidence, for example, by being allowed to do things on their own like feeding themselves and using the toilet. They also learn self-confidence when they are allowed to initiate activities with their parents and are supported in their efforts. Self-esteem, on the other hand, is learned not from one's own activities but rather from the "reflected appraisals" of others. Handsome children often have high self-esteem because of the positive responses to their appearance. But all children can acquire self-esteem if they are treated with respect and consideration. We do this when we are polite to children and say, "please," "thank-you," "you are welcome," and "excuse me" to them when we would use these expressions with adults. Children treated in this way come to think of themselves as valuable and worthy of respect.

The same results are not always achieved by participation in sports. Too often, children who perform poorly in sports may develop feelings of inferiority rather than of self-confidence.

As far as self-esteem is concerned, children who participate in sports are not always treated with respect and consideration either by their teammates, coaches, or parents. It is not unusual for less talented players to spend most of their time on the bench. And too venereal disease, and so on, they were always a small proportion of the population. What is new today are the numbers, which indicate that pressures to grow up fast are social and general rather than familial and specific (reflecting parental biases and needs). The proportion of young people who are abusing drugs, are sexually active, and are becoming pregnant is so great that we must look to the society as a whole for a full explanation, not just to the parents who mirror it.

Parallelling the increased sexuality of young people is an increase in children of what in adults are known as stress diseases. Pediatricians report a greater incidence of such ailments as headaches, stomachaches, allergic reactions, and so on in today's youngsters than in previous generations. Type A behavior (high-strung, competitive, demanding) has been identified in children and associated with heightened cholesterol levels. It has also been associated with parental pressure for achievement.

Another index of the stress encountered by today's children is their overall health. Researchers say that kids these days are on their way to being the most unfit ever.

- 64 percent of today's children aged six to seventeen fail to meet the President's Council on Fitness and Health standards of a healthy youngster; 35 percent have at least two heart disease risk factors; and 42 percent have high levels of cholesterol.
- Only 36 percent of these children participate in daily physical activity programs. In elementary school, half the students attend such classes once a week, and figures drop sharply after that.
- The number of children aged six to eleven who are obese has increased 54 percent in the last 20 years. For those between twelve and seventeen, the figure has grown 30 percent.[18]

The pressure to grow up fast is also reflected in the statistics regarding school violence. A 1993 Center for Disease Control and Prevention (CDC) survey[19] found that nationwide:
- 16.2 percent of students had been in a physical fight on school property during the year preceding the study.
- Approximately one third of the students had personal belongings stolen or deliberately damaged on school property during the preceding year.

many parents react negatively, and sometimes with violence, to a child's misplay or a coach's decision.

Nor is it the case that participation in organized team sports is the only, or necessarily the best, way for children to cooperate and compete. Children in a developmentally appropriate early childhood program, for example, learn healthy cooperation every day. When they participate in group projects, dramatic play, and group games they are also learning to work together.

Likewise, in a good early childhood program, children learn not only how to cooperate with other children but also to compete with themselves. Always trying to do better than what you have done before is the healthiest form of competition. Although this form of competition can be learned in organized sports, it can also be learned by engaging in many other types of social activity.

Children who participate in team sports also run the risk of learning the wrong kind of competition. Too many parents get too involved. When their child's team loses, parents have been known to yell at or even punch the coach or to yell at or even slap a child. Although many coaches encourage their team to congratulate the winners and to be good sports, this is not always the case.

Clearly, I see little value and considerable risk in engaging young children in organized team or individual sports. I believe there is no reason to involve a child in such sports until at least the age of six or seven. Before that age, young children can acquire any of the alleged benefits of organized adult sports from regular participation in a quality, early-childhood program.

Academic Pressure

Parents also hurry children when they insist that they acquire academic skills, like reading, at an early age. Indeed, some programs now promise parents that they can teach their children to read as infants and toddlers. The desire of parents to have their children read early is a good example of parental pressure to have children grow up fast generally. This pressure reflects parental need, not the child's need or inclination. In the second half of the book we will examine this parental need in more detail. Here we need to look at the evidence that shows that children who are being pushed to read early are indeed being urged to grow up fast. It is certainly true that some children gravitate to reading early, seeking out books and adults to read to them. Such children seem to learn to read on their own with little fuss or bother. But such children are in the minority. Studies by my colleagues and myself, and by other investigators, find that only 1 to 3 children in 100 read proficiently (at the second-grade level) on entrance to kindergarten. If learning to read was as easy as learning to talk, as some writers claim, many more children would learn to read on their own. The fact that they do not, despite their being surrounded by print, suggests that learning to read is not a spontaneous or simple skill.

The majority of children can, however, learn to read with ease if they are not hurried into it. Our youngest son is a case in point. He is the youngest of three boys and is very outgoing, social, and verbal. He was telling full-length stories at the age of three. He is one of those youngsters who, when you ask him a question, gives you a full and richly detailed answer. Because of his verbal skills, I thought he might want to learn to read at the age of four. We read a lot of books together, and I asked him if he wanted to learn to read or try reading the book on his own. He did not. At least one reason, I think, was that I would no longer need to read to him and we would lose that time together.

Because my wife went back to school, we placed him in a very fine private school where, by the way, there was no pressure for him to read early. In fact, he would sit under the table and do math problems when the other children were reading. The teacher allowed him to work at arithmetic and didn't press the reading. In second grade, he became interested in reading and began bringing books home from school. Now, as a college senior, he is an English major. I am not sure that this would have been the case had he been forced into reading.

Studies of children who have been introduced to reading later rather than earlier support our experience with our son. Carleton Washburn, the famed educator, conducted an elaborate study in the 1930s with children in the public schools of Winnetka, Illinois. He compared classes of children who were introduced to formal reading instruction in first grade with those who were first introduced to it in second grade. Although the children who started earlier had an initial advantage on the reading tests used to assess pupil progress, this advantage disappeared by the time the children were in grade four.

Perhaps the most interesting and intriguing part of the study was a long-term follow-up that was made when the subjects of the study were young adolescents and were attending junior high school. Observers who did not know which children had been in which group were introduced into the classrooms; they were to look at all facets of the young people's reading behavior. The observers found that the adolescents who were introduced to reading late were more enthusiastic, spontaneous readers than were those who were introduced to reading early.[21]

These data are also supported by educational information from other countries. In England, studies comparing children who attended informal (late reading) elementary schools and those who attended the formal (early reading) elementary schools reported similar findings. In Russia, formal education and instruction do not begin until children are age seven, and yet Russian children seem far from intellectually handicapped. Early reading, then, is not essential for becoming an avid reader, nor is it indicative of who will become successful professionals.

Other studies suggest that children confronted with the task of learning to read before they have the requisite mental abilities can develop long-term learning difficulties. In one high school, for example, we compared the grades of pupils who had fall birthdays (in September, October, November, and December) and had entered school before they were five with those whose birthdays were in April, May, June, and July and who entered school after they were five. For boys in particular, there was, on the average, an advantage in terms of school grades to entering kindergarten after attaining age five rather than before attaining that age.

If there are benefits to a gradual introduction to reading, are there costs paid by those who were trained to read early? To be sure, it depends upon the child. A child who has learned to read because he or she wanted to pays no serious penalty in school. We found, however, that most early readers do not identify themselves, perhaps for fear of being considered difficult or different. To some teachers, children who read early are a kind of threat, either because they have to do something special for them, or because they feel that someone else has usurped their prerogative to teach the child to read. A teacher of this sort—fortunately there are not many—could display a negative attitude toward an early reading child that might make the child's life in the classroom difficult.

I once encountered a more serious example of the dangers of hurrying children into reading at a school in Chicago where a very energetic teacher was training four-year-old and five-year-old black children to read. To accomplish this, the children spent long hours doing drills and exercises. There was little time in their school day for much else. I must say that when I sat with individual children and had them read to me, I was impressed at the ease and fluency with which they read the storybooks. What also impressed me was the quietness of their voices.

When I visited a first-grade group who had been through that kindergarten program, they showed the benefits in terms of reading progress. But when I had the children read to me individually, the quietness of their voices was extraordinary. They were not reading aloud but whispering, so that I had to strain to hear. Although they had learned a skill, it had been at great cost, and I interpreted their low voices as a sign of embarrassment and fear. They experienced no pleasure in reading aloud or in my praise or approval of what they were doing. It almost seemed that reading had been foisted upon them, at great cost in time and effort, without their having any real understanding of the value of what they were learning. They showed the apathy and withdrawal that are frequent among children who are pushed too hard academically. (This topic will be explored more fully in the next chapter).

In this connection it is necessary to say something about television programs such as *Sesame Street* and *Electric Company*. These and other educational programs for children allow young people to become acquainted with letters and sounds and numbers. But in our own studies, and in those of others, we have found that what is crucial to beginning to read is the child's attachment to an adult who spends time reading to or with the child. The motivation for reading, which is a difficult task, is social. Without that social attachment and motivation, what children see on *Sesame Street* becomes entertainment more than education. And current reading achievement scores give little evidence that such television programs have had any large-scale or long-term effects on this generation's reading achievement.

Parental pressure to hurry children academically in the early years can also be seen as a downward extension of the parental concern expressed with adolescents. "Ability grouping," for example, has been fought for decades. Parents whose teenagers operate at a slower pace than the norm insist that these young people be expected to do the same work as their faster-moving peers so that they will not fall behind. The failure of some parents to recognize the limits of their children's abilities at the high school level has its counterpart in the insistence by some parents that their children be taught to read early. In both cases, parents seem to want their children to grow up faster than what seems reasonable for the children in question. Children should be challenged intellectually, but the challenge should be constructive, not debilitating. Forcing a child to read early, no less than forcing an adolescent to take algebra when simple arithmetic is still a problem, can be a devastating experience for a young person who is not prepared intellectually for the task. A young man of seven who was struggling with reading told me, "I can't read, I guess I'm a flop in life."

The Child as Status Symbol

Another prevalent form of stress encountered by today's parent, particularly the mother, is role conflict. Within the short space of twenty-five years, the role of the middle-class woman has been profoundly altered. In the 1950s, a woman who worked was looked down upon as someone who did not "care enough" to look after her husband and children. Today, however, a quarter century after the feminist revolution, a middle-class woman who chooses the life of the housewife is often regarded as unambitious (and therefore less intelligent than her working counterparts) and generally lacking in self-respect and female pride. The situation is complicated by the fact that with the higher divorce rate, more and more women have to work.

Thus many women are caught in a conflict between their desires to perform well the traditional role of mother (and wife) and what may well be an equally strong inclination to embrace the new professional and social possibilities that have fortunately opened up for women in our society.

Women who choose to stay at home may thus come under considerable (not necessarily entirely conscious) stress for having opted for this traditional role. In her book *The Cinderella Syndrome,* Colette Dowling captures well the emptiness and restlessness of some of these women. Despite a certain pride in their husbands' positions and income, many women "admitted to a certain eventlessness in their days. They couldn't quite break off from their bridge groups, though they described them as boring. In the empty house, when they weren't shopping or entertaining or chauffeuring the kids, they read romances."[12]

Bragging Rights

Such women are stressed, whether they realize it or not. It is likely that bridge and romance novels are escapes from reflecting about what they might really want to do with their lives. For some mothers in this situation, children serve as the only, or major, justification of an otherwise somewhat empty and boring existence: "If my children can bring me attention and respect, then I don't have to feel so bad about staying home." Unfortunately, this rationale overlooks the fact that children, under these circumstances, are all too often not permitted to be just children but are pushed to be mini-achievers. While parents have traditionally taken pride in their offsprings' achievements and have been concerned about their education, it is a unique characteristic of contemporary society that we burden preschoolers with the expectations and anxieties normally (if wrongly) visited upon high school seniors. Today, parents brag not only about the colleges and prep schools their children are enrolled in but also about which private kindergartens they attend. Helen LaCroix, director of admissions at Chicago's Frances W. Parker School, has said that "it's become a little more difficult to get into a private kindergarten than to enroll in college."[13]

Parents wish, and with good reason, to have their children win admission to the classy preschools that not only provide superior education but, more importantly, facilitate entry into the "better" prep schools and colleges. However, parents (and children) too easily become trapped in the fallacious inference expressed by Darla Poythress of Atlanta's Trinity School: "Parents believe if they don't get their kids in [on the Ivy League track] at the kindergarten level, they won't get them in at all."[14] Yet there is no evidence that gaining a child admission into a fine kindergarten has any real bearing on prep school or college admission. Moreover, the cost of matriculation at any fine private college is escalating at such a rate that many parents may not be able to afford to enroll their children, particularly not after putting them through expensive preschools and grade schools.

The anxiety generated by the school admissions sweepstakes has a symbolic significance. "Look at us," it says, "how concerned and committed we are as parents to be doing all this for our children." Hauling the kids to school and back, attending PTA meetings and school events, now become the full-time "occupation" of a young mother who feels justified in not getting a job.

Certainly, women should have the option to work at home if they wish to and be able to do so without any social stigma. Ideally, this will occur when the gains of the women's movement have been more firmly consolidated than is yet the case. But for the present and the foreseeable future, many young mothers are stressed by their conflicting desires to stay home and to have a career. For mothers who cleave to the housewife role, it is often tempting to invoke the children—and their precocious academic accomplishments—as the justification for their not working. In doing so, however, mothers—and fathers—are placing too heavy a burden on their children.

The Child as Partner

What about the mother who opts for a career *and* a family? The number of working mothers in the United States has increased substantially in the last few decades. In 1948, only 26 percent of married women with children ages six to sixteen were engaged in, or seeking, work. Today, the percentage has doubled. The majority (60 percent) of mothers of school-age children now work. The figures for working mothers of younger children are equally impressive: half the mothers of young children under age two now work full-time or part-time outside the home—a 108 percent increase since 1970.

For many women, work is a gratifying and fulfilling experience, and many find that if they cannot "have it all," as Betty Freidan said they should, they can still have the best of the work and wife-mother roles. Nevertheless, judging by the outpouring of books and magazine articles recounting the tribulations of working mothers ("Are You Jealous of the Other Woman in Your Baby's Life?," "How Working Mothers Work It Out," "You, Too, Can Cope with Added Stress"), many women are finding work stressful.

Working women are less likely to have extended family networks to rely upon for child care and are likely to be less concerned with the intellectual stimulation their children are receiving as with their physical care and protection. Finding quality child-care workers and facilities, particularly for infants and young children, is a constant effort and a constant stress.

In addition, women, far more than men, carry the dual burden of professional work *and* housework. A recent study showed that in 1965, men averaged about 9 hours a week doing household chores and caring for children. Ten years later, men were spending 9.7 hours a week in such activities. Women, in contrast spent 28.8 hours per week in housekeeping and child-care activities in 1965, and 24.9 hours per week in 1975. The decrease probably reflects the fact that more women were working professionally and therefore had less time to spend at home.

Working parents, particularly mothers, are of necessity more stressed by time constraints than are nonworking parents. In such families, the children have to adjust to parental schedules rather than the reverse, as is usually the case with the nonworking mother. The children must be awakened early, dressed, fed, and taken to a caretaker, day-care center, or nursery school. Arranging car pools is time consuming, as is picking up children and dropping them off. (And there are always those irresponsible parents who are habitually late, forget the schedule, fail to show up, and so forth.)

Young children have limited powers of adaptation, which are sometimes exceeded by the pressures of adult scheduling. I recall one situation in which a mother wanted to have her daughter attend a prestigious nursery school in the morning and a day-care center in the afternoon. The child became increasingly upset, and after we discussed the matter, the teacher encouraged the mother to place the child in the day-care center full-time (the school was only half-day) because the stress of transition and readaptation was too much for the young girl to tolerate.

Although the programmatic hurrying of young middle-class children appears new, it is in fact a downward extension of a kind of hurrying that has been going on for a long time at older age levels. At the elementary school level, for example, it is not unusual for some children to go to hockey practice, or swimming, or gymnastics training before school. After school, these same students may take music lessons or participate in a church or civic social organization activity, such as putting on a play. The heavily scheduled preschool child of today is a downward extension of the heavily programmed elementary schoolchild. In a real sense, we are hurrying young children to be hurried like older children.

Older children in homes with working parents, in turn, must learn at an early age to fend for themselves. They learn to get up on their own, choose their own clothing, make their own breakfasts, clean up after themselves, and get to school on time. Now surely these are reasonable demands to make on children and do not, *ipso facto,* constitute hurrying; it may even be said that many children in two-parent homes with only one working parent would benefit from being expected to do more for themselves.

Demands and expectations can quickly get out of hand, however. A young patient of mine illustrates the hurrying that arises when parents overburden children in this fashion. The father of the boy owned a motel and the mother was the cook in the small restaurant associated with the motel. Their son usually took out the trash and occasionally helped the chambermaids with making the beds. On Saturdays, when he wanted to play with his friends, the boy's father insisted that he work at the motel—to flatten the cans that had accumulated in a week of refuse so that the price of trash removal would be lower.

This young man (age fourteen), like most children of working parents, appreciated the economic circumstances that required him to pitch in. It was only when the demands on him became unreasonable—far out of proportion to what the parents needed their son to do—that the boy could be said to be the victim of hurrying in the sense that he was burdened with adult responsibilities and expectations too early. Only then did he begin to show signs of emotional stress.

It is not always easy for working parents to separate what is reasonable from what is not. If a child can start dinner, then why not have him or her prepare the whole meal? If the child can keep one room tidy, why not the whole house? The temptation to pile heavy domestic burdens on the child is strong for parents under stress. Helping parents is one thing; taking over their jobs and responsibilities is quite a different matter.

Another way parents treat children as partners is to allow them to become decision makers. Asking children to make age-appropriate decisions, such as what they want for dinner, is one thing, while expecting them to make inappropriate decisions, such as choosing the parent they will spend their holiday with, is another. Decision making is hard for anyone, but it is particularly hard when it is done alone—that is, when one is a single parent—without benefit of counsel and shared responsibility. There is stress in the choosing and stress in the anticipation of consequences. "What if I quit my job?" or "What if I tell my former husband to leave the children alone?" It is natural to wish to talk such matters over with someone, but children, especially young ones, lack the experience and intellectual maturity to be of much help. Children who are placed in this uncomfortable situation recognize that they are being asked to share responsibilities for which they are unprepared, and they may resent it.

The Child as Therapist

Separation and divorce, perhaps the most pervasive and endemic source of stress in America today, affect one in three marriages. Thus, almost half of American children under eighteen are likely to live in single-parent homes. Though stressful to both parents (as to children), divorce and separation mean something different for men and women.

For women, the stress of a marriage in trouble or ended (by death or divorce) is compounded by the fact that many women are not prepared to survive economically. The National Advisory Council on Women's Programs report *Neglected Women* points out that one in three American women lacks the basic skills needed to earn a reasonable living. They are "products of past educational and social patterns which do not apply to today's society."

When a woman finds herself alone and responsible for a family, her initial reaction may be one of shock and panic. For one thing, having custody of the children, the woman now feels she must fill the role of both mother and father, and solo parenting is made more difficult because there is no one to share the load with or lean upon in time of stress. One mother who put her children in day care told me, "If I didn't get out of the house for a while, I would go crazy."

There are other stresses as well: a woman's concern about whether she is still attractive to men, or how to go about meeting men; her anxiety that she may have to spend the rest of her life single, which is to say entirely alone once the children are grown. Continued association with old friends (especially couples) from one's married days often proves more difficult for the single woman than for her bachelor ex-husband. New friends can be made, of course, but they are usually other single, divorced, or widowed women who may be under so much stress themselves that they have little support to give to others. Going to a movie or play or concert suddenly looms as a problem if the woman is not in the habit of going alone (or simply doesn't want to). In sum, needing to support children financially and emotionally, without herself enjoying those kinds of support, is perhaps the most severe stress encountered by a female in our society.

Not surprisingly, therefore, single mothers are developing the familiar pattern of egocentrism and hurrying that is characteristic of parents under stress. One common way that single mothers hurry their children to grow up is to treat them as confidants. In some ways this is a natural phenomenon: a young mother, living alone, begins to confide in her eight-year-old daughter. The mother may tell the girl about the "crazy" man at work who always walks around talking under his breath, or she may express some of her frustrations about co-workers or office tribulations. Such ventings may lead to anxious mutterings about the state of family finances, and then, in turn, to reports of her feelings about the men she may be dating. When a mother meets a man she is interested in, the daughter learns about him, meets him, and is perhaps asked to venture an opinion about him and/or about her mother's relationship with him.

The child in such circumstances is asked to meet a parental need in much the same way as when children are hurried into school or sports. In this instance, children are hurried into mature interpersonal relations because the parent is under stress and needs a symbolic confidant. We say "symbolic" because, of course, at eight or ten years of age, the child lacks the experience and intellectual and emotional security to be of much practical use to the mother. Rather, the child serves as sympathetic listener, which is, indeed, part of what the mother needs. Unfortunately, though, it is by no means clear that this is what the child needs. As five-year-old Deana told me, "I like Mommy's friend who smells nice but I don't like the furry one who smells bad," then wistfully, "sometimes I wish she wouldn't ask me."

Single fathers also use children as confidants. Usually they do not have custody and so realize, often for the first time, how much they not only miss but literally need their children. The man's self-esteem, like the woman's, may be at a low point as a result of separation or divorce, and he may be feeling sorry for himself. When he sees the children on weekends, he may complain to them about how much money he has to give to their mother and how little this leaves him to live on. Or he may express his resentment about the arguments that caused the break-up, or his jealousy over their mother's new relationships. The children are caught in the middle of these adult conflicts. Treated as confidants whom father wants as allies, they are still expected to remain impartial (and devoted) to mother.

Many single fathers also present their children with a new romantic attachment too soon after a separation. Sometimes the father leaves the family to be with another woman, a situation that happens less often with the mother. The simple act of Daddy leaving home is already an enormous shock to children. To be confronted with another woman at the same time is confusing (particularly to younger children) and challenges their implicit assumption that family relationships are binding. If the mother-father relationship can be changed so abruptly, cannot the parent-child relationship undergo the same trauma?

Single fathers who fail to visit their offspring or who fail to contribute financially to their children's upbringing stress youngsters in a different way. Despite the mother's frequent efforts to present the father in the best possible light, the children feel rejected. They are thus confronted early with the fear of abandonment. They have to grow up fast to cope with those fears.

The Child as Conscience

Not unusually, parents, in their search for symbolical relief from stress, cast the child in the role of moral arbiter. While this may also happen in complete families, it is more common in single-parent homes. This phenomenon is well illustrated by two case histories taken from my clinical practice.

Alice Knoepfel (not her real name) was an attractive divorcee of thirty-six who had two teenage children, a boy and a girl. The family lived in a large home in an upper-middle-class suburb. Soon after the divorce was final, the mother began dating a man of questionable reputation and business connections who was the opposite of her staid, professional husband. Alice became pregnant. Her lover insisted that she undergo an abortion, but she refused and had the baby. Alice did not explain her pregnancy to her children; she simply expected them to accept the situation. In fact, she expected more—she expected them to condone her behavior, to give it explicit moral sanction. In time, her teenage son moved in with his father, and her daughter got pregnant, had an abortion, dropped out of school, and moved in with her boyfriend.

In another case, Harry Tartakower (not his real name), a forty-two-year-old mathematics professor, deserted his wife and two children (ages five and nine) for a graduate student with whom he had fallen in love. Soon after moving into the home of his new girlfriend, Harry invited his two children to come see him. He made it clear that he expected them to accept his new living arrangement. He and his girlfriend were affectionate in front of the children and did not conceal the fact that they were sleeping together. The children were unprepared for this dramatic shift in their father's behavior and could hardly believe his attentions to a woman other than their mother. They were in a state of shock when they returned home, and only through counseling were they able to express the anger and frustration they felt toward their father.

Both Alice and Harry tried to treat their children as adults so as to derive from them moral approbation for actions that they knew the community did not approve of. In these instances, children were thus asked to serve as symbols for the larger moral society—despite the fact that they neither fully understood nor especially approved of what their mother or father had done. By expecting children to comprehend and condone behavior that most adult members of the same society frown upon, Alice and Harry not only hurried their offspring to grow up but also placed them under an impossible psychological burden of conflict.

The children, moreover, feel the burden and resent it. As one seven-year-old told me, speaking about his recently divorced parents, "My dad tells me things about my mom and wants me to like him more than her. And my mom tells me things about my dad, and she wants me to like her more than him. They get mad if I say anything good about the other one. I get tired of being asked which one I love the most. After a while you get used to it and don't say anything."

All of us today are under a great deal of stress from our rapidly changing society. Some parents are so stressed that they become egocentric and either forget or find it impossible to use the knowledge we have about the nature and needs of children. Such parents need the support, the companionship, and the symbolic achievements of their children to relieve their stress. And the expectation that children make moral judgments and evaluations, lend a comforting ear, and make decisions is not always or necessarily harmful. Indeed, young people need to learn to make judgments and decisions. The question is not whether children should be asked to make judgments and decisions and listen attentively but rather the *appropriateness* of the particular demand given the child's age, intelligence, and level of maturity. Asking a child to decide between two fast-food restaurants is probably a good idea; requiring a child to alleviate a parental burden by selecting one of two nursery schools is unfair. By making such demands, parents relieve some of the stress on themselves by stressing their children.

3
....
The Dynamics of
Hurrying: Schools

....

Many of our schools reflect the contemporary bias toward having children grow up fast. They do this because such schools have become increasingly industrialized and product oriented. Teachers are unionized, textbooks are standardized on a national level and testing has become mechanized (machine scored) and all pervasive as a consequence. In many communities, teachers and principals are held accountable for children's academic achievement as demonstrated by their performance on standardized tests. And, in some states, teachers are also being tested to determine their competence to teach.

The industrialization of our schools is not surprising, for universal schooling in the United States was introduced, in part, to prepare children for the new ways of living and working brought about by the machine age. What is surprising about our schools today is that they continue to follow a factory model at a time when factory work, as it was once known, is becoming as obsolete as farming without a tractor.

Our schools today suffer from the same structural problems that made our industries an easy mark for foreign competition. School systems are often top-heavy administratively and excessively hierarchical and authoritarian. The creativity and innovation of teachers is deadened by overly close ties to the uniformity of educational publishing and testing. Finally, effective change in education is often blocked by school boards whose decisions may be dictated more by concerns of personality and politics than by those that are properly pedagogical.

At a time when American industry is "restructuring," education is "reforming," which means more basics, more hours, more homework, more testing—more of everything that is creating the problem. It is a classic case of the cure being worse than the disease. Our schools, then, are out of sync with the larger society and represent our past rather than our future. While schools are always (and necessarily) behind the times because they transmit accumulated knowledge and skills, the discrepancy is particularly great today because of the knowledge explosion and the technological revolutions that occur with machine-gun rapidity. Our children do poorly in school today, in part at least, because they are repeatedly made aware that what they learn outside of school is more up to date than what they learn in school.

The factory model of education hurries children because it ignores individual differences in mental abilities and learning rates and learning styles. Children are pressured to meet uniform standards as measured by standardized tests. Those who cannot keep up in this system, as indicated by the tests, are often regarded as defective vessels and are labeled "learning disabled," or ADHA (Attention Deficit, Hyperactivity Disorder). Yet many of these same children can easily demonstrate how much knowledge they acquire from television and how quickly they learn skills needed to operate electronic games. Our tests don't measure this kind of knowledge or those computerlinked skills.

Another example of how schools hurry children is the progressive downward thrust of the curriculum. When school is looked upon as an assembly line and when there is pressure to increase production, there is a temptation not only to fill the bottles faster but also to fill them earlier. Why not put in as much at kindergarten as at first grade? Why not teach fourth-grade math at grade two? Indeed, as one professor mused, why not teach philosophy at grade three? The pressure to teach subject matter at ever earlier ages will be illustrated in this chapter by what has happened with sex education. But it could be equally well demonstrated by efforts to teach computer programming to young children, or to instruct them in "thinking skills."

A continuing issue in education has to do with kindergarten, and whether to retain or not retain.

A final illustration of how our schools hurry children is the return to the outmoded practice of rotation. Rotation involves moving children from classroom to classroom for different subjects. This practice makes inappropriate demands for adaptation on elementary school children. Yet this is often justified in terms of children's needs for specialized instruction.

There is a growing awareness that the "reform" measures of the 1980s—longer school days and years, more homework, teacher evaluations, merit pay, and the like—are not working. The process of education is ineffective, so the solution can hardly be to impose more of it upon children. True educational reform will require the kind of tough restructuring that has made some of our industries competitive once again. Such restructuring is never easy, and may well be painful to many. But the alternative, an educational system that cannot match the effective education in other countries, is equally unpleasant.

Assembly-Line Learning

The standardized, machine-scored test that we are so familiar with today is a relatively recent invention. Standardized tests were first introduced around the turn of the century by French psychologist Alfred Binet and his colleague Henri Simon. Binet had been commissioned by the French government to find a way to identify mentally retarded children at an early age so that they could be placed in special institutions. To develop his test, Binet went to teachers and asked them to describe the sorts of skills they had observed in children at different ages. On the basis of these teacher comments, Binet constructed his test items, which dealt with language, understanding, reasoning, and motor skill.[1]

Binet standardized his "scale" by testing the items on large numbers of normal children. Any item that was passed by about 75 percent of a particular age group was assigned to that age level. If everyone at a particular age level passed the item, it was considered to be too easy for that age group. And if only half or fewer of the pupils passed the item, it was considered to be too difficult. This manner of assigning items to a particular age (and later grade) level resulted in what has come to be known as a "norm-referenced" test. A child's performance on such a test is always interpreted with respect to a norm group.

Binet assigned six tests to each age level from age two to adult (after age sixteen, no further age discriminations were made). A child's score was reported not in points but in terms of what Binet called Mental Age; two months credit was given for each test a child passed. The child's total score was the total number of months of credit he or she attained; expressed in years and months, this total month score constituted the child's Mental Age. Hence a child who received sixty months of credit would have a Mental Age of five, regardless of his or her chronological age.

Binet insisted upon the Mental Age concept because he wanted to keep the measurement of intelligence in psychological units. He was very wary of using numbers to describe intelligence and did not approve of the Intelligence Quotient (IQ) concept introduced by William Stern. The IQ concept proposed a measure of "relative brightness," how bright children were vis-à-vis their age mates, rather than an absolute measure of brightness such as the Mental Age. The Intelligence Quotient was defined as IQ = Mental Age (MA) ÷ Chronological Age (CA) × 100. A child with a Mental Age of 60 months and a chronological age of 60 months would thus have an IQ of 100. A child whose MA was greater than his or her CA would have an IQ of more than 100; a child with a CA greater than his or her MA would have an IQ of less than 100.

Intelligence tests were useful in screening retarded children, but Binet was very much aware of their dangers and wrote: "We should at least spare from this mark [a test score that would send a child to an institution for the retarded] those who do not deserve it. Mistakes are excusable, especially at the beginning. But if they become too gross we can injure the name of these institutions."[2] Not to mention the costs to the children involved. Unfortunately, Binet's hope was not realized, and as we shall see, we are still making mistakes with tests.

During the First World War a new innovation in testing was introduced: the group test. A group-administered test, the Army Alpha, was used to screen recruits who were not bright enough to be soldiers. (One finding was that the average recruit had, according to the test norms, a Mental Age of thirteen.) The introduction of group intelligence tests led the way to the proliferation of group tests of vocational aptitude, personality, and school achievement.

The next technological innovation in testing was the introduction of machine-scored tests. Specifically, the IBM score sheet, which could be electronically read and scored, had momentous implications for schools. Once machines took over the drudgery of scoring tests, the way was open for their extensive use in the schools, as well as in industry. There are few innovations in education that have had any staying power, but the machine-scored test is the exception and has become a major force in contemporary education.

Indeed, machine-scored group tests, probably more than any other single influence, have heightened the factory quality of our schools, pushing them to turn out ever more uniform products. This emphasis has grown dramatically over the last twenty years as dissatisfaction with the schools and with children's attainments has become more pronounced on the part of both parents and legislators. This dissatisfaction was greatly increased by the publication in 1983 of an Office of Education assessment of American high school education entitled "A Nation at Risk," which warned of a "rising tide of mediocrity" and included the following among its findings:

- International comparisons of student achievement completed a decade ago revealed that on nineteen academic tests, American students were never first or second and, in comparison with students from other industrialized nations, were last seven times.
- The College Board's scholastic aptitude tests (S A T s) demonstrated a virtually unbroken decline from 1963 to 1980. Average verbal scores fell over fifty points and average mathematics scores nearly forty points.
- Many seventeen-year olds do not possess the "higher order" intellectual skills we should expect of them. Nearly 40 percent cannot draw inferences from written material; only one fifth can write a persuasive essay; and only one third can solve a mathematic problem involving several steps.[3]

This report, along with others, gave impetus in the early 1980s toward an educational "reform" movement. But there was controversy about which direction such educational reform should take. On the one hand are those authors, such as those who wrote "A Nation at Risk," who are concerned about our economic competitiveness and see the primary function of schooling as instilling the skills and knowledge young people will need to enter an increasingly technologically advanced and competitive workplace.

On the other hand are those authors who see education as preparation for life and find fault with education not because it fails to instill basic skills, but rather because it fails to ground students in the literary, philosophical and historical foundations of society. The most recent exponents of this position are Alan Bloom (*The Closing of the American Mind*)[4] and E. D. Hirsch (*Cultural Literacy*).[5] It should be said that this argument between the educational pragmatists and the educational purists has been going on for centuries.

Still other workers, such as Howard Gardner at Harvard and Robert Sternberg at Yale, are working toward reform in a somewhat different direction, namely in our conception of intelligence and intelligence tests. Gardner argues that there are multiple intelligences, including those for the arts, and that schools and tests focus on only a few of these different forms of intelligence. Sternberg, in contrast, argues for three basic types of intelligence. He believes that some people may excel in conventional thinking, others in novel thinking, and still others in practical thinking. Both Gardner[6] and Sternberg,[7] unlike the humanists such as Bloom and Hirsch, believe in testing but argue that the available tests are much too narrow.

Not surprisingly, the pragmatists, those focused on improving basic skills and on testing, seem to have won the day. While some aspects of educational reform have been beneficial, they have, for the most part, followed the factory rather than the liberal education model. And that is the major reason educational reform in the 1980s has added to the hurrying of children. For, in addition to long overdue increases in teacher salaries, now come the traditional solutions to low factory production. In too many communities educational reform has meant the raising of standards, the introduction of more homework, the elimination of recess, and proposals for longer school days and longer school years.

The major aim of this type of school reform is clearly to increase test scores as a measure of an improved product. The hurricane of testing that reform has unleashed is well described by Edward B. Fiske:

> *American schools are going test-crazy. The scores emerging from those sheets full of X's and penciled-in circles are increasingly being used to promote and hold back students, hire and fire teachers, award diplomas, evaluate curriculums, and dole out money to schools and colleagues.*[8]

Nonetheless, the reforms instituted to increase test scores are not working. The most recent National Assessment of Educational Progress (1996) on the knowledge and abilities of nine-, thirteen-, and seventeen-year olds indicates that while there have been some modest increases in basic skills from 1971 to 1996, only a few students meet reasonable standards for their age groups. The results from the reading scores provide a dismal example. Only 39 percent of seventeen-year olds read well enough to understand the material they will encounter in high school textbooks. And about half of the same age group does not understand junior high mathematics, such as finding averages.

In addition, the great emphasis on tests and test scores has pushed school systems as well as individual administrators toward questionable practices. A case in point is what has been called the "Lake Wobegon effect"—named of course after humorist Garrison Keillor's description of the imaginary town of Lake Wobegon where "all the children are above average." The Lake Wobegon effect refers to a study, conducted by physician John B. Cannel, of fifty state education departments, forty-nine of which reported above-average performance for their students![9]

The issues here are many and complex and have to do with test norms, the choice of tests by school systems, and the meaning and interpretation of test scores. One of the most critical questions is to what extent teachers are preparing children to take the tests. Is the Lake Wobegon effect a reflection of the fact that teachers know what tests will be given and use instructional time to teach the answers to the test? What do test results mean under these circumstances? Although many in the testing industry believe that the Lake Wobegon effect can be explained away, it has initiated serious debate and discussion about test norms and about better and clearer communication of test scores to parents.

When tests become the focal point of education, they add to the pressures on children in another way. Testing is stressful at all age levels, but it adds to the pressure when test results are widely publicized in the local newspapers and on local television shows. And when teachers and administrators appreciate that student tests scores are read as a measure of *their* competence, they concentrate on how well the students do on tests rather than on how well they learn. Under these circumstances children discover very quickly that passing tests, rather than meaningful learning, is what school is all about.

In this regard, what Kenneth Kenniston wrote in 1976 holds equally true today:

> *We measure the success of schools not by the kinds of human beings they promote but by whatever increases in reading scores they chalk up. We have allowed quantitative standards, so central to the adult economic system, to become the principal yardstick for our definition of our children's worth.*[10]

The testing mania can also have some tragic effects for schools and for children. For example, one school principal, so pressured to keep up the high grades and reputation of the students and school, illicitly got copies of the tests to be administered and had teachers coach the children on the answers. The truth came out, and the principal resigned once the story made big print. The tragic part of the whole episode was that the principal ran an excellent school and the children were already testing at high levels. Although one cannot excuse the principal for this action, we can all appreciate the stress of constant pressure to demonstrate high test scores.

Even young children are being caught up in this testing craze. In the last few years, testing has been pushed down to earlier and earlier grades. In 1987, the state of Georgia passed legislation that makes testing mandatory for admission to kindergarten and promotion to first grade. In some schools in New York City, children entering kindergarten may be tested four times before November. In addition to testing, many kindergarten children are now graded and given homework. It is a bit much for children at that age. As one frightened five-year old asked her mother before going to school on the day of a test, "Will you kill me if I don't get an A?" While some states, such as California, North Carolina, and Mississippi, initially resisted the testing epidemic, they, too, have now succumbed.

Why, some readers may ask, does testing, homework, and grading hurry young children? Aren't we coddling them by allowing them to do nothing but play during the early years when the mind is so ready and eager for learning? I will deal with this issue in more detail in Chapter 6, but a brief answer can be given here. Young children believe that adults are all-knowing and all-wise. When we confront them with tasks for which they are not ready—such as tests, workbooks, and homework—these children blame themselves for failure. "If this all-wise, all-knowing person tells me I should be able to do this and I can't, there must be something wrong with me." We are sending too many children to school only to learn that they are "too dumb" to be there.

Accountability and test scores are what schools are about today, and children know it. They have to produce or else. This pressure may be good for many students, but it is bound to be bad for those who can't keep up. Their failure is more public and therefore more humiliating than ever before. Worse, students who fail to achieve feel that they are letting down their peers, their teachers, the principal, the superintendent, and the community. This is a heavy burden for many children to bear and is a powerful pressure to achieve early and grow up fast.

The effect on young people of these new reforms is the opposite of what was intended. The high school drop-out rate, which had been level for many years, is on the rise again. In part this is a result of having raised the standards for graduation without giving young people the wherewithal to meet those standards. The emphasis on the early identification of children with learning problems forces children to think of themselves as defective before they have had a chance to show what they can do. The introduction of remedial reading programs at first grade shows how widely this epidemic of early identification has spread. Once a child is marked with the "special needs" stamp, that stamp is more likely to be re-inked than erased.

There are problems at the other end as well. The present day recognition of the special needs of gifted and talented children is long overdue. Nonetheless, the introduction of classes and programs labeled as "gifted and talented" has provided an untapped granary for feeding parental ego. The desire to say that a child is in one of these "gifted and talented" programs has pushed many parents to put their children in such programs even when they really do not belong and cannot keep up. Such youngsters are doubly humiliated by their failure within the "gifted and talented" class and then by having to leave it and rejoin the regular class.

The pressures resulting from the abuse of testing have other negative effects as well. What schools teach children, more than anything else, is that the end result, or grade, is more important than what the grade was supposed to mean in the way of achievement. Children are much more concerned with grades than with what they know. So it isn't surprising that when these young people go out into the work world, they are less concerned with the work than with the pay and the perquisites of the job. Recent surveys have shown that contemporary youth are much more materialistic than earlier generations. While the media contributes to this materialism, the attitudes inculcated by the schools, contribute as well.

Even more discouraging is the dishonesty and cheating that are fostered by the over-emphasis on testing. If it is the grade you get rather than what you know that counts, then the most important thing is to get the highest grade. The many recent scandals involving young stock brokers and newspaper reporters selling information are only the tip of the iceberg. Again, why should this seem surprising to us (as it seems to be)? If young people are treated as products, as worth only as much as they score on a test, then they need have no other moral or ethical scruples than any other industrial product would have. Treated as objects, young people can hardly be held either ethically or morally accountable.

The Japanese Example

One of the major contemporary arguments for factory solutions to our educational problems comes from the many recent comparisons of our schooling with that of Japan. Japanese children start earlier than our children, they go to school for longer hours and for a longer school year, and they do much more homework than American children do. If this were not enough, more than half of Japanese children go to after-school tutorial programs, known as "juku," often for several hours a day in addition to the time spent in public school. Not surprisingly, Japanese students are far superior to American students according to most measures of academic achievement, particularly in mathematics. As one Japanese official put it, "In the 1950s you had 'Sputnik' shock and in the 1980s you are having 'Toyota' shock."

By any standard I have discussed in this book, Japanese children are hurried. Yet they don't seem to show the stress symptoms that American children do, and they actually seem to thrive on the pressures of their intense educational program. Doesn't Japanese education give the lie to my whole hurrying = stress argument? Not really. Japan was one of the first countries to have *The Hurried Child* translated into their language.

At the start of the 1988 school year, seven Japanese school children and a school teacher committed suicide. Notes from several of the children indicated that school pressure was what they were escaping. As we shall see, excessive academic pressure affects Japanese children as much as it does American youngsters.

Nonetheless, to understand why Japanese children are not hurried in the same sense that our children are, we need to look a little more closely at Japanese education in its cultural context. First of all, Japanese society is very different than our own:

*The Japanese value harmony, reflexive obedience, conformity,
and self-sacrifice on behalf of the group. We prize pluralism,
independence, rugged individualism, and creativity. Theirs is a
hierarchical society in which education, like most government functions, is highly centralized. We favor local control whenever possible.
They are a homogeneous population. Americans come in more colors
than a bruise.[11]*

For our purposes, an understanding of what makes the pressure
of Japanese education tolerable, we need to look at the critical
factor—or person—that modifies the hurrying = stress equation,
namely the Japanese mother:

*No one doubts that behind every high scoring Japanese student—
and they are among the highest scoring in the world—there stands a
mother, supportive, aggressive, and completely involved in her
child's education. She studies, she packs lunches, she waits for
hours in lines to register her child for exams, and waits again for
him in the hallways for hours while he takes them. She denies herself
TV so her child can study in quiet and stirs noodles at 11 pm for
the scholar's snack. She shuttles youngsters from exercise class to
rhythm class to calligraphy and piano, to swimming and martial
arts. She helps every day with homework, hires tutors, and works
part-time to pay for juku. Sometimes she enrolls in "mother's class"
so she can help with drills at home.[12]*

The success of Japanese education is, in large part, due to the
efforts and self-sacrifice of Japanese "Education Mothers" or
"Kyoiku Mamas." Japanese children are able to tolerate the stress
and pressure of the educational system because their mothers are
always there for support and encouragement. Unlike the "pushy"
mother in America—who is often looked down upon with deri-
sion—a "Kyoiku Mama" is looked upon as engaged in a demanding and prestigious profession. And the social pressures on these
mothers is enormous:

*Much of a Japanese mother's sense of personal accomplishment is
tied to the educational achievements of her children, and she*

*expends great effort helping them. . . . In addition, there is consider-
able peer pressure on the mother. The community's perception of a
woman's success as a mother depends in large part on how well her
children do in school.*[13]

But it is not only Japanese mothers who pay the price:

*Several cross-national studies have revealed that the level of self
esteem among Japanese children is much lower than that of children
in other countries. The self-rating scores given by Japanese elementary and junior high school children are especially low in domains
such as school achievement and intelligence. . . . For many Japanese
school children, pursuit of excellence does not result in good feelings
about themselves, or allow them to appreciate the scholastic accomplishments of others. This situation is one of the chief reasons for
recent problems in schools, such as physically and psychologically
abusive acts towards peers, aggression directed to teachers, vandalism, and suicide.*[14]

One last point about Japanese education and hurrying: In Chapter 8 I describe one reaction to hurrying as "premature structuring." Children pushed to grow up fast may attain more than other
children during the period in which they are hurried, but there-
after they may go slower and not attain the same high levels of
achievement as those who have moved more slowly. This seems to
be what happens in Japan. Although the Japanese graduate a
higher proportion of high school students than we do (90 percent
versus 76 percent), more of our students go on to college than do
Japanese high school graduates (58 percent versus 29 percent).

Even more important, from the standpoint of premature structuring, is the quality of Japanese university education. It is at the
college and university levels that Japanese education is generally
conceded to be inferior to that in the United States. The college
years are often referred to as a "four-year vacation" with little attention to academics and little pressure on students to do more than
have a good time. In contrast, many American students come into
their own at the college and university level. They may not have
moved as fast but they go further.

A clear-cut measure of the capacity of our students to go further than the Japanese comes from a comparison of the numbers of Americans and Japanese who have won Nobel Prizes. The number of Nobel prizes awarded to any given country would seem to be a reasonable measure of that country's ability to produce creative individuals. The first Nobel prizes were awarded in 1901, and in 1969 an award for economics was added. In the eighty-six years over which the prizes have been given, Japan has received a total of five! Two of these awards were in physics, one was in chemistry, one was in literature, and Eisaku Sato won the Peace Prize in 1974. When we compare these with the hundreds of Nobel Prizes won by Americans, we have a good index of the negative effects of premature educational structuring.

The problems of American education will not be solved by modeling our system after those that are "successful" in other countries. We should have learned that lesson in the 1970s when British "informal" instruction was our educational role model. The only residues of that adolescent "crush" are a number of schools without walls. The walls were removed from these schools because when the British talked about "open" education they were talking about the school child's mind, while we understood them to be talking about the school child's building.

Our problems in American education arise because we are not sufficiently American, not because we are insufficiently British or Japanese. Our classrooms are not as individualized, and our curriculums are not as flexible, as our values of individualism and self-reliance demand. True educational reform will only come about when we make our education truly democratic, *appropriate* to children's individual growth rates and levels of mental development.

Sex for Beginners

Just as there is controversy over the current management emphasis in schools and its resulting pressure on children, there is also controversy over the new sex education and its impact on children. The idea of sex education is not new, of course. Around the turn of the century, G. Stanley Hall discovered, via his questionnaires, that adolescent women believed that they could become pregnant by kissing; he thus advocated sex education posthaste. In the same way, boys had many misconceptions of the harm (brain rotting, early death, and so forth) that would be produced by masturbation. Early sex education was meant primarily to correct misinformation.[15]

This emphasis on correcting misinformation continued well into the 1950s when sex education—billed as "preparation for marriage and family life"—was most often part of home economics courses. By then, the sex education curriculum had expanded to include information about the dangers of venereal disease and premarital pregnancy. In addition, some aspects of sexual anatomy and its functions were taught in courses on human biology. Such material, however, was reserved for junior and senior high school students.

In the late 1960s, sex education in the schools, in response to social changes and the growth of the women's movement, began to explore some of the human aspects of sexuality. Issues such as clothing and provocative behavior, dating, peer pressure, and the personal consequences of being sexually active were discussed. Again, most of these programs were geared to students at the high school level. Such programs are probably the most frequent in our schools today except that they are now increasingly taught at the junior high level rather than at the high school level.

Still, the kind of sex education that is controversial is not the benign health education described above, but a much more explicit and value-laden program that has been adopted in many schools, partially in response to the AIDS epidemic. The new sex education programs—over 80 percent of children in schools across the United States now take some sex education course[16]—are the products of concern of mental health workers, psychologists, social workers, organizations such as Planned Parenthood, and recently, even the surgeon general of the United States. Of common concern to these groups are the results of increasing amounts of sexual activity among teenagers; unwanted pregnancy, the threat of AIDS, and the spread of other sexually transmitted diseases. The new sex educators want not only to educate and inform but also prevent some of the negative consequences of premature and unsafe sexual activity.

The new sex education programs also include material with another goal—sexual adjustment and awareness. These programs aim to help young people feel more comfortable in expressing the many facets of their sexuality, to be more sensitive to the needs of their partners and accepting of other lifestyles, and to enjoy their sexuality as a normal and healthy part of their lives. Many proponents of this kind of sex education, such as Surgeon General C. Everett Koop, believe that the presence of AIDS demands that children be taught, and taught early, the realities of sexual activity. He says, "There is now no doubt that we need sex education in the schools and that it must include information on heterosexual and homosexual relationships."[17]

The new courses on sex education include much more than anatomy; they deal with such issues as dating behavior, abortion, contraception, homosexuality, masturbation, mental illness, and death and dying. As Harvey Fineberg, dean of the Harvard School of Public Health, says, "AIDS will definitely change the nature of sex education as we know it. It will lead to more open, explicit discussions about condoms and other strategies for safe sex. . . . we are at a point where sex education is no longer a matter of morals—it's a matter of life and death."[18] The teaching technique is usually discussion, which is often triggered by educational films such as *Who Happens to Be Gay*, about homosexuals, or *We Were Just Too Young*, which depicts a teenage couple trying to rear a child with little money and frequent separations.

The following excerpt conveys the flavor of some of the discussions that can occur in a sex education class. This one is from teacher Thomas Lundgren's seventh-grade "Family Life and Health" course:

> *The course separates the sexes for two or three days a year because girls do not want to discuss sanitary protection in front of boys, and boys are just as embarrassed to talk about wet dreams in a mixed class. When students talk about the emergence of heterosexuality and homosexuality, Lundgren says, "we tell them we're just giving them an educated guess, and use an analogy with right-and left-handedness, that sexual orientation is something that is established very early in life."*

Lundgren talks about condoms ("No glove, no love" is a popular class mnemonic), and abortion is a fact of life.[19]

The problem is, of course, that what may be appropriate for seventeen-year-olds may not be appropriate for younger children. Inevitably, however, the conviction that "earlier is better," which so dominates today's educational climate, means that such programs will be and are being used with preteen and young teenagers who may be given more information than they want or need. The real question is not whether sex education should be provided in the schools but, rather, whether what is offered in the name of sex education is meaningful and useful to the age groups for whom it is provided. Unfortunately, the answer is often "no," and many young people are exposed to programs and information that reflect adult anxieties about teenage sexuality much more than the very real concerns and anxieties experienced by the young people to whom the programs are directed.

For some, questions about the effectiveness of school-based sex education for children at any age remain. When asked in an interview that appeared in *Psychology Today* whether sex education cleared up children's distorted ideas about sexuality, renowned child therapist Bruno Bettelheim replied: "No, because correct information about sex does not do away with incorrect information. That's a prejudice. New information is just grafted onto the misinformation and leads to greater confusion. Right here in Palo Alto, a colleague's daughter came home from school and said 'We saw a movie that shows where babies come from.' Her mother asked her where babies come from and the little girl said 'Babies are brought by the nurse to the mother, I saw it in the movie.'"

Asked what good sex education might be like, Bettelheim replied: "In my opinion, sex education is impossible in the classroom. Sex education is a continuous process and it begins the moment you are born. It's in how you are bathed, how you are diapered, how you are toilet trained, in respect for the body, in the notion that bodily feelings are pleasant and that bodily functions are not disgusting. You don't learn about sex from parental nudity or by showering together. That's nonsense. How you feel about sex comes from watching how your parents live together, how they enjoy each other's company, the respect they have for each other. Not from what they do in bed to each other."[20]

And as far as classes in sex education are concerned, Bettelheim says: "I think even such classes are a danger and that they are implicated in the increase in teenage sex and teenage pregnancies. You cannot have sex education without saying that sex is natural and that most people find it pleasurable. Sex education cannot teach respect for the integrity of one's body. The problem in sex is sexual anxiety, and you cannot teach about sexual anxiety because each person has different anxieties."[21]

So there is far from total agreement as to whether sex education in the schools is beneficial to *any* age group, much less to young people approaching adolescence. One has to conclude that sex education in the schools reflects adult anxiety about young people's sexuality. The "prejudice" that early sex education will produce children with "healthy sexuality" is open to serious question—even if experts agreed what healthy sexuality is, which they do not. Sex education in the schools, given at ever younger ages and without clear-cut theoretical or research justification, is another way in which some contemporary schools are encouraging their pupils to grow up fast.

To Retain or Not to Retain

The entrance of mothers of young children into the workforce has meant that many more children than ever before are in one or another out-of-home setting for at least part of the day or week. It has been estimated that some 85 percent of children have been in out-of-home placements before entering kindergarten. Young children are in nursery schools, day-care programs, and home care programs as well as in specialized education programs such as Montessori and Waldorf. Quality of care, intellectual stimulation, and the social and emotional guidance such programs provide varies tremendously. The fact that a child has been in an out-of-home program does not, therefore, guarantee that he or she will have the same richness of experience as another child in a different program.

The demand for quality, early-childhood programs, however, far exceeds the supply. Many public elementary schools have responded to the need for out-of-home care by offering full-day kindergartens, which has created a lot of controversy. Many parents do not want their five-year-olds in a program for a whole day. On the other hand, if they do not place their child in the program, they feel that he or she might fall behind. To complicate the matter, although the full-day kindergarten is first and foremost a child-care initiative, it is often given an educational justification. It is the educational, rather than the child-care rationale, that will receive funding. Accordingly, although a developmentally appropriate day kindergarten should be a half-day of hands-on learning experiences in the morning and nap and quiet time in the afternoon, this often does not happen. The kindergarten is now seen as preparation for first grade and a place where children learn their letters and numbers.

The large number of preschool children in out-of-home settings, together with the widespread popularity of full-day kindergartens, has changed expectations of what children should know upon entering first grade. Prior to the 1960s, when less than 40 percent of children were in early-childhood programs or attending half-day kindergarten, the first grade had to be open and flexible. Children of the same chronological age were at vastly different levels of intellectual, social, and emotional development. First-grade teachers had to deal with children who might be academically advanced but socially immature, and vice versa.

With the prevalence of early childhood programs, expectations with regard to first grade have changed. Today, literacy and numeracy skills are regarded as the prerequisite to success in the first grade. Yet as I suggested above, this expectation is unwarranted. First of all, early childhood programs vary tremendously from little more than baby-sitting to rich, intellectually, socially, stimulating program. Second, although early childhood is a period of rapid intellectual growth, young children grow at different rates. Children of the same chronological age and IQ may nonetheless be at very different places in their ability to acquire literacy and numeracy skills.

The growing number of public schools that require children to know their letters and numbers prior to first grade has created a crisis. A large percentage of children of an age to enter first grade do not have the requisite numeracy and literacy skills. Consequently, in some school districts, 10 to 20 percent of kindergartners are not promoted to first grade. They are either retained in kindergarten or placed in a "transition" class. The redefinition of the entering first grader as one who has attained basic reading and math skills results in many children not moving ahead with their age mates.

For some children, retention, that is, remaining in kindergarten for another year, may the least damaging decision. This is true because the curriculum in the first grade is always geared to the most advanced students. As a consequence, there is the so-called "age effect" the youngest children do more poorly than the older ones. This "effect," however, is simply a reflection of the fact that older children are more likely than younger children to have attained the new mental abilities required for learning the basic tool skills. Younger children, particularly boys, are likely to struggle in an academically demanding first grade.

The decision to retain a child, however, should be made with care and should take into account the child's maturity, the intellectual demands of the first grade, and, not least important, the individual child's feelings about the matter. I recall talking about the possibility of retention with one five-year-old who decided to stay with the kindergarten teacher she liked. She voted against the alternative, a transition class, because a girl who "glommed onto her" was in it. Retention is not bad or good in principle and the decision should always be made on the basis of the social, emotional, motor, and intellectual maturity of the child and the nature of the first grade he or she will be entering.

Another accommodation for children who do not fit the mold of the reinvented academic first-grader is to place the child in a transition class that has both kindergarten and first-grade features. Like retention, the decision to place a child in such a class should be made only after consideration of the particular transition class and the individual child. If the class is small, if it is not a dumping ground for children with nonacademic problems, and if the teacher is well trained, the transition class can be an excellent choice for children who are not quite ready for first grade. Even if these conditions are met, however, the child's feelings still need to be considered. If he or she views being in a transition class as a sign of failure, or if he or she desperately wants to be with peers in the regular classroom, these feelings need to be taken seriously. Even the best transition class may not benefit a child who resents the placement. Transition class placement always has to be made on an individual basis.

A third accommodation to the problem of kindergarten children who are not ready to move into an academic first grade is multiage grouping. In multiage groupings, children at two or three age levels are in the same classroom. For example, a classroom might have both kindergarten and first-grade children, kindergarten, first-, and second-grade children, or first- and second-grade children. Such groupings, reminiscent of the one-room schoolhouse, have a number of advantages. For one thing, depending on the group, only half or a third of the children are new to the classroom; this eases their incorporation into the group. Second, teachers get to know the children better when they have them for more than one year and are better able to adapt the curriculum to their needs and abilities. Third, children are able to work with others at the same ability level, quite apart from chronological age.

Like the other options, multiage grouping is not a cure-all and presents its own challenges. Most teachers have not been trained to work with children at different skill levels and may find working with such a wide range of abilities and skills somewhat daunting. Although multiage grouping has the advantage of having the same teacher with children for two or three years, this can, in some cases, be a disadvantage. If there is a mismatch between the personality of the child and that of the teacher, this will be aggravated if the child remains in the classroom for a second or third year. Finally, some parents worry that academic standards for older children will be lowered (dumbed down) by having younger children in the classroom. These obstacles are not insurmountable, but successful multiage grouping takes a lot of work and dedication.

There is a great deal of controversy about the retention issue. Some educators claim that these children who are less mature than their age mates should be given the "gift of time" that retention or transition classes permit. Other educators present research evidence to show that children who are retained or in transition classes do not do better academically than those who are socially promoted. They point out that children who are held back, and are larger than their age mates, may suffer lowered self-esteem. I have spoken to parents who were gratified with the effects of having held their child back and others who wished they had not done it.

The problem becomes particularly difficult if the child's birth date comes close to the cut-off date for entering kindergarten or first grade. Although there are no sure tests for whether a child will succeed in first grade, my belief is that social skills are more important than academic skills. To be successful in first grade a child must have three basic social skills:

1. He or she must be able to listen to an adult and to follow instructions.
2. He or she must be about to start a task and to bring it to completion on his or her own.
3. He or she must be able to work cooperatively with other children, to take turns, stand in line, and share.

If a child, even with a birth date close to the cut-off, has these skills, learning literacy and numeracy skills is easy. On the other hand, a child who knows his numbers and letters but does not have these social skills is going to have a hard time.

There is no simple answer to the problems created by the academic demands of the contemporary first grade. In making the decision whether to retain a child, the important point to remember is that readiness is not in the child's head. Readiness is always a relation between the child and the class he or she will enter. There are still many first-grade teachers who are flexible and open. A child might do well with such a teacher yet do poorly with another. Knowing the classroom a child is going to enter is just as important as knowing his or her level of social, intellectual, and emotional maturity.

These practices can be used to address the particularity and irregularity of individual children. The appropriateness of any given child for any given practice, however, cannot be made on any general principle, but only after careful evaluation of the child and the classroom (both teacher and children) he or she is to join.

Readiness is not in the child's head, but rather, should always refer to the match between the child and the classroom he or she is to enter.

Rotation at an Early Age

In addition to testing and questionable subject matter, and first-grade issues, schools are engaging in other practices that hurry children. One of these is growing number of schools that are rotating elementary school students from one teacher and classroom to another for instruction in different subjects. This new focus on subject matter and away from the pupils being taught has occurred at other times in our history, particularly when education was under attack and "educational reform" was in the air.

During the early and middle decades of this century, rotation at the elementary school level appeared under a number of different labels, such as the Platoon System, the Dalton Plan, and the Winnetka Plan. Implicit in these plans was the idea that elementary education could be more effective if modeled after the junior and senior high schools. By the early 1940s, however, the ineffectiveness of rotation at the early grades became increasingly apparent and was gradually given up.

The modern outcry for educational reform was first heard in the late 1950s in response to the Russian Sputnik. It resulted in a wave of "new" curricula from the universities washing over the public schools. The wave finally receded in the 1970s but left a generation of children and parents still choking on the expert generated curricula in language, math, and science. These new curricula (such as variable-base arithmetic known as the "new" math) were given up because they were too difficult for the age groups to whom they were presented—not to mention for the parents who had to help with the homework!

Yet the next wave of modern educational reform, "back to basics," presented itself as "getting tough on kids" after a decade of presumed educational permissiveness! The realities were just the opposite. In fact "back to basics" meant going back to teacher-written and child-centered curricula. Far from being tougher on children these new "back to basics" curricula were easier! A simple example will help to make this point clear. With the new math, when a first grader was presented with the problem 2 + 2 = he or she was instructed to "make this sentence true." When we got back to basics, children were once again instructed to "find the sum." Back to basics, under the guise of getting "tough" on students, was successful at least at the elementary grades because it presented children with age-appropriate, meaningful curricula.

But the "back to basics" wave of contemporary educational reform in its turn receded with the publication mentioned earlier in 1983 of a "A Nation at Risk," which starkly documented how poorly our secondary students did in comparison with those from European and Asian countries. Still another tidal movement for educational reform was underway. A guiding theme of this new movement is "effectiveness."

It is in this spirit of making schools more "effective" that depart-mentalization has reemerged. Here lies the irony. Under the rubric of educational reform, practices long ago discarded are being res-urrected to make schooling more effective. And this despite the fact that the available research on departmentalization (Slavin, 1987) shows this practice to be *ineffective* at the elementary school level.[22]

Before looking at the reasons early departmentalization hurries children, we need to listen to some of the arguments for such a practice. The major justification for rotation is that subject-matter areas have become so specialized that it is no longer possible to be a generalist. No one teacher, so the argument goes, can be expected to keep abreast of the changes in theories and research in reading, math, social studies, and science. Children are clearly the beneficiaries when they are taught by an expert rather than by a generalist.

Specialization is clearly the direction other professions have taken with resultant increases in status and remuneration. In med-icine, for example, since no single physician can be expected to master all of the ongoing research, say both on cancer and on heart disease, we have specialties in cardiology and oncology. Attorneys likewise specialize in corporate law, in criminal cases, in probate, or in tax law. To be sure, there are still some general practitioners in both law and medicine but they have less status than the specialists. The same is already true in education. Departmentalized high school teachers are often better paid and have higher status than elementary school teachers. Perhaps these discrepancies will disappear if elementary school teachers become specialists as well.

Unfortunately, an instructional practice that may benefit teachers may not benefit children. This is the case for rotation. The reason becomes clear as soon as we look more closely at the medical and legal analogies given above. The use of these analogies implies that the child is a patient or client of the teacher and that the child will necessarily benefit from the teacher's expertise. But the child is really not a patient or client of the teacher, the child is a student of the teacher. To correctly follow the medical or legal analogy, we have to ask whether, and at what stage, the beginning medical or legal student is taught by specialists.

Before students can apply to medical school or to law school they must first complete a bachelor of arts or science degree. To attain this degree the student is required to take introductory, survey courses in the sciences, mathematics, and humanities. It is only when students move into the junior and senior years of college that they begin to take specialized courses. But even these are still more general than those taught at the graduate level. Most survey courses at the college level are taught by generalists, not by specialists. In short, specialization is for advanced students, not for beginners.

What is true at the college level is equally true at the elementary and secondary levels. A child entering school does not need to be taught by a specialist in reading or math. This is true because teaching entry-level skills requires much more knowledge about the students being taught than it does specialization in the subject matter. Like the instructor teaching introductory courses at the college level, the task of the elementary school teacher is to "capture" students and get them excited and interested about learning the subject matter as well as to teach them the basics.

By the time students reach junior high school or high school, they can begin to profit from specialization. Because they have become proficient learners, less of the teacher's attention needs to center on their personal characteristics. A high school teacher who really knows a subject can therefore be an effective instructor even if he or she is not an expert on individual students. This is much less likely to be the case for an elementary school teacher. To be sure, teachers at all levels of education should be aware of individual students as well as being knowledgeable about subject matter. But the balance shifts progressively from student to subject as the students become more advanced.

Departmentalization at the elementary level cannot, therefore, be justified on the basis of young children needing or benefitting from specialized content. Nor cannot it be justified on grounds of educational efficacy. Consider the time it takes nine-year-old children to put away their materials, move to another classroom, and set up shop at another set of desks. If this process is repeated four or five times a day, the children have spent more time in getting up and getting down than they have in learning!

In addition, elementary school children have not yet attained an integrated sense of themselves as persons, the sense of personal identity the late psychoanalyst Erik Erikson says is achieved in adolescence. At the elementary school level, children benefit from an adult who has seen them in different learning situations and at different times of the day. This adult can then reflect back to them their individual wholeness and continuity. This reflection back to the child is particularly necessary today when, with so many two-parent working families, parents are less able to play this role. With rotation, no single teacher gets to know a child well enough to be a mirror to him or her.

Even if we accept for a moment that specialization is beneficial to young children, where is it written that it is the children who must rotate? It is interesting that in all the discussion about and comparisons with Japanese education, one important practice is never mentioned. In Japan, it is the teachers, not the students, who rotate. Even at the high school level, each class has its own room. The teacher, even at the high school level has an individual desk in a large teacher's room. The Japanese arrangement reflects a belief that keeping young people together and rotating teachers is not only more efficient but also has many social benefits. The class develops a cohesion and sense of mutual support that benefits both learning and adaptation to the larger society.

Departmentalization and rotation at the elementary school level hurries children. It hurries them both on a day-to-day basis by requiring so many additional adjustments to new teachers and classrooms, and it hurries them on a long-term basis by depriving them of a teacher who knows them sufficiently well to reflect back to them their continuity and wholeness as persons. Such reflections help young people attain an integrated sense of identity as adolescents. Finally, rotation at an early age deprives children of an important educational marker. When rotation goes on at the elementary school level, children can no longer look forward to it at the junior high and high school levels as a marker of greater maturity and independence. It has lost its value as a rite of passage.

Many parents who read these pages will conclude that I am yet another advocate of permissiveness in the sense of being soft on kids; but this really is not the case. I believe in discipline, in hard work, and in learning basic skills. I do not believe that children should be left to their own devices, nor that rules are made to be broken. I am opposed to schooling practices that not only will not work but that may harm children.

A high school student told me recently that she had four hours of homework each day. Then she demanded, "Don't you think I am being hurried?" I asked whether her homework was read and commented upon, and she allowed that it was. I asked whether she had some study hall hours during the day when she could do some of her homework. She allowed that indeed she did. My response then, was "No, you are not being hurried. Your homework is meaningful and not excessive given your schedule."

A certain amount of stress and pressure are important and healthy for children to realize their full powers. It is only when the stresses and pressures become inappropriate and extraordinary, as they are in many of our schools today, that expectations and demands become hurrying and the stress unhealthy. Many of the current initiatives in education that are labeled "reform," put children at risk for no demonstrable purposes.

The point is that "quick fixes" in education never work. We know what good education is. Substantial learning is taking place in many urban, suburban, and private schools that provide well-trained and committed teachers, reasonable class size, and adequate materials and support. Pressuring children to get certain marks on tests that at best measure rote knowledge is hardly the way to improve the education of our children. What good is it if children can read but not understand what they read or if they know how to compute but not where, when, or what to compute?

Our educational establishment suffers from the same ills as did our industrial establishment: it has become too product-oriented and has ignored the workers. By pressing for ever faster, more efficient production, the needs of the workers—self-esteem, pride in their work, and a sense of accomplishment—suffer. The result is shoddy workmanship, absenteeism, and lack of commitment to the job and the industry. The school's response, to push children even harder, is bound to fail.

Industry is beginning to recognize that workers are people who have a need to participate in decision making and to learn different facets of the industry they are involved in. Companies such as Chrysler that are using these new approaches are finding that quality is up and absenteeism is down. If we have to see our schools as factories, then we should learn from our modern-day factory experience. Hurrying workers and threatening them do not work. Treating them as human beings who want to take pride in their work, who don't want to be confined to the same routine, and who want the opportunity to express their opinions and to have those opinions taken seriously, does work.

Such an approach, in industry or schooling, is not permissive—it is democratic in the best sense of the term. Children need direction and limits, but they also need to be able to make choices that are appropriate for them to make and to take appropriate responsibilities. And teachers need to be empowered to have a say in the governance of the schools in which they teach. Democracy is the balance between total control and total freedom, and what we need in education, as in industry, is true democracy. Only when the values upon which this country was founded begin to permeate our educational and industrial plants will we begin to realize our full human and production potentials.

A closing word about dynamics: Schools and school personnel are currently under pressure to produce improved test scores of pupils. We have seen that when people are under stress they become egocentric and do not—cannot—appreciate other people's needs or interests. Hence the new "measurement-driven programs" ignore what we know about children for the same reason that parent schedules hurry children—the adults who are involved cannot put to use their knowledge about children and education. If we take some of the pressure off schools and school administrators, we will take some of the pressure off children.

4

••••••••••

The Dynamics of Hurrying: The Media

••••••••••

Media—including television, radio, newspapers, magazines, and movies—extend our senses, as Marshall McLuhan[1], the Canadian media analyst, has suggested. The progression from silent films to "talkies," from black-and-white to color films, and the contemporary transformation of classic black-and-white films into computer-generated color, all attest to the movie industry's efforts to extend our senses. Likewise, the trajectory from black-and-white to color television, and to ever larger (and smaller portable) screens as well as the progression toward improved sound and visual (DVD) quality speak to the television industry's exertions to extend and enhance our sensory experience in space and time.

In contrast to the extension of our senses by the media, education seeks to transmit our cultural past, to stock our memory. Schools are charged with transmitting accumulated knowledge and skills, and, as such, necessarily represent our cultural past rather than our cultural future. As we have seen, despite our knowledge about children's development, all too many schools still regard children as empty bottles on an assembly line of grades—each grade fills the bottle up a little more, the bottle representing the child's memory. What the schools fail to appreciate is that the "bottles" are already overflowing with information about the present and future that is provided by the media that now includes the Internet.

Television

Increased Access. Television, including that now available on the internet, is unique in that it gives us unmediated access to live events in all parts of the world. No other media can do this. The presentation of news is a good example of television's speciality. Newspapers and films necessarily present news events after they happen. Radio can report events as they happen but the events are colored by the words and the voice of the broadcaster. Few broadcasters are as believalbe as Orson Welles who, in his famous radio program, "The War of the Worlds," convinced his listeners that Earth was being attacked by Martians. More commonly, radio requires us to retranslate words into sensory images and thus stimulates the imagination.

Television, however, engages our senses immediately and does not always require the verbal mediation of a broadcaster to be conveyed or understood. Even young children don't need to understand the verbal description of tragedies taking place on television—the horrible images speak for themselves. Because television information does not require verbal encoding or decoding to extend our experience, it is very accessible to young children and sometimes hurries them into witnessing terrifying events never before witnessed by this age group.

Several years ago, this fact was brought home to me in a very unsettling way. Shortly after the story of the young mother who had drowned her two sons by driving the family car into a pond hit the news wires and television programs, I began receiving phone calls from worried mothers all over the country whose children had heard the story and seen the car dragged out of the water. Their children were asking them questions like, "Mommy, are you going to drown me?" I encouraged these mothers to reassure their children, hug them, and tell them how much they loved them and that they would never do anything to hurt them. Even so, I am sure this story impacted children everywhere, learning fears and doubts not easily erased.

With television, therefore, children no longer have to be able to read, or to translate a broadcaster's words, in order to observe events that are happening in distant places. Television is now to the child what radio is to the adult. With radio, the adult has access to news, drama, and entertainment at home without the intermediate step of reading. With television, children have access to news, drama, and entertainment without having to translate words into images. The images are already there.

Television, then, has special appeal to young children because it allows them unmediated access to previously inaccessible information. Indeed, statistics show that young children watch television more than any other age group and the amount of time young people spend watching television decreases with increasing age.[2] This phenomenon is, in part, a function of schooling. Adolescents spend less time in school than grade-school children, but they still watch less television. Television has somewhat less appeal for adolescents. Teenagers' mental abilities make it more challenging to extend their senses by means of the more complicated media of radio or print.

Lessened Parental Control. Although television removes many of the intellectual barriers to information once confronted by young children, it also lowers another barrier that is not limited to any particular age group. This is the barrier of parental discretion and monitoring. Parents usually have some idea about which books, magazines, and movies they want, or do not want, their children to read or to watch. But with television it is often impossible to know what is coming in advance of the event. In many ways, television renders us relatively impotent to control the information flow to our children. With the introduction of VCRs, cable television, and the V chip, this is much less true than it was in the past. Nonetheless, many parents are so conditioned to not exercising control over television that they may still feel helpless and fail to make use of the monitoring tools that are available.

Homogenization. Television not only makes information more accessible to the young and lessens parental control, it also serves to homogenize social class, ethnic, cultural, and age differences. As early as 1966, theater critic Louis Kronenberger wrote:

> *What I think must be said is that television is not just a great force in modern life, but that it virtually is modern life. What, one might ask, doesn't it do? It gives us—be we rich, poor, snowbound, bedrid-*

den or slow-witted—the time, the weather, the small news, big news,
sport news, now in spoken headlines, now in pictured narrative,
now at the very scene of the crime or the coronation itself. It plays,
sings, whistles and dances for us, takes us to movies and theaters,
concerts and operas, prizefights and ball games, ski jumps and ten-
nis tournaments. It delivers babies, probes adolescents, psychoana-
lyzes adults. It dramatizes floods, fires, earthquakes, takes you to the
top of an alp or the bottom of an ocean or whirling through space;
lets you see a tiger killed or a tiger kill. It becomes a hustings, or a
house of worship; guesses your age, your weight, your job, your
secret, guides you through prisons, orphan asylums, lunatic asy-
lums; lets you see a Winston Churchill buried or a Lee Oswald shot.
It teaches you French, rope dancing, bird calls and first aid; pro-
vides debates and seminars and symposiums, quizzes and contests
and it tells you jokes, gags, wheezes, wisecracks, jokes and jokes.[3]

Television extends the senses of everyone; it does not discriminate. According to McLuhan, television "retribalizes" us in that:

electric circuitry has overthrown the regime of "time" and "space"
and confronts us instantly and continuously with the concerns of
all other people. It has reconstituted dialogue on a global scale. Its
message is Total Change, ending psychic social economic and politi-
cal parochialism. The old civic, state and national groupings have
become unworkable. Nothing can be further from the spirit of the
new technology than "a place for everything and everything in its
place."[4]

Although McLuhan probably overstates his case (human inertia
being what it is), the homogenization of human experience is certainly a fact. For example, an estimated 1 billion people watched the
2000 Olympics in Sydney. Such a universal experience, and it is but
one of many (American television series are popular all over the
world, as well as singers and rock groups from England, Ireland, the
United States, and many other countries) is bound to have a homog-
enizing impact. Even in remote, small islands in the Caribbean, the
inhabitants give evidence, in their clothing and food choices, of the
homogenization of styles and tastes promoted by television.

The homogenization across social, ethnic, and geographical boundaries is also true for age boundaries. Obviously, television programs are not rigidly age-graded. To be sure, children's programs like *Barney* and *Telletubbies* are geared to the very youngest age groups. Likewise, the Saturday morning programs of cartoons and adventure programs are directed at children. But even young children watch programs designed for older audiences. A case in point is the program *Dawson's Creek,* which is watched by children although it is aimed at late adolescents. This show, and others like it, deals with sexual activity, drugs, and emotional disturbance. Through the medium of these serial dramas, children are initiated into issues and problems that are age-inappropriate.

The reasons for this homogenization, as television commentator Jeffrey Cowan suggests, are largely economic:

> *To some extent, the sameness and exploitaitiveness of television—to which so many viewers have a legitimate objection—is a function of the industry's curious economic structure. Unlike other media, such as books and newspapers—which derive their income from consumers as well as advertisers—television relies solely on advertising for its revenue. Since the vast majority of companies that advertise on television want to reach an 18 to 40 year old urban audience, there is little incentive to develop programming that appeals primarily to people who are older than forty-nine, younger than eighteen or who live in rural areas. If middle-aged or elderly people in a small town in rural America feel that television ignores their tastes and offers little that is nourishing to children, they are right.[5]*

Targeting a limited age group not only deprives children of age-appropriate programming, it also forces them to watch programs meant for more mature audiences.

The Fantasy-to-Reality Teeter-Totter. Family sitcoms are often watched by children. These sitcoms, however, alternate between fantasy and realism. These shows have value in that they expose children to alternative lifestyles. Nonetheless, the more realistic sitcoms can sometimes be troubling, particularly to young children.

During the 1950s and 1960s fantasy families dominated the television screen. Shows like *Leave It to Beaver, My Three Sons,* and *Father*

Knows Best presented homes that were well furnished and compulsively clean. Parents were always available for advice, guidance, and to set limits. The issues were often appropriate to children and teenagers, such as dealing with winning and losing, getting homework done, and dating. Even the shows that foreshadowed into the realism of the 1970s by depicting single parents, such as *The Courtship of Eddie's Father* and *The Partridge Family,* or blended families such as *The Brady Bunch,* still presented ideal homes and dealt with child-centered issues.

Then came the 1970s. The changes in television families during this decade are well described by Peggy Charren (founder of the Action for Children's Television advocacy group) and historian Martin W. Sandler, who wrote at the end of that steamroller decade:

> *With the social upheavals of the last ten years, TV Families underwent great changes. Today's so-called situation comedies deal with real-life problems: marital infidelity, unemployment, impotence, divorce, alcoholism. Norman Lear revolutionized the genre with shows that tore apart old TV cliches.* Maude *is to sentimental family fare what* M*A*S*H *is to* Dr. Kildare.

> *Virtually the only healthy marriages on television exist in the past or on fantasy shows. As television critic Jeff Greenfield has noted, Marriage on television today is a cross between a bad joke, a bad dream, and a nostalgia trip. Finding a contemporarily, happily married couple on television is like finding an empty taxi in midtown Manhattan at 5 PM—possible but not very likely. More often than not, prime-time TV marriages are troubled with the typical soap opera woes, infidelity, incompatibility, and incurability. Single parents abound on shows ranging from* The Love Boat *to* Mork and Mindy *to* Hill Street Blues.[6]

Yet the more things change, the more they remain the same. By the tail end of the 1980s, television had returned to the fantasy family sitcom of the 1960s. As dramatist Nora Ephron wrote in 1988:

> *Dr. Cliff Huxtable, aka Bill Cosby, is sitting in his living room. His wife, Clair, walks in from the kitchen. "Are you free Thursday at four?" she asks. Huxtable pauses a beat. "Yes," he says.*

It's Friday afternoon. Huxtable's son-in-law, Elvin, comes into the kitchen. Clair, dressed for success in a stunning beige blouse and skirt, takes a roast out of the oven and bastes it. "Would you like to stay for dinner?" she asks.

And so it goes in the sitcom dual career home. Huxtable, an OB-GYN, knows he is free Thursday at four without consulting his appointment book. His wife, a partner in a law firm, who has three of five children still living at home and no household help, has time and energy on a weekday to cook a delicious dinner. One thing is clear: The American viewer continues to love the fantasy world of the family sitcom. The Cosby Show *[was] still at the top of the ratings [as was]* Family Ties. *These shows are relentlessly upbeat and fun.*[7]

If the 1980s were a return to fantasy, during the 1990s family sitcoms again reverted to realism. In *Roseanne,* a working-class family struggles with child-rearing, economic, and gender issues. In *Everybody Loves Raymond,* a couple lives across the street from their intrusive in-laws and the plots revolve around the conflicts of this living arrangement. In *King of Queens,* a working-class couple lives together with her widowed father. Among other things, the show deals with the problems of accommodating a parent into a grown child's household. *Seventh Heaven* is about a somewhat dysfunctional family in which the parents try to reconcile occupational demands with child rearing; their children cope with often unconventional disciplinary practices.

What remains common across these decade-to-decade swings from fantasy to realism in television programming generally, and in family sitcoms in particular, is the targeting of the eighteen to forty-nine age group. In so doing, television producers often treat children as grown up. Although this is harmless in many cases, in shows such as *Everybody Loves Raymond, Malcolm in the Middle, Who Wants to Be a Millionaire? Survivor,* or *Jeopardy!* it may set a precedent for children watching other adult shows such *ER, NYPD Blue, JAG,* and *Touched by an Angel.* Owing in part, perhaps, to viewing such shows, even young children seem quite knowledgeable about the major issues of our time—drugs, violence, crime, divorce, single parenting, inflation, and so on. What they are able to do with this information is quite another matter. Television exposes children to experiences they could never have had without it. But exposure is one thing, and understanding is another. Making experiences more accessible does not make them any less confusing or any less disturbing.

Therefore, one consequence to children of television homogenization and the decade-long swings between fantasy and reality is to create what might be called *pseudo-sophistication*. School-age children today know much more than they understand. They are able to talk about nuclear fission, tube worms at 20,000 fathoms, space shuttles, chat rooms, and surfing the Net. They also give the impression of being conversant with the topics of sex, violence, and crime. But much of this information is largely verbal. One has only to listen to preteens talk about *Dawson's Creek* to appreciate their superficial understanding of the complex interactions of the program. Adults, however, are often taken in by this pseudo-sophistication and treat children as if they were as informed as they sound.

Ironically, the pseudo-sophistication that is the effect of television hurrying children encourages parents and adults to hurry them even more. But children who sound, behave, and look like adults, nonetheless, still feel and think like children. Of course, this is not unique to children. As we age, we sometimes do not feel as old as our bodies tell us we are. Psychological aging and physical aging are often not on the same tracks. A young girl, made-up and dressed in a seductive outfit, still feels and thinks of herself as a young girl, not as a young woman.

Advertising. Yet another way in which television hurries children is through advertising. This has become especially true in the 1980s with the deregulation thrust of the Federal Communications Commission (FCC). In 1984, the FCC overturned a ten-year policy against "full-length" commercials on children's television. Whereas before the commercial message was clearly marked off from the program, this is no longer true for many children's programs. The commercialism of children's marketing is exemplified by the Golden Marble awards given to the most successful advertising campaigns directed at children. The products promoted by these advertisements, however, do not promote the well-being of children. One of the past winners was for promoting the *Alien Autopsy* action figure. Other products that promote high fat, high sugar, and heavily salted foods to children have also won awards. The following disturbing statistics for what has happened in the decade of the 1990s was compiled by the Media Center at the Judge Baker Child Guidance Center in Boston:

- Children consume forty hours of media a week and 20,000 commercials a year.
- Corporations spend more than $12 billion a year marketing to children—well over twenty times the amount spent ten years ago.
- One-third of twelve-year-old girls try to lose weight through dieting, vomiting, laxatives, or diet pills.
- Discontent about body image is directly related to how often girls read fashion magazines.
- The most frequently advertised and best-selling toys are linked to media.
- Children play less creatively with toys linked to movies and television.
- Children are more vulnerable to advertising than adults.
- Advertisers work with psychologists to develop marketing strategies aimed at children.
- The United States regulates advertising to children less than most other democratic nations.[8]

Over the last three decades, therefore, advertising has become more age-conscious, but programming has not. Children in the United States today influence the spending of $500 billion each year and are bombarded with commercials for products that range from violent toys to junk food. Children are much less able to recognize commercials than adolescents and adults, and, therefore, are more influenced by them; advertisers hurry children into psychologically and nutritionally unhealthy consumerism.

The Television Mirror. Television hurries children in still other ways. Television, it has been said, is an electronic mirror that reflects a vague or ambiguous image. As society is complex and many faceted, broadcasting reflects a variety of images. These are never precisely focussed and completely clear. . . . Looking at a blurred or vague image, different individuals see different things . . . television programs mean different things to different people and mean different things to one person at different times, depending upon attitude and mood.[9]

From this standpoint, television serves as a way of finding out who and what we are. By identifying with a television character we find out more about ourselves or try and make ourselves more like the character we identify with. How children are portrayed to children thus reflects how society views children and also provides images with whom children identify and seek to emulate. My middle son always wanted to be like Danny, the red-headed cut-up of the Partridge family.

What, then, can we say about children as they are depicted on television? One feature characterizes them all—they are precocious:

> *The children [on television] are too well behaved and are reasonable beyond their years. All the children pop in with exceptional insights. On many of the shows the children's insights are apt to be unexpectedly philosophical. The lesson seems to be "Listen to little children carefully and you will learn great truths."[9]*

There are additional messages in these television depictions of sagacious children (the most recent being, at this writing, Malcolm, in the show *Malcolm in the Middle,* who has uncanny insights into adult issues). To children they provide models of emotional and intellectual precocity, thus constituting a kind of hurrying to behave in wise, mature ways. And to adults, this kind of depiction may add to expectations that children be more wise, more sage, and more understanding than we have a right to expect.

Magazines and Books

Television has had a major impact on other media that reach children, such as books and magazines.

Television can be credited with the virtual destruction of the very bottom layer of American popular culture—the comic book, the pulp magazine, the radio serial, the hillbilly movie. Newton Minnow's wasteland has been in fact a flood over an abyss which used to be filled by garbage a good deal worse than the featureless rubble of routine television.[10]

Clearly, a comic book like Bugs Bunny cannot compete with the cartoon *Bugs Bunny*; nor can the Power Ranger comic compete with the *Power Ranger* program. The demise of comic books, however trashy they may be, is unfortunate in a way because many children learned to read by reading comics. The comics provided a motivation for reading that was as strong as the child's desire to be up on Saturday morning to watch the cartoons.

In the 1960s the comic book began to be replaced by *MAD* magazine, which has been in existence for almost fifty years, just about making it about the same age as television. As *MAD* magazine discovered, the new [television] audience found the scenes and themes of ordinary life as funny as anything in the comic strip "Lil Abner" (depicting life in the backwoods village of Dogpatch). "*MAD* magazine simply transferred the world of ads into the world of the comic book and it did this just when the TV image was beginning to eliminate the comic book by direct rivalry."[10] What is unique about *MAD* magazine it that it provides children not with fantasy but rather with satire. Al Feldstein, former editor of *MAD* magazine, wrote:

> *What we did was to take the absurdities of the adult world that youngsters were facing and show kids that the adult world is not omnipotent, that their parents were telling the kids to be honest, not to lie and yet were cheating on their income tax. We told them there was a lot of garbage out in the world and you've got to be aware of it. Everything you read in the papers is not necessarily true. What you see on television is mostly lies. You're going to have to learn to think for yourself.[11]*

What is significant about *MAD* magazine is that satire is really only understood when children become adolescent. In a September 2000 issue, under the heading "Letters to Britney Spears," is the following from a seven-year-old girl: "Dear Britney, what size breast implants should I get now?" In a December 1999 issue under the title "Monica's Closet," was the following from a distressed woman:

"My life is spinning out of control, I've come to a sad realization." "What's that?" "I'm too old to be a Bimbo."

MAD magazine, then, is for adolescents, not for children, although the age of readers has been dropping. Originally the magazine was targeted for older adolescents (ages fifteen to seventeen) and college students, but in recent years the mean age of the readership has been about thirteen. And as the readership has grown younger, the material has grown racier. In the February 2000 issue, under the heading of "An 8 Step Guide for WB Network Teen Wanabes": "When having an affair with your teacher it is considered bad form to ask for a higher grade in addition to the sex."

What has to be understood about *MAD* magazine is not so much its content as its form. Children who have been hurried to grow up fast have many feelings, fears, anger, and anxieties that they are often unable to express. Humor has always been a way to express dangerous feelings—almost every joke has some aggressive or sexual content. Thus, *MAD* magazine provides young people with some comic relief from the pressures of growing up fast. By making sexuality, drugs, and hucksterism into a joke, young people are able to distance themselves from some of the stresses of being exposed to too much too soon. *MAD* is a stress relief valve but, unfortunately, only for bright children and adolescents who have the mental ability to appreciate the satire.

Magazines for girls have also reflected women's changing values. In the 1970s and 1980s, magazines such as *Seventeen* offered serious articles about politics, the environment, and careers as well as the usual articles on health, beauty, and relationships. In the 1990s, however, there was a reversion to articles on grooming, diet, "How to Get Your Guy," and fewer serious intellectual pieces. In addition, the models in these magazines have become progressively thinner; many of the models appear anorexic. Again, these models reflect advertising efforts and pressures. Perversely, clothing styles for young girls have gotten more sexy; styles for adolescent girls sometimes look more childlike.

Over the last three decades, there have also been cyclical changes in children's books. Like television, during the 1970s there was a dramatic shift toward a new realism and a breaking down of many traditional taboos. Books for young children such as those of

Ezra Jack Keats, *Whistle for Willie* and *Hi, Cat!* depict in rich colors and sensitive words episodes in the life of ghetto children. And books by Maurice Sendak created a stir, particularly *In the Night Kitchen,* in which the young hero's penis is clearly evident. One cannot really quarrel with sensitive, artistically pleasing books such as these other than to say that the new realism is present even in books for young children. Unfortunately, there are few writers for young children as sensitive and gifted as Keats and Sendak.

The 1970s new realism also produced a lot of tasteless junk for children. For example, in one story by Carl Withers, *Eenie-Meenie-Minie-Mo,* some black bears fall into white paint. Their mother doesn't know they are hers until the paint happens to wash off. The story was, I imagine, meant to convey the message that "black is beautiful," but why is washing off whiteness required for this recognition? Bringing in whiteness simply confounds the issue for children who need to be valued for themselves and not in contrast to those of another color.

In the 1980s, the children's book field saw a swing back to fantasy and away from realism comparable to what happened in television. This is particularly evident in what has come to be called the Young Adult book field, books that help teenagers make the transition from child to adult literature. The realism of the 1970s has given way to treacle romances and low-quality Sci-Fi. Like the family sitcoms of the 1980s, present-day teen romances seem to express a nostalgia for the past: "The romances seem to want to press kids back to the 1950's," said Donald R. Gallo, a professor of English at Central Connecticut State University. "The characters are predominately white suburban Protestants speaking standard English in nuclear families with traditional values. You rarely see even subsidiary characters who are minorities."[13]

Author Walter Dean Myers reinforces Professor Gallo's point.

In 1974 there were more than 900 children's books in print on the black experience. This is a small number of books considering that more than 2,000 children's books are published annually. But by 1984, this number was cut in half. For every 100 books published this year (1986) there will be one published on the black experience.

Walking through the aisles at this year's American Library Association meeting in New York was, for me, a sobering and disheartening experience. Were black writers suddenly incapable of writing well? Of course not, but we were perceived as no longer able to sell well.[14]

Perhaps this reaction against the realism of the 1970s was predictable. Our society seems to go to extremes, which means that the correctives need to be equally extreme. The return to the romantic image of the family and one-color society is perhaps a reaction to the too-abrupt introduction to the real world of the previous decade and the heavy pressure to grow up fast. In the meantime, these schlock romances seem to feed young people's intense need to fantasize about less troubled, less hurried family and adolescent life.

Another thrust of the 1970s was also blunted in the 1980s and 1990s, namely, efforts to have a kind of "unisex" literature. In the 1980s and 1990s, the literary preferences of children and adolescents remain gender linked. Boys, librarians say, prefer books on the military, racing, trains, airplanes, mysteries, reptiles, all kinds of sports, and ghosts and monsters (especially books based on old horror movies like *The Mummy* and *The Wolf Man*).

Boys tend to speak less of subject than of sensibility. According to eleven-year-old Casimo Nozkowski, "Boys like really funny books, like Daniel Pinkwater's *Invasion of the Fat Men.*" I asked a number of boys, including my nine-year-old son Bruno, about what kinds of books they liked. Bruno, echoing the answers of many of the boys, said proudly, "Boys like disgusting books." The name mentioned most often in this context was Thomas Rockwell's *How to Eat Fried Worms*—as its title suggests, this is a novel that confronts the ultimate challenge.[15]

Girls, in contrast, prefer mystery and romance. In addition, boys prefer shorter books than do girls. Girls get involved with books, whereas boys expect the books to involve them. Boys, too, often will not read books that seem to be addressed to women. In my own case, I deprived myself of the pleasures of reading Jane Austen until middle age because of an unconscious prejudice, picked up in adolescence, that she was a woman's author and hence too "mushy" for a boy to read.

Sex differences in young adult literature are shown in yet another way. Coming-of-age stories about girls are usually published as juveniles, while those about boys originate on the adult lists. This pattern may have been set up by early prototypes, but it has held true long enough so that it appears to reflect general social attitudes about the differences between boys and girls. In 1942 the landmark girl's romance *Seventeenth Summer* by Maureen Daly was published on a children's book list; nine years later, the adolescent boy's classic, *The Catcher in the Rye* by J. D. Salinger, was brought out by Little, Brown as an adult novel. Since then, stories about girls have continued to accentuate romance and have usually been marketed as children's books. Stories about boys, on the other hand, such as Golding's *Lord of the Flies* and Knowles's *A Separate Peace* are apt to examine broader issues and be included in the publisher's general trade catalogue.[16]

In the second edition of this book I came to appreciate that whether the book dealt with realism or fantasy, the most important thing was the quality of the story. I wrote:

> *I understand, now, however, that the issue is not really fantasy versus realism. What is most important is that the books be of high quality. What we call a book, fiction or non-fiction, may have nothing to do with how the young person reads it. Good writing, whether fiction or non-fiction, enriches our experience and the nature of that enrichment is always unique. We can never know what a young person will take from a book. But whatever it is, the extent of enrichment will be proportional to the quality of the book.*

> *Regardless of the cycles in the focus of children's fiction, reading will remain a healthy counterpoise to hurrying and stress. Reading is under children's control and they can make their own choices and proceed at their own pace. Young people can and do find books that are nicely suited to where they are in their social and emotional development. In the large world over which young people have so little control, the smaller world of books is a welcome oasis.*

I wrote these words before the appearance of R. L. Stine's remarkably successful Goosebumps books that first appeared in the mid-1990s and sold more than 300 million copies. Although not great literature, Stine's prose is simple and attuned to the language of the age group he writes for. He also appeals to children's attraction to being scared in safe ways, that is, by reading. But what really reinforced the words written earlier, however, was the publication of the Harry Potter books by English writer J. K. Rowling. About a young boy who engages in wizardy, these books have taken the world by storm. As Paul Gray wrote in *Time* magazine:

> *But then the whole Harry Potter hubbub seems outlandish—the proliferating pages that fans are posting on the Web, the word of mouth testimonials from parents marvelling that their non-reading children (even boys) are tearing through the Harry Potter books, and begging for more, the confessions of a growing number of adults that they find the books irresistible. . . .*
>
> *And, in fact, it is not very hard to figure out the rules governing the Harry Potter books. Place appealing characters in interesting, perilous situations, and leave the outcome in doubt for as long as possible. Nothing new here, nothing that story tellers as far back as Homer did not grasp and gainfully employ. But, as devoted Harry Potter fans have learned, knowing a magic charm is not the same as performing magic. Rowling's secret is as simple and mysterious as her uncanny ability to nourish the human hunger for enchantment: she knows how to feed the desire not just to read a story, but to live it as well.[17]*

The Movies

Like television and books, movies have alternated between fantasy and realism in topics, in language, and in characterization. In the 1990s there seems to be plenty of both. With respect to movie fantasy, there are animal stories such as *Babe, Dinosaur, Ants,* and *Chicken Run.* At the same time there are plenty of realistic movies. It is hard to believe in this era of *Something About Mary, American*

Beauty, and *Boys Don't Cry* that there was once a media censorship group, the Hayes Office, that operated in the 1930s, 1940s, and 1950s. The Hayes Office banned scenes with a couple in bed together and forbade the use of words like "hell" and "damn" from being used by actors and actresses onscreen. The 1960s saw the overthrow of most moralistic prohibitions and by the 1990s audiences had become so accustomed to four-letter words and nudity in films that they are neither surprised nor appalled by what is shown on the screen.

By the 1990s, parents have become so numbed to the swearing, nudity, overt sexual activity, and violence in movies that we have become less vigilant about letting our children watch this material. Additionally, the advent of cable television and rented CDs has made monitoring young people's film watching even more difficult for us. Film ratings, like PG, R, and X, are ambiguous at best, and neither parents nor children seem to take them too seriously. Since even X-rated films are available to children at home on late-night cable television, theater restrictions are something of a joke.

Films, however, affect young people in a somewhat different way from television and books. In films, there is a rather clear delineation between the actor or the actress and the role portrayed. This may have to do with the fact that Hollywood markets "stars" in a way that television does not. What may influence children even more than what they see on the screen, therefore, are the real-life escapades of youthful heroes and heroines. Whether or not Leonardo DiCaprio is romantically involved offscreen may be more significant to his fans than the roles he plays onscreen. Thus, in effect, series television hurries children much more than film. On television there is much less distance between actor and role, largely because the role is always the same, whereas in films, for the most part, the roles change. With television, children identify with the role, whereas with film, young people are more likely to identify with the actor. It is how an actress like Keri Russell (the star of the TV show *Felicity*) behaves on the show that provides her fans with a role model to emulate.

It has to be said that the new realism in the media is somewhat adulto-centric. It presumes that children have acquired the same sexual repressions and inhibitions as adults and that the new realism is as liberating for them as it is for grownups. But this is hardly the case. Children today are viewing all facets of sexuality at an age when they should be learning some repressions. The attitude of parents and the culture in general is that sexual activity is okay. Hollywood deliberately uses heavily sexualized materials to attract adolescent filmgoers and children often watch these films as well. Freud was very clear that while too much repression is unhealthy, too little is not healthy either. The media in general, films in particular, encourages sexual expression at just the age children should be learning some healthy repression.

One might argue, of course, that in our new openness regarding sexuality we are becoming a little more European. Films in Europe have always been more explicitly sexual than in the United States, as is true for European literature. Europeans, however, regard sexuality as a normal part of everyday life, and although it is not flaunted in front of children, sexuality is not regarded as something dirty or to be hidden, either. Just as many children in Europe are allowed to have a little wine with meals, they are also exposed to some facets of sexuality as a preparation for adulthood.

What is so troubling about the presentation of sexuality in the American media today is its "overdone" quality. Too many films and TV programs rely heavily on seductive dress and sexual innuendo for humor and drama rather than on well-written scripts. Perhaps the TV show *Baywatch*, with its barely clad, bosomy girls and well-muscled young men, is the most recent flagrant example of the genre. It shows that we really haven't progressed as far as we think we have or would like. Nudity in the media is present and explicit, as is sexual activity. But I am not sure that we are more comfortable with our sexuality today than we were in the past, despite our current openness about it. Our puritanical attitude that it is "dirty" still persists. Many more young people, for example, watch *Baywatch* than admit to watching it.

Perhaps this is what pushes young singers like Britney Spears (whose audience is young teens and preteens) to strip down to a skin-colored bikini in her performances. Her's is a defiant act, flaunting the puritanical mores that continue to exist beneath our apparent liberalism. The real issue that has to be faced in the pressure of media to hurry children into adult awareness of sexuality is whether or not some amount of repression is healthy for the process of growing up. Freud thought so, and not just because he was a Victorian. Freud realized that repression of some instinctual propensities was necessary for social life. If we did not repress some of our sexual and aggressive impulses, we would still be living in a jungle. Even today, sexual liberation is not sexual license. Granted, we are more free and open about our sexuality, but we still are constrained by social rules that limit sexual behavior. The essence of civilization is rule-regulated behavior.

Realism in the media in general, and films in particular, should not be equated with "anything goes." Part of growing up is learning to control impulses and to behave in socially prescribed ways, which requires time and effort by us as parents. When our children are exposed to sexual behaviour before they know the rules, they are likely to be overwhelmed and totally withdraw or, what is more common, to be pressured by the peer group into behavior for which they are not really ready.

The explicit sex and violence that pervades the media puts a greater monitoring burden on parents. And it does so just when we are least able to bear it. That is to say, the monitoring demands on us have increased just as the time available for such oversight has decreased. Recent surveys indicate that parents are working more and have less time for child rearing than in the 1970s and 1980s. The amount of time is also reduced because of the number of two-parent-working and single-parent families.

But we do need to monitor. And it is necessary, not out of some misguided notion that childhood is a period of innocence that has to be shielded but, rather, because children do need to be socialized and it is our job as parents to teach them the socially prescribed rules of behavior. The rules and limits we set are gradually internalized, and eventually become automatic so that the child can behave without awareness of them. The real danger of growing up fast is that children may learn the rules of social license before they learn the rules of social responsibility. This inverted sequence increases the potential for uncivil behavior.

Music

For the most part, we are a visually oriented culture that is more concerned with what we can see—sex and violence on television and in the movies, for instance—than with what we can hear. But music, as Tipper Gore pointed out so vocally a number of years ago, can influence a young person just as much as any visual media. Philosophers and theologians have long been aware of the power of music: Plato in his Republic wanted music censored because he feared its citizens "would be tempted and corrupted by weak and voluptuous airs and led to indulge in demoralizing emotions."

Music promoted for young people is directed not so much to the conscious as to the unconscious or subliminal level of awareness, and this is too easily dismissed. Perhaps more important, music directed at young people today is aimed not so much at hurrying them into adulthood as it is at providing an escape from pressures to grow up fast. The music industry offers young people role models whose concerns, pleasures, and fantasies—family pressures, school, sex, drugs, cars, and the endless party—speak to them directly.

Young people are the market for the music industry, unlike television, for whom they are only a small share of the market. Music advertising is aimed directly at adolescents, and it is not unusual to see a pop star selling anything from soda to beer, and appearing not only in concert but on television and in the movies. The amount of time young people spend listening to music is estimated at six hours a day. According to the Recording Industry Association of America, in 1996, sales of singles, LPs, CDs, and tapes exceeded $8 billion. The purchases of young people between the ages of ten and nineteen accounted for over 30 percent of total music sales.

Music is available at any time of the day or night, and it is not unusual to see a teenager plugged into a Walkman while doing his or her homework. The introduction of music videos and cable channels such as MTV provides yet another way for children to listen—and watch—music. More recently, the ability of young people to download music from the Internet has provided yet another music venue that is open to young people. The pressure to listen and buy the "right kind" of music is just one more way that children are hurried, and who listens to what can early become a social standard among them.

Music for young people, like other forms of popular entertainment, suggests release from stress (caused by parents, school, responsibilities, and the like) through several different outlets, most commonly sex, escapism (which often means drugs), fantasy, and rebellion. There is a great deal of powerful and often subliminal sexual stimulation implicit in the lyrics, rhythm, and appearance of popular performers. The late classicist and historian Allan Bloom wrote:

> *Rock music has one meal only, a barbaric meal to sexual desire— not love, not eros, but sexual desire undeveloped and untutored. It acknowledges the first emanations of children's emerging sensuality and addresses them seriously, eliciting them and legitimating them, not as little sprouts that must be carefully tended in order to grow into gorgeous flowers, but as the real thing. Rock gives children, on a silver platter, with all the public authority of the entertainment industry, everything their parents used to tell them they had to wait for until they grew up and would understand later. . . . Young people know that rock has the beat of sexual intercourse. That is why Ravel's* Bolero *is the one piece of classical music that is commonly known and liked by them. In alliance with some real art and a lot of pseudo-art, an enormous industry cultivates the taste for the orgiastic state of feeling connected with sex, providing a constant flood of fresh material for voracious appetites. Never was there an art form directed so exclusively to children.*[18]

Teen idols rely, in part, on their "sex appeal" for their popularity. A decade ago, Madonna, whose audience consisted mainly of young girls, often performed in lingerie and sang, among other things, about virginity and teenage pregnancy; in "Papa Don't Preach," a pregnant teenager informs her father that she will keep her baby. A singer like Madonna presents an image of both good girl and bad girl, and no doubt many of her young fans identified with her themes of sexual freedom, parental pressures, and exploration, even if they didn't fully understand them.

Today, Britney Spears, who appeals to the same audience, also appears in sexually provocative outfits. Her songs, however, are more romantic and less rebellious than Madonna's. In this way her songs reflect what is also happening in young women's magazines and literature. Her best-selling album, *Oops, I Did It Again,* describes how she encouraged a boy to fall in love with her, but sees it as a harmless mistake for which she does not have to apologize. Britney Spears's subject matter is much more developmentally appropriate than Madonna's; perhaps that is why she seems to have even more appeal among preteens than Madonna had.

Because young people also use singers and groups as markers of their development, they go through groups at a rapid pace. Young teenagers today might listen to New Kids on the Block, Back Street Boys and N' Sync, but older teenagers turn up their noses at these singers and listen instead to rock groups such as Blink 182 and Destiny Girls. There is now a whole industry devoted to creating new rock groups like N' Sync to meet the identity needs of each new cohort of young preteens and teens.

Sex is not the only outlet that rock music provides for teenagers. Drugs, rebellion, and violence have always been major themes in rock and roll. Heavy-metal groups, with names like Iron Maiden, AC/DC, and Motley Crue, play heavily on these themes. Although these groups were popular a decade ago, they have recently been resurrected and put out new albums in 2000:

> *Heavy metal has long been rock's rude underbelly, scorned by adult taste makers while it's beloved by fans; by now it is the entrenched music of young America, especially white male suburban teenagers. As other pop fashions come and go, the formulas of heavy metal endure: Drums crash, guitars blare, singers cackle and howl, lyrics break taboos. . . . Heavy metal's main subject matter is simple and virtually universal. With grunts, moans and subliterary lyrics, it celebrates teenagers' new found feelings of rebellion and sexuality, family and menial work. Most heavy metal fantasizes a party without limits.[19]*

Heavy metal, like rap music (which now finds its audience among both black and white teenagers) is meant to be played loud. It is music any parent could hate, and it expresses in its aggressive beat, its loudness, and its subject matter teenage feelings of frustration and anxiety. Heavy-metal music and other kinds of rock and roll have often been criticized for promoting the use of drugs and violence against women, and although there is no evidence to suggest that there is a correlation between the two, heavy metal, like other forms of popular music, does run the risk of hurrying young listeners to be prematurely concerned with issues that are not yet real for them, and glamorizing drug use, fast cars, and easy sex.

Sex, drugs, and partying will always be major themes in rock and roll, and it is rare to find groups that try to solve conflict in alternative ways. A decade ago, though, a new crop of female singers—then-seventeen-year-old Debbie Gibson and sixteen-year-old Tiffany, for instance—arrived to sing about love, not sex. Their songs were romantic and chaste, and they found wide popularity among young female listeners. Other groups and performers have responded responsibly to the threat of AIDS and to the negative effects of drug use by suggesting alternative ways of living and getting high.

Rock music in all its forms seems to provide young people with escapes from the pressures of growing up fast, from feelings of meaninglessness, and from the emotional loneliness such pressures produce. Free-floating anxiety is reduced through some of rock's themes; loneliness lessened through sexual activity and conquest, and the pain of reality through the escapes of drugs, rebellion, and fantasy. Today rock music shares the young audience with folk and ballad music as a reflection of the fact that today's youth are less rebellious than those of past generations. Nonetheless, rock music groups will still be used by young people as markers of their growing maturity, and as a means of staying young in a world that would make them old too soon.

5

The Dynamics of Hurrying: Lapware, Brain Research, and the Internet

Demands on children to grow up fast come not only from social change but also from new technologies and research findings. In the first edition of this book, published in the early 1980s, television was the major technology encouraging the perception of children as miniature adults. By the early 1990s, however, when the second edition was printed, computers and video games were equally significant innovations that promoted hurrying. As we enter the millennium and the third edition goes to press, software for infants, brain research, and access to the Internet are the latest technological and scientific advances to be used as justifications for putting inappropriate intellectual and social pressures on children.

Computer Programs for Infants and Young Children

The introduction of new technologies seems, inevitably, to create the temptation to use them with ever younger age groups. This has certainly been the case with computers. Nonetheless, I think it is a temptation that parents should resist. At the outset, I want to make clear that I in no way want to demonize computers. Computers are here to stay and they are becoming an ever more integral part of all facets of our lives. Nonetheless, computers are very complex machines that often pose a challenge for even the most experienced adult users.

To be sure, many children and adolescents are often exceptionally adept at computer use. School-age children have attained a level of intellectual maturity that enables them to deal with, and to manipulate, symbols. Most children do not acquire these mental skills until the age of six or seven and then become progressively efficient in their use. But infants and young children are not efficient symbol users and manipulators. A premature introduction to this symbolic world, before the child has mastered the world of things, might well do more harm than good. The computer, like other technologies, is simply a tool. Used intelligently, it is extremely powerful and beneficial. It is the misuse of this extraordinary machine that can do harm to children.

Lapware for Infants and Toddlers

The idea that earlier is better, which has been applied to everything from reading to sports, has now been extended to computer use. In the early 1990s, the typical educational software product was written for seven- to twelve-year-old children. Since then, the age group for whom software is being written is getting younger and younger. In 1999, sales of software labeled as appropriate for children ages three to six totaled $309 million[1]. In 1998, software for infants from six months to two years of age was introduced with the term "lapware." These programs allow an infant or toddler to sit on the parent's or caregiver's lap and tap a keyboard, move a mouse, or hit a large button while watching on-screen images and listening to computer-generated songs. The first lapware was called Jumpstart Baby. In this program, the infant is guided through a nursery environment and eight learning activities by a host named Teddy. Babies are introduced to concepts of cause and effect, music, colors, shapes, animals, and clothing.

Jumpstart Baby soon had competition. In 1998, BABYWOW was developed for infants from nine months to three years old and is a collection of more than 300 images and 2,000 words. The research basis for this program are a few studies that suggest a correlation between the number and variety of words a child hears and his or her IQ. Another program, BABYROM, targeted for children from six months to four years of age, purportedly allows children to discover geometric shapes, colors, letters of the alphabet, numbers, and body parts. According to PC Data, 770,000 copies of software for infants was sold in 1999.

Not surprisingly, there is a lot of controversy about the efficacy and value of these programs. Many researchers are opposed to these programs and argue that they are based on misinterpretations of infancy research. Clifford Nash, a professor at Stanford University who specializes in the interaction between people and computers, argues that young children learn best when they are playing with real objects, like puzzles and teddy bears, along with other children and adults. He contends that it is the tactile and social experiences that are crucial to early development.[2]

Robert Calfee, also a professor at Stanford University who, ironically, has served as a consultant to software companies, questions whether the claims made for these products have any research support. For example, those marketing Jumpstart software claim that is "the most comprehensive solution for preparing kids for success in school and the real world." And the promoters of the Reading Rabbit[3] series, aimed at children from eighteen months to three years, claim that the series "builds important skills children need for future development." But Calfee says that he has gone through the research literature diligently for evidence of the benefits of using computers with infants and toddlers, and found nothing. This is really not surprising. The products have only been on the market for a year or two, so their long-term effectiveness could hardly be demonstrated.

The professional chorus against lapware is quite loud. John Breur, author of *The Myth of the First Three Years*[4], says that claims for the benefits of lapware are vastly overstated, "It's an abuse of neuroscience, and its misleading to parents. We all feel anxious enough already. . . . Children get all the stimulation they need from things they encounter in the everyday world—crawling in grass, playing with pots, hearing you speak."[5] Other researchers warn of the dangers of overstimulation. Infant researcher Arnold Sameroff, professor of psychology at the University of Michigan, says that when infants are overloaded with stimuli, they turn away, close their eyes, or start to fidget and cry. And John Shonkoff, chairman of the National Academy of Sciences Committee on Integrating the Science of Early Childhood Development, says that "artificial pressures from a super-enriched environment—particularly when anxious parents are standing by, can be detrimental."[3]

Not all professionals are in agreement, however, about the ineffectiveness or even harm of lapware. Alvin Poussant, director of the media center of the Judge Baker Center in Boston and an internationally renowned authority on kids and the media, contends that the jury is still out on whether or not computer use is harmful to kids. He agrees that children should not spend too much time on the computer, but adds that "there just hasn't been enough research, the damage to children is just speculative at this point . . . even the name 'lapware' insinuates that parent and child will be sitting together at the computer. At this stage interaction is a critical part of development." He also argues that it gives the infant a chance to learn more about the parent. "Young children are endlessly curious about the lives their parents lead. Allowing a child to 'act like Mom' and tap on a key board gives her a wonderful opportunity to look into your world."[3] Likewise, Claire Lerner, a child development specialist with Zero to Three, a Washington-based advocacy organization, says that although she does not believe the software is necessary, limited interaction with it is acceptable. "I think it is another toy that has limitations because it is so stimulating that a child doesn't have to do a lot to be engaged with it." Lerner, like Poussant, cautions against overuse of the computer. "I think it is limiting their opportunity to develop some critical skills they need to be successful in school . . . that is why real world learning is so important and can never be replaced by a computer."[4]

Along with the majority of professionals, I believe that there is little scientific justification for lapware and that it poses more risks than it does benefits. The promoters of these products play on our parental guilt and anxiety about our children's ability to compete in an increasingly technological and global economy. These concerns are understandable, but they are also a little misguided. What infants need most, and what will give them the best foundation for whatever world they are going to live in, is not provided by any computer program. What they need most is a healthy sense that the world is a safe place, that their needs will be met, and that they will be cared for and protected by the grown-ups in their world.

Those who promote computer programs for infants, however, suggest that skills are what infants need to learn. The following is the sales pitch for a lapware program called Colors, designed for infants and young children.

Does your child know his primary colors? Colors sounds and graphics will capture the young one's attention and before they know it they are learning. Colors is designed as "infantware." Colors requires almost no mouse or keyboard interaction thus making it accessible by even the youngest of children. Colors will aid your toddler in learning his or her primary colors. It also helps them associate letters and the written word with the spoken word.[5]

Let us examine this claim that Colors will teach infants and toddlers the primary colors and help them associate the printed letters and words with the spoken one. First of all, it is well established that infants can identify colors during the first few months of life without the aid of any computer program. By about two months, babies can tell red from green and by four months they can respond selectively to red, green, blue, and yellow.[6] Like adults, infants also prefer red and blue to the other colors.[7] I would argue that writers for Colors do not know much about infant visual development or, if they do, that they are taking credit for teaching the infant something he or she already knows.

The program also claims that it will teach infants and young children to associate printed letters and words with the spoken word. Here again, the assertion is totally at odds with the abundant research regarding literacy attainment by young children. First of all, an infant's visual system is relatively undeveloped. It is only after about two years that toddlers have the visual acuity to discriminate between different letters. The ability to identify words as visual entities comes even later. It is only during their third year that some children learn to name letters and to associate a few words with the appropriate verbal labels. Second, children do not begin to associate letters with the sounds that they represent (phonics) until at least age four or five. Finally, the first words children learn are not color words but rather function words that are tied to concrete actions such as "stop" and "go." The understanding that printed letters and words are symbols for sounds and spoken words is an extraordinarily complex achievement that most children do not acquire until ages five or six.[8]

These facts reveal the major problem with lapware, and indeed with much of the software for infants and young children. Basically, those writing the software do not understand child development, or choose to ignore the abundant research and market these products to gullible parents. As a result, the programmers make the two mistakes that were illustrated above; namely, they either instruct the child in something he or she already knows, or they attempt to teach the child skills that are far beyond the child's developmental reach. For both of these reasons, buying and using lapware for infants is a waste of both money and time.

Harmful Side Effects. These programs are more than just wasteful, however; they are potentially harmful. An infant's visual system is not fully developed until the end of the second year. We don't know what the effect of watching a computer screen may be on a visual system that is not adapted to that type of stimulation or overstimulation. Indeed, the American Academy of Pediatrics has suggested that children should not watch television until the age of two. In addition, encouraging the child to concentrate on visual stimuli could lead him or her to neglect information coming from the other senses. The first year of life is the time when an infant should concentrate on sensory integration. Auditory discrimination, for example, must be assimilated to visual discriminations for a child to move successfully into reading. A too early concentration on the visual could impede the development of the other senses and the all-important process of sensory integration.

A potentially more harmful side effect of lapware programs is their impact on the parent-child relationship. One of the characteristics of such programs is that they suggest to the parent that there are "right" and "wrong" responses the infant or toddler can make to the screen. Without even being fully aware of it, parents may emotionally reward the baby when he or she makes a "right" response and emotionally withdraw when he or she gives a "wrong" response. Parents may even get frustrated and angry at the infant's "wrong answers." This puts the infant in an unnecessarily stressful situation in which actions that are meaningless to him or her are randomly rewarded or punished. Lapware thus has the potential to impair an infant's developing sense of trust and security, which is essential for the baby to explore his or her world with pleasure and confidence.

Computer Programs for Young Children. By the age of three most children are well along in both their sensory motor development and integration and in their language development. At this age, some exposure to the computer and carefully selected computer programs is much less risky than it is at the earlier age levels. But even for this age group, some of the exaggerations of the lapware developers are again in evidence. For example, those who advocate software for preschoolers argue that it teaches them that they have control over their own learning. Yet toddlers who insist on feeding themselves and who teach themselves to walk and to talk certainly do not need a computer program to discover that they have control over their own learning.

A study carried out by Patricia Bishop[9] is revealing. Bishop had parents and teachers observe how children four years of age and younger responded to eight different computer programs. The observers were generally pleased with what they saw. The reasons they gave for introducing computers to children at a young age were predictable, but had little to do with what they had actually observed! "Teaching young children computer skills gives them a head start for the skills they will be learning at school." Computer programs "allow children to make choices and encourage them to become confident self motivated learners."

Although these hoped-for outcomes seem reasonable, there is no data to support them. There is no evidence, for example, that early exposure to computers gives infants an academic head start at a later age. Indeed, a lot of evidence is to the contrary. Consider, *Sesame Street* has now been on television for more than thirty years. As a result, children today learn their numbers and their letters earlier than any other generation of young children.[8] Yet the same children are not reading earlier or better nor doing math earlier or better than children who were never exposed to *Sesame Street*. Indeed, some scholars argue that children's reading and math skills are worse today than they were before television.[10] If early exposure to academics on television does not promote reading and math skills, why should early exposure to similar programs on computers do so?

As to the other supposed benefits, they can easily be acquired by other means. There is abundant evidence that children can learn to make choices and to become self-motivated, confident learners without computers. Attending a developmentally appropriate early childhood program, where children can interact with children and adults, will give a child all of these skills and more, with less stress[11]. In addition, it is simply a fact that many computer skills are learned more quickly, and more effectively, at a later age than at an early one. An eight-year-old will pick up keyboard and mouse skills more rapidly than an infant, and be less likely to develop bad habits and misunderstandings.

Computers for young children are, then, not an unmixed blessing. Although some exposure of children over the age of three to well-designed, age-appropriate programs may do no harm, it is unlikely that such exposure will have important or lasting benefits. There is no evidence that early exposure to computers gives children an edge in computer literacy, self-confidence, or self-esteem. In this regard it is well to remember that Bill Gates, founder and CEO of Microsoft, did not have a computer as an infant and young child. Nor did the majority of individuals who currently design the hardware and write the software for computers. All of the purported benefits of exposing infants and young children to computers can easily be acquired through other means and with less risk.

The Authority of the Brain

In our information society, the brain has become, at least for parents and educators, the ultimate scientific authority. Over the past decade, neuroscientists have learned an enormous amount about the growth and functioning of the brain. Most of this research, however, has been done on animals: rats, cats, and primates. New knowledge has been obtained in three main areas: *synaptogenesis, critical periods, and the effects of enriched environments.* These advances reflect new technologies that make it possible to get accurate counts of brain cells, to measure brain activity, and to identify areas of the brain that are associated with different mental functions. Much of this information has now been popularized in the media and has created a new enterprise zone of infant stimulation practices.

Before reviewing and evaluating some of these practices, it might be helpful to briefly summarize some of our new knowledge about brain growth and activity.

Synaptogenesis. At birth, an infant has far fewer synapses (connections between neurons) than an adult. During the first few years of life, however, synapses proliferate exponentially, with the result that the brains of infants and young children have vastly more synapses than the brains of adults. This early explosion of synapses is followed by a period of synaptic pruning, largely regulated by experience. As a result of this progressive thinning, adult brains have fewer synaptic connections than children's. However, it is the pattern of connections, rather than their number, that makes adult brains so much more capable than those of infants.[12]

Critical Periods. In the course of brain growth, particular skills and abilities must be acquired during specific age periods. To illustrate, the critical age for the attainment of some visual skills, such as tracking and shape discrimination, is the first year of life.[13] The window for higher-level functions, such as planning and foresight, does not open until adolescence.

Benefits of Enriched Environments. Animal studies suggest that an environment rich in sensory stimulation and full of opportunities for motor activity is more conducive to brain growth than an environment that lacks these possibilities.[14] It should be noted, however, that such studies often compare stimulus-deprived animals with those who have experienced a rich environment. They tell us nothing about whether animals who are already reared in a rich stimulus environment will make additional progress with overstimulation.

Although these findings are suggestive, neuroscientists are cautious about extrapolating from these animal studies to human brains and to human behavior.[15] Several responsible, balanced books for the lay public such as *Magic Trees of the Mind,*[16] *Teaching with the Brain in Mind,*[17] and *The Growth of the Mind*[18] detail these cautions. Unfortunately, others writing for parents have not shown similar restraint. Popular magazine articles such as "Fertile Minds"[19] and "How to Build a Baby's Brain"[20] and national television programs such as *Building Brains: The Sooner the Better* and *Your Child's Brain* offer interpretations that go far beyond what the data warrant.

There is both some good news and some bad news deriving from this heightened, brain-driven interest in young children's learning and development. Many of the suggestions for infant stimulation, supposedly stemming from brain studies, in fact were arrived at from years of clinical experience and developmental research. For example, in a recent monograph titled *Rethinking the Brain,* the author argues that the following are "key findings" of recent brain research:

- Human development hinges on the interplay between nature and nurture.
- Early care and nurture have a decisive and long-lasting impact on how people develop, their ability to learn, and their capacity to regulate their emotions.
- The human brain has remarkable capacity to change, but timing is crucial.
- There are times when negative experiences or the absence of appropriate stimulation are more likely to have serious and sustained effects.
- Evidence amassed over the last decade points to the wisdom and efficacy of prevention and early intervention.[21]

These ideas are neither new nor are they derived from neuroscience research. They are based on decades of clinical work and thousands of developmental investigations. Presenting such well-entrenched developmental principles as building on brain studies presumably lends them more authority and makes them more persuasive. Although misleading, invoking the authority of the brain to support healthy child-rearing practices is excusable. If the authority of the brain encourages parents and child caregivers to employ more developmentally appropriate child-rearing practices, then no serious damage has been done, and some benefits may well result.

There is, however, also some bad news from this new appeal to the authority of the brain. Although Shore, like Diamond and Hopson, Greenspan, and Jensen, calls upon the authority of the brain in support of well-established practices, writers for the popular press are not bound by similar scruples. For example, in a *Time* article, writer Madeline Nash[19] has no hesitation in offering parents advice based on our new knowledge of how rapidly the brain grows during the early years: "Loving care provides the baby's brain with the right kind of stimulation. Neglecting a baby can produce brain wave patterns that dampen happy feelings. Abuse can produce heightened anxiety and stress responses."

After describing how the brain progressively refines the circuits for reaching, grabbing, crawling, walking, and running, the author suggests that parents do the following:

> *Give babies as much freedom to explore as safety permits. Just reaching for an object helps the brain develop hand-eye coordinations. As soon as children are ready for them, activities like drawing and playing the violin and piano encourages the development of fine motor skills.*[19]

How are we, as parents, to interpret these recommendations? What constitutes neglect and abuse? If we do not respond every time a baby cries, is that neglect? Are we abusing our child and causing bad brain wave patterns if we restrain the infant from engaging in a potentially dangerous activity? Likewise, how are we to know when a youngster is ready for drawing and playing the violin and the piano? If we don't give our child these extracurricular lessons are we harming our offspring's brains? Recommendations such as these are clearly irresponsible. They are too general to be helpful and yet specific enough (violin and piano lessons) to create parental anxieties. Unfortunately, this is but one example of many articles in the print media that attempt to translate brain research into child-rearing practices. The results are often more confusing and stress provoking than they are helpful.

Neuroscientists are much more restrained in their interpretations of brain research. For example, Susan Fitzpatrick, a neuroscientist at the McDonnel Foundation, has this to say about the rash of extrapolations from brain research to education: "Anything that people would say right now has a good chance of not being true two years from now because the understanding is so rudimentary and people are looking at things in such a simplistic way."[22] Likewise, Greenough, one of the leading researchers on the effects of enriched environments on animal brains, cautions that there is no reason to believe that there are critical periods for socially transmitted skills such as reading, mathematics, and music and these can be acquired at any age. Other researchers point out that the emphasis on the infant brain ignores the important findings to the effect that the mature brain has the ability to change and reorganize.[23]

My own sense, after reviewing this material, is that parents should move slowly and with care when employing any type of infant stimulation that bases its claims on the authority of the brain. On the other hand, we do have a solid basis for encouraging parents to talk and sing to the infant, and to have simple and safe crib toys such as rattles and play gyms readily available. Brain research is fascinating and telling us more about this remarkable organ than we ever knew before. But we are still a long way from being able to translate the microscopic events of the brain into macroscopic child-rearing practices.

The Internet

The most recent challenge to our ability to monitor the information our children receive comes from children's use of the Internet. It is remarkable how quickly the Internet has taken over all facets of our lives. The Internet was created in the early 1960s as part of the Defense Department's effort to set up a computer network that would continue to operate after a nuclear attack. This fear followed the Russian launch of the *Sputnik* space capsule. Later the network was opened for communication among four California universities and was called ARPNET. The linking of these sites was a great success and was rapidly expanded from four universities to twenty-three. One of the most popular features of the ARPNET was e-mail—the system that we all now know—which allowed scientists to rapidly correspond and exchange data with one another. By 1973, these universities crossed the Atlantic and connected to universities in England and Germany.

It was in the late 1970s and early 1980s that the general public began to gain access to ARPNET. News groups were formed among users who wanted to exchange information about particular topics. In 1982, the term Internet was introduced and quickly replaced ARPNET. During this period new, standardized protocols were written that made access easier both for corporations and individuals. By 1990 there were some 300,000 Internet users, including universities, corporations, and individuals. In 1991, the federal laws were revised and commercial use of the Internet was permitted, including the selling of products. In 1991 the World Wide Web was invented, allowing easy navigation among Web sites. By 1995 the Internet was completely free of government regulation, had 150 countries connected, and had more than 10 million users. And the number will grow exponentially even between the writing and the publication of this book.

The computer, which seemed like such an important technological innovation, is now often used simply as a portal for Internet access. Children and adolescents are increasingly using the Internet for e-mail, to engage in chat room discussions, to do research for school, to download music, and to buy goods online. As with computer programs, there are many wonderful sites for children that are both educational and entertaining. Unfortunately, like computer programs, there are many other sites which have little or nothing to commend them. Although the computer industry is to be applauded for making the Internet widely available, there are negative as well as positive consequences. Adult sites find their way onto the Web in astonishing numbers. Indeed, among the top ten keywords used in Internet searches are "erotic," "sex," and "nude."

In addition to pornography, there are other mine fields for children and their parents on the Web. For example, hate groups and cults have sites. The two young men responsible for the Columbine High School shootings in Colorado, for example, had regularly logged on to hate group sites. There are also sites that give detailed instructions on how to build bombs. Even seemingly innocuous chat rooms can be offensive and dangerous: Some contributors to chat rooms use the vilest and filthiest language imaginable.

The chat rooms can also be used by child predators. The *Orlando Sentinel*[24] reported that a fifteen-year-old boy, Sam Manzi, was sexually assaulted by a forty-three-year-old man he had met on an America OnLine chat room. Manzi was subsequently accused of sexually assaulting and murdering an eleven-year-old boy. The Internet can be dangerous.

Family Use and Attitudes Toward the Internet. The Internet poses a serious dilemma for both parents and educators. On one hand, the Internet is a fantastic educational and informational source. Yet it can also expose young people to vile language, pornography, and all sorts of hate material. In light of this conflict, a study on children's Internet usage was conducted by the National School Boards Foundation, the Children's Television Workshop, and the Microsoft Corporation. The study surveyed 1,700 American households with respect to their use of the Internet and their attitudes regarding the new technology.[25]

Perhaps the key finding of the study was that both parents and children agree that Internet usage is beneficial for children, despite the potential for exposure to negative social influences.

The study also gave evidence of how widespread Internet usage is among young people. Of the families surveyed, more than half had at least one child who regularly used the Net. Among teenagers, three out of four adolescents were on-line. Other findings of the survey were that, in the opinion of the polled families:

- Education is the primary reason families buy computers and connect to the Internet.
- The Internet does not detract from other healthy activities, like reading and sports.
- The Internet does not isolate children from their families, peers, or communities.
- Girls are just as involved in the Internet as boys.
- Schools can contribute to breaking down the digital divide separating information "haves" and "have-nots."[26]

Most parents used a commonsense, balanced approach to monitoring their children's Internet usage. They provide two helpful guidelines for all parents: Monitor the sites your children watch and limit the time your children spend on-line and set usage rules.

Filters. To help parents monitor the sites their children log onto, a number of special software programs have been created that can be installed in your computer and that will work with your Web browser. Most of these filters work in much the same way. You enter words into the program that are most likely to link to offensive material such as "sex," "erotic," "nudity," "bomb," "hate," and so on. Once you enter these words into the program, the child working from your computer will be unable to access any pages that contain these words. Of course, these filters only work when your child types in one of these words, and does not control instances, all too common, when an innocent Internet address calls up an offensive link.

Like most of our new information-age technologies, the Internet is a mixed blessing. It is a tremendous resource for getting all sorts of information rapidly and in our own homes. And it is an extraordinarily helpful educational resource as well. At the same time, it poses a number of risks for children and adolescents. The price of our new technologies, like the price of liberty, is eternal vigilance. But if we use common sense, set reasonable usage rules, and do some monitoring, we can probably get the best out of the Internet and avoid some of its less savory offerings.

Part II
· · · · · · · · · ·

Hurried Children: Stressed Children

6
·········
Growing Up
Slowly

·········
The concept of hurrying implies
that there is a slower, more normal and healthier pace to growth
and development than many American children currently enjoy.
This chapter will describe some of the achievements, and some of
the limitations, of the major stages of development—infancy, early
childhood, childhood, and adolescence. In addition, the chapter
will spell out some of the effects hurrying has upon the "normal"
course of intellectual, emotional, and social development.

Swiss psychologist Jean Piaget has described four major stages in
the development of children's thinking. Piaget argued that at each
stage children do not copy what they encounter but actively construct reality out of their experiences with the environment. The
realities constructed by children are, in a sense, a series of progressive approximations to adult reality and so do not coincide
point for point with the adult vision of the world. Moreover, prior
to adolescence, children lack the mental abilities to think, reason,
judge, and make decisions in the way that adults do. These capacities are developed in stages as well. In short, both the content and
the form of children's thinking changes with age.[1]

In recent years evidence has been accumulating in support of
the stages described by Piaget. The tests he devised have now been
used in more than half the countries of the world with amazingly
comparable results. Children all over the world go through these
stages at least up to adolescence. In addition, recent studies suggest
that children's success on tests and with curricula is related to the

"fit" between the child's stage of mental development and the stage presupposed by the tests and curricula. This means that educational practice can be improved by a better match between the child's level of development and that imbedded in the tests and curricula.

The Piagetian stages, however, will be only the framework for the description provided below; included as well is a discussion of children's social-emotional development. Once we see and understand the strengths and the limitations of each stage of development, the meaning of hurrying and its dangers will become more obvious.

The Sensorimotor Period

From birth until about two years of age, infants are concerned with constructing a world of permanent objects, attaching themselves to significant others, and establishing what the late Harvard professor Erik Erikson called a sense of "trust."[2] These three attainments constitute the major intellectual, social, and emotional developments of the infancy period.

With respect to permanent objects, young infants have no idea that objects continue to exist when they cannot see, hear, feel, taste, or smell them. What we as adults experience as objects, cups, saucers, dogs, cats, and so on, are in part concepts that we have constructed. We know that a particular cup does not exhaust the class of cups and that cups exist all over the world regardless of whether we are able to see or touch them. But our knowledge about cups, like our knowledge about dogs, cars, houses, and boats, is not innate; we did not come into the world with this knowledge but had to acquire it.

How does this acquisition come about? Traditional psychology said that children looked at the cup and abstracted its common properties or features. The problem with this position is that it presupposes the knowledge it seeks to explain. If children could distinguish a cup well enough to abstract its common features, they would already have the concept they were supposed to be obtaining. The abstraction theory of knowledge acquisition is circular.

Piaget argues that objects such as cups are not perceived as distinct entities by children but, rather, must be constructed by them. Only as children look at, touch, drop, push, and grab a cup do they begin to construct it. Their conceptions are based on their actions on the cup, their active explorations of its properties, not on passive looking and abstracting. This is the reason it is so important for infants to actively explore objects by touching, feeling, tasting, grabbing, and dropping them. Through these activities, infants, by the end of the first year, are able to construct a pride of permanent objects, like cups, that they know exist even when they are not looking at them.

This development is easy to demonstrate with both animate and inanimate objects. When Piaget's daughter Jacqueline was eight months old, Piaget held a cigarette case in front of her and then proceeded to let it fall to the floor. Jacqueline did not follow the trajectory of the case but continued to look at his hand. She had not yet formed a concept of a cigarette case as a permanent object that would enable her to follow it when it fell. By the time she was nineteen months old, however, Jacqueline gave evidence that her conceptualization of objects was now well advanced. Piaget placed a coin in his hand and then placed his hand under a coverlet where he let the coin drop before removing his hand. Jacqueline first looked in his hand and then immediately lifted the coverlet to find the coin.[3]

A similar construction occurs with respect to people. Young infants do not believe that people, any more than objects, continue to exist when they are not present to the senses. In one study, for example, infants of three months and ten months of age were compared for their reactions to a few days of hospitalization for minor surgery. When the three-month-old infants returned home, they showed few adjustment problems and quickly fell back into the routines they had followed before they left. In contrast, the ten-month-old infants showed signs of acute anxiety, clung to their mothers, and did not settle down for several weeks. It is not surprising that fear of strangers and reluctance to be with baby sitters also appear at this time.

According to English psychologist John Bowlby, infancy is also a time when children form their primary attachments to caretakers.[4] These attachments—the mother is usually the prime attachment figure—depend in part upon the infants' construction of the mother as an object. But they also reflect much more: they reflect a basic need for attachment, to relate in an emotional way to another person. The child's attachment to the mother is a powerful motivation of much of the child's learning. Attachment makes it possible for the infant to enjoy love and caring (which mean nothing if they come from someone to whom the infant is not attached) but also to fear separation and loss.

In addition to specific attachments, infants must also establish a sense of trust that outweighs their sense of mistrust. This healthy outcome depends very much on the infant's experience with caregivers. The infant who finds the world a dependable place, whose needs are met in a timely and consistent fashion, acquires a sense of trust that is stronger than his or her sense of mistrust. And this sense of trust, that caregivers are good and reliable, is gradually extended to adults in general. Conversely, an infant whose caretaking has been sporadic, who has been neglected, may develop a sense of mistrust of the world as a fearful and dangerous place in which no one can be depended upon. While a modicum of mistrust is a healthy safeguard against undue confidence in others, too much can end up being self destructive.

Infancy, therefore, is a very important time because it is the period when children not only develop their basic concepts about the world, but also when they form their most critical attachments and social orientations. These achievements, like those that come later, take time and effort and cannot be rushed. Becoming an adult person does not happen all at once, and the quality of the person that develops will depend, in part, upon the quality of time and effort expended during infancy. This does not mean that infants should not be placed in day-care centers or left with sitters. It does mean (as we shall examine in detail when we consider contracts) that infant needs should not become subordinate to parental needs.

The Preoperational Period

The years from about two to six are momentous ones in the child's development toward full personhood. From the intellectual standpoint, it is a period when children acquire the symbolic function and can now represent, in conventional or original ways, the objects and relations they have constructed during the years of infancy. The acquisition of language permits children to express their intellectual discoveries and their wants and feelings with words. In addition, as they become socialized and recognize their relative powerlessness, discover dangers, and encounter unpleasant people and experiences, they begin to express fears and anxieties in dreams and in symbolic play. The fascination that super heroes (such as Superman) have for some children is a case in point. Super heroes demonstrate the weaknesses and limitations of the average adult. They help children overcome the belief that parents are all powerful and all knowing.

In addition to the symbolic function, young children also acquire elementary reasoning powers in relation to symbols. They begin to form concepts of classes and relations that go beyond the specific acquisitions of the infancy period. But children at this stage also make characteristic mistakes having to do with the one and the many. When young children see a dog and say "dog," it is not clear whether they mean "look at that black cocker spaniel," the specific dog, or "look at the dog," at a particular example of the class of dogs. When young children call a strange man "Daddy," they give evidence of a confusion between words that stand for one object, "Daddy," and those that stand for many, "man."

The attachment to, and investment in, symbols helps explain the difficulty many young children display when asked to "share" persons and objects they consider their own. Young children resent a new baby in the family because, in part, they conceive of the symbolic "mommy" as belonging to them alone, a part of their symbolic "me and mine." The same is true for toys; preschoolers have trouble sharing but not because they are selfish in the adult sense. Rather because young children think of their toys as part of themselves, sharing a toy is like sharing part of their being.

The symbolic function also gives rise to a kind of word magic. Young children believe that if they are called by a bad name, such as "stinky," they are gifted with the property along with the name. Preschoolers also believe that events that happen together cause one another. A child often becomes attached to a blanket or a teddy bear that on one occasion was associated with comfort and good feelings. From then on, the child believes the teddy or blanket "causes" good feelings and reaches out for it at times of stress. It is this kind of magical thinking that makes children believe that they are responsible for parental separation or divorce. The young child believes that something he or she said or did at the time of separation "caused" the separation. Such thinking can contribute to lifelong feelings of guilt and remorse.

Early childhood is also the period, in Eriksonian theory, during which the balance is struck between children's sense of autonomy and their sense of shame and doubt. If children are encouraged, once they give evidence that they are ready, to take charge of their eating and toileting, this strengthens their sense of autonomy. On the other hand, if children are pressured to feed or toilet themselves before they have the requisite motor abilities, they will have embarrassing accidents. Such accidents together with parental disapproval, strengthens children's sense of shame and doubt at the expense of their budding sense of autonomy. Whether a child acquires a healthy sense of autonomy or moves into childhood burdened with an overwhelming sense of shame and doubt depends on the care parents take to match their expectancies to the child's developing competencies.

Around the age of four or five, children must deal with their sense of initiative versus their sense of guilt. Children of this age have acquired considerable motor control, language ability, and intellectual competence. They are curious about their world and eager to explore it, and their curiosity is expressed in endless "Why" questions, such as "Why does the sun shine?" or "What happens when you get to the end of the earth?" Children at this age also like to take things apart (like old clocks, toasters, or radios) to see how they work.

A child's sense of initiative, curiosity, and exploration is strengthened when parents take time to answer the child's questions, when they provide materials and opportunities for exploration and discovery, and when they do not get unduly upset by the resulting clutter and debris. On the other hand, if a child's questions are answered cursorily or not at all, if parents are too busy to provide exploration opportunities and become angry at the "mess" created by the child's effort to take apart old clocks, telephones, and radios, this increases the child's guilt to the detriment to the child's sense of initiative.

Young children need time to explore and investigate in a responsive environment if they are to acquire a sense of initiative stronger than a sense of guilt. When preschoolers are hurried from one caregiver to another, or from one lesson to another, they may be deprived of the opportunity to explore their environment freely. Likewise, if parents are too busy or too tired to answer the child's questions, the child may feel guilty about asking them. When the child's efforts at initiative are blocked or shot down, the child's sense of guilt will be the predominant orientation acquired at this stage. An overwhelming sense of guilt established in early childhood may result in a lifelong orientation of tentativeness and fearfulness about initiating new projects.

The Concrete Operational Period

At around the age of six or seven, children attain a new set of mental abilities that Piaget calls "concrete operations." Like the symbolic function attained in early childhood, concrete operations enable children to do many things they could not do before. In particular, they are now able to operate upon symbols in the way that they learned to act upon and manipulate objects in infancy. For example, once children attain concrete operations, they are able to classify in a hierarchical way. They now grasp that boys and girls are included in the class of children; that cats, dogs, and mice are animals; that pianos, violins, and tubas are all musical instruments. Children can now manipulate symbols for things in the way that they once manipulated the things themselves.

There is an important difference between the manipulation of things and the manipulation of symbols. The manipulation of symbols is mental and goes on in children's heads; it does not involve their hands. To illustrate, if a four-year-old is shown a finger maze (a large wooden maze that permits the child to explore alternate paths manually), the child proceeds to explore it with his or her finger, moving it along the different paths until the one that leads to the exit is discovered. When the maze is given to a six-year-old, in contrast, the child does not explore it manually at all but explores it visually until finding the correct path, and only then putting his or her finger to the maze. In exploring the maze visually, the child is mentally manipulating the maze with the aid of symbolic rather than manual activities. Symbolic manipulation vastly extends the range and variety of explorations the child can perform.

The capacity to manipulate symbols mentally makes possible a whole new level of achievement that was not possible for preschool children. Unfortunately, however, our language does not give us markers for these new achievements and so they are often missed.

Consider the child's conception of number. Young children may be able to correctly identify two or three things and correctly use the terms two and three. But for them, two and three are simply names, comparable to the number on a football player's jersey. It is only at the age of six or seven that children attain a true sense of number. At that age they recognize, for example, that a set of twelve objects, such as the forks, knives, and spoons used to set the table for four people, remains twelve whether they are arranged on the table or bunched together in the dishwasher.

Advanced reading, like advanced number understanding, is quite different from beginning reading, although again our language provides no markers of the difference. We talk about children reading or not reading as if children either read or do not read. But there are many different levels of reading attainment. The young child who has memorized all of the words in a book has learned to sight read, but like learning the numbers two and three sight reading is a much easier mental activity than decoding new words using syntactic structure to infer meaning. That level of reading does not usually emerge until after the age of six or seven.

These levels of competence are often ignored when children are hurried. When parents do not distinguish between beginning and advanced levels of number and reading skill, they can mistake one for the other.

"If," I hear some parents I say, "she knows her numbers (can count to ten), why isn't she doing arithmetic?" Or, "If he can read this sentence (such as "I have a turtle" in a book with one sentence per page), why can't he start on Robinson Crusoe?" Learning to efficiently manipulate symbols mentally takes time and can't be rushed if the child is to become truly competent.

Concrete operations make possible new interpersonal as well as intellectual attainments. Children at this stage, for example, have the capacity to learn and operate according to rules, the basis for all lasting social exchange. Learning to operate according to rules requires a kind of syllogistic reasoning that's made possible by concrete operations. For example, in order to learn to use please or thank you correctly on particular occasions, the child must reason as follows:

"Whenever someone gives you something, you must say thank you."

"This person has just given me something."

"Therefore, I must say thank you."

The child is not aware of going through this reasoning process; it is part of what Piaget calls the "intellective unconscious." Much of our thinking is unconscious, and we are usually only aware of the results. This is one reason we have so much trouble understanding the difficulty children encounter in learning such things as rules. Once we have mastered rules and syllogistic thinking, we are no longer aware of using these processes in our interpersonal exchanges. It seems to us, for example, that children should learn to say please and thank you after being told to do so a few times. To adults, saying please and thank you seems to be a simple matter of memory, not reasoning. We say to children "Remember to say please" or "Remember to say thank you" as if learning rules were a matter of memory alone.

The ability to learn rules makes formal education possible. Most of what children learn as they acquire the basic skills of reading and arithmetic are rules. They learn phonic rules (long a with a silent e) and spelling rules (i before e except after c) and arithmetic rules (when you add horizontally, $49 + 55 = 104$, you move from left to right; when you add vertically, you move from right to left). Mastering the basics means acquiring an enormous number of rules and learning to apply them appropriately. Hurrying children academically, therefore, ignores the enormity of the task that children face in acquiring basic math and reading skills. We need to appreciate how awesome an intellectual task learning the basics really is for children and give them the time they need to accomplish it well.

Learning rules also makes it possible for children to play games that presuppose complex rules and to create their own games and rules. One of the dangers of organized team sports for this age group is that they no longer have the opportunity to create their own games and rules and thus to acquire a healthy sense of the relativity of rules. I recall seeing a group of boys racing along the street when one yelled, "Last one to the corner is a nerd." One unfortunate youngster was tripping over his sneaker laces and had to stop to tie them. He shouted to the first boy, "Not included!" To which came the swift reply, "No say-backs." Learning to create rules—even simple rules for otherwise uncomplicated street games—and to abide by those you have created is an important part of rule learning and of mature social behavior.

Children who have attained concrete operations are also able to enter the culture of childhood, which is, in effect, a body of rules that has been handed down by oral tradition over hundreds of years. Sayings such as "Step on a crack, break your back" or "Rain, rain go away, come again another day" or "Finders, keepers; losers, weepers" make up part of the language and lore of childhood. Learning the sayings, the superstitions, the jokes and riddles of childhood are the initial stage of social interaction among peers who share common ways of looking at and dealing with the world. Hurried children are often deprived of this rich cultural heritage and the opportunity to interact with peers on a level that is unique to childhood and removed from adult concerns.

I am not advocating a romantic view of childhood that suggests that this period is free of conflict and anxiety. There are conflicts and anxieties that are appropriate to this age period—concerns about peer acceptance and about academic and athletic competence—that have to be faced and dealt with. What is crucial during this period is that young people learn to deal with peers on an equal footing as persons with reciprocal needs and interests. This is different from dealing with an adult where the relationship is unilateral—wherein adults have authority over children but not the reverse.

One consequence of single-parent families and of families in which both parents work is that adults and children sometimes interact on a mutual footing. Calling parents by first names, as is common today, reflects this development. Perhaps that is why, in part anyway, we have organized sports at the elementary school level. The family once provided the superordinate-subordinate system of relationships while peers provided that of mutuality and equality, but the reverse seems to be happening today. Parents deal with their children as equals, whereas peers, at least in sports, have to recognize that some age mates (for example, the captain of the team or the quarterback) have more authority than others. Through such inversions peers can come to have more authority than parents.

From a social attachment point of view, childhood marks the first partial separation from parents and the beginning of new attachments to other adults and peers. This comes about, at least in part, because of concrete operations. Young children tend to think of their parents as all-powerful and all-knowing, godlike creatures. When children attain concrete operations, however, they have the mental capacity not only to reason but to check symbols against experience. They begin to distinguish between, for example, fantasy and reality and give up the belief in Santa Claus and the Easter Bunny. (It is perfectly okay for young children to entertain these ideas; giving them up provides children with a useful marker of intellectual development—"I don't believe in that anymore.") But they can now also discover that parents make mistakes and say things that the child knows are not true.

This discovery that adults are not perfect and the resulting deflation of their godlike state is nicely described by art critic Edmund Gosse in his childhood memoirs:

> *The theory that my father was omniscient or infallible was now dead and buried. He probably knew very little; in this case he had not known a fact of such importance that if you did not know that, it could hardly matter what you knew.*[5]

Once parents are removed from the pantheon of gods, children are able to elevate other adults to that status. During the elementary school period, children often idealize sports figures, movie stars, and young musical performers. They also begin to talk about being "in love" with a peer, about having "boyfriends" or "girlfriends" although in fact there is not much boy-girl interaction during this period.

Another consequence of the dethroning of parents is a phenomenon that I have called "cognitive conceit." When children catch their parents in an error (as Gosse did), they assume that if the parent did not know that simple fact, then the parent doesn't know anything.

Furthermore, the children also believe that if they know something the parent does not know, then they must know everything. They must be smarter than their parents and, by extension, adults in general. It is not surprising that children of this age tell jokes and favor stories that put adults in a derogatory or stupid role. Homer Simpson, the bumbling, forgetful, impulsive, work-avoiding character of *The Simpsons* provides a nice portrait of the child's view of the adult. Interestingly, Homer's children are portrayed as more adult and mature than he is.

Cognitive conceit is thus one outgrowth of the school-age child's beginning emancipation from parents. Although cognitive conceit is a normal phenomenon of childhood and usually does little harm other than providing children with amusement (they love to laugh at adult errors of any kind), it can have more serious consequences. Hurrying children into decision making that is more appropriate for adults plays into the child's cognitive conceit. When adults ask children to help them make critical decisions in their lives—about moving, remarriage, changing jobs—the children's sense of cognitive conceit, of being smarter and wiser than adults, is reinforced. This can give children an inflated notion of their own wisdom and power and can bring them grief later.

The beginning detachment from parents also makes possible, in late childhood, the establishment of what psychiatrist Harry Stack Sullivan called *chumships*—close friendships between children of the same sex wherein the pair share their most intimate feelings and thoughts. Sullivan believed that it is essential for children to establish a sense of intimacy that would be the basis for all future relationships with persons of both the same and the opposite sex. The hurrying of children can sometimes have the consequence of robbing them of the opportunity and time for chumships.[6]

Finally, from an Eriksonian point of view, the period of childhood is the time when children establish either a firm sense of industry that they can do a job and do it well—or an abiding sense of inferiority, a sense that whatever they undertake will end badly. Because of the changed attachment conditions and because children now spend long hours at school, parents are no longer the primary arbiters of the child's sense of industry or inferiority. This has both positive and negative potentials.

If, for example, children have parents who undermine their sense of industry—by, say, complaining about everything they do around the house, jumping upon their every mistake, and ignoring what they do well—their sense of inferiority may come to outweigh their sense of industry. However, should these children encounter a teacher who senses their capabilities, gives them opportunities to work, and reinforces their achievements, the children may acquire a healthy sense of industry in spite of, rather than because of, the treatment they received from their parents.

Unfortunately, the reverse is also possible. Parents who make every effort to instill a healthy sense of industry in their children may find their efforts undermined by a school that is too bent on hurrying children into academics to acknowledge individual differences. Children who are confronted with demands to do math or to read before they have the requisite mental abilities may experience a series of demoralizing failures and begin to conceive of themselves as worthless.

Such children not only acquire a sense of inferiority that overwhelms their sense of industry but also may acquire what Martin Seligman of the University of Pennsylvania calls "learned helplessness."[7] When humans or other animals are confronted with a series of situations over which they have no control and wherein any efforts they make toward control are ineffectual, they become quiescent and no longer make efforts to master their environment. As we shall see later, children who experience repeated school failure are likely to acquire the orientation of learned helplessness as well as an abiding sense of inferiority. While parents can prevail against the school's impact in this regard, they may not be successful.

Childhood, then, is a period when children have attained concrete operations, can learn rules, and are ready for formal schooling. It is also a period when children are beginning to detach themselves from parents and during which time other adults and peers become more important. Particularly in late childhood, close "chumships" pave the way for future intimate interpersonal relationships. Finally, childhood is also a period when the balance between industry and inferiority is determined by the child's experiences at both home and school.

Formal Operational Period

As children become adolescents, around the age of eleven or twelve, the physical changes in height, body configuration, and facial proportions are so dramatic that they often mask the equally dramatic changes that are going on in children's thinking. Indeed, Piaget's discovery of the new mental abilities occurring in early adolescence constitutes one of his truly momentous discoveries.[8] While it has long been recognized that by age six or seven children attained the "age of reason," it was not recognized that there are quite distinct levels of reasoning. In effect the reasoning engaged in by children is of a different order than adolescent reasoning. It constitutes nothing less than a Copernican revolution in how children see the world.

In addition to the intellectual changes, emotional and social changes occur as well. Attachments to parents and to others become more complex and undergo fundamental transformations. Relative dependence is transformed into relative independence in the emotional, intellectual, and social domains. And adolescence is also the period that Erikson describes as critical for the establishment of a sense of personal identity that must overshadow a sense of role diffusion. All of these achievements of the adolescent period can be affected by hurrying.

The intellectual attainments of adolescents are considerable. Just as the child is able, thanks to concrete operations, to manipulate objects by means of symbols, the adolescent learns to manipulate symbols with high-order symbols. For example, when we talk about a noun or a preposition, we are using symbols for symbols. The language of grammar is a second-order symbol system in which the terms represent classes of symbols rather than classes of things. It does not, therefore, make a lot of sense to teach children grammar, since they cannot really deal with it in any intelligent way until they have attained the new mental abilities that Piaget terms "formal operations" and that permit young people to deal with symbols for symbols.

However, children can certainly use grammar correctly before they can think about it in an abstract way. Young children, for example, use correct word order, tenses, plurals, and so on before they can talk about what it is they are doing. Language itself is a symbolic process. To talk about language rather than things requires a new level of language comprehension and, in effect, a new language—the language of the grammarians. But this language can only be understood by those with formal operational thought. The ability to do something does not imply the ability to talk intelligently about what is being done.

Piaget gave an interesting experimental demonstration of this phenomenon when he asked children of various age levels to first walk on all fours and then to describe what it was they were doing. Although young children were much more adept at walking on all fours than were older children and adults, they were much less adept at verbally describing it. Only the adolescents and adults could say, "First I move my right hand, then my left hand, then my right knee, then my left knee." Right and left are symbolic relations, and to talk about them successfully requires formal operations.[9]

Algebra is still another illustration. In an algebraic equation—$(a + b)^2 = a^2 + 2ab + b^2$—the letters represent numbers. Algebra, like grammar, is a second-order symbol system that represents a first-order symbol system. Second-order symbol systems permit the manipulation of first-order systems. Metaphor and simile are of second level because they are symbols for symbols. A proverb such as "Shallow brooks are noisy" is a metaphor because its symbols, shallow brooks, do not represent the actual things, shallow brooks, but rather other symbols—shallow individuals. Most young people do not really appreciate simile and metaphor until they are adolescent. Thus children read Alice in Wonderland and Gulliver's Travels as straight stories, and adolescents read them as allegory.

Much of our thinking is also symbolic, so that although children think, it is not until adolescence and the appearance of formal operations that young people think about thinking. It is at this time that words which symbolize thought products and activities begin to appear in young people's vocabulary. Teenagers, in contrast to children, begin to talk about what they "believe" and "value" and about "faith" and "motives." Thinking about their own and other people's thinking is a unique achievement of adolescent mental operations.

Formal operations also enable adolescents to conceptualize or reconceptualize past and future in new ways. Parents, for example, are often amazed and distressed to hear themselves bitterly castigated for some slight the young person incurred as a child—"you bought him a new bike and you didn't buy me one"—which was not remarked upon at the time. But in adolescence such memories are elaborated and embellished with the aid of formal operational thinking. Now young people can conceptualize and attribute motives to their parents' behavior that they only intuited before. Many painful memories of childhood are resurrected and reinterpreted in adolescence. Hence young people begin, in adolescence, to pay their parents back for all the real or imagined slights parents committed during childhood that were suppressed or repressed— but not forgotten.

This is an important point in the context of this book. Children who are hurried as children may not understand or resent the hurrying until they become adolescent. Then they may begin to be angry and resentful at parents for reasons the parents find hard to fathom. Many of the problems and behaviors of adolescents have their roots in childhood experiences that are only resented at the time but reacted to later. This "sleeper" effect of hurrying occurs because the new mental operations adolescents acquire enable them to recast their early experience in terms of parental motivations and intentions.

Thanks to formal operations, young adolescents also construct what I call an "imaginary audience." Now that teenagers can think about their own and other people's thinking, they nonetheless make a characteristic error. They confuse what they are thinking about with what other people are thinking about. Because of the dramatic changes taking place in their bodies, in their feelings and emotions, young people concentrate upon themselves. Consequently, they assume that others are as concerned with their appearance, their feelings, and their thoughts as they are. This is the imaginary audience, the belief that others are as concerned with us as we are.

The imaginary audience, which is most prominent in early adolescence, has powerful motivational force. The characteristic self-consciousness of young adolescents derives, in large measure, from the imaginary audience. You become self-conscious when you assume that everybody is looking at you and thinking about you.

For example, young adolescent males who, as boys, had to be forced to take baths and wash themselves begin showering and washing their hair every day of their own volition. The hours spent by young people in the bathroom and the affinity of this age group for mirrors of whatever kind and in whatever place also speak to the power of the audience.

The presence of an imaginary audience helps to explain why some young adolescents react more strongly to separation and divorce than children or older adolescents. The young adolescent may believe that everyone not only knows about the divorce but also about some of the more unpleasant reasons for it. The young person feels embarrassed that everyone knows about the family's personal life and bitterly resents his or her parents for what is experienced as a humiliating public exposure.

A common, indeed universal, imaginary-audience fantasy is that which involves imagining the audience's reaction to our own demise. When we are feeling low, sad, sorry for ourselves, we take pleasure in such audience constructions. It is a way of "stroking" ourselves when there is no one else to do it for us. Recall the passage from Tom Sawyer in which Tom sneaks back to his home, after having run away with Joe and Huck, to discover that he and his friends are thought to have been drowned:

> But this memory was too much for the old lady and she broke entirely down, Tom was snuffling now himself—and more in pity of himself than anybody else. He could hear Mary crying and putting in a good word for him from time to time. He began to have a nobler opinion of himself than ever before. Still he was sufficiently touched by his aunt's grief to long to rush out from under the bed and overwhelm her with joy—and the theatrical gorgeousness of the thing appealed strongly to his nature too—but he resisted and lay still.[10]

While we all engage in such fantasies at times, we are usually aware of what we are doing. But my impression, in encounters with adolescents who subsequently committed suicide, is that the imaginary-audience fantasy can play a part in such acts. Indeed, children who are hurried by being exposed to a real audience at an early age—perhaps because of the negative or positive achievements of their parents that puts them into the tabloids and in the public eye—may construct more powerful imaginary-audience fantasies than children who have been less exposed. Such young people are more at risk for suicide. If a young person feels at the mercy of an all-powerful audience and feels that the audience is disapproving, he or she may commit suicide in an effort to punish the audience and make it suffer for the mistreatment that it meted out. The following case history (from my personal file) illustrates this sequence of events:

> *A young man of sixteen, Harry Y., committed suicide by stealing drugs from a doctor's office, taking them, and then concealing himself in the ticket booth at the high school stadium so that he could not be found. He had been born in Germany to an army sergeant who married a German girl. When Harry was five his father, in a jealous frenzy, murdered his wife and killed himself. Harry went to live with an aunt in Colorado. The aunt had a poor marriage herself and Harry was taken in largely because of the government checks that came for his support. From an early age, Harry was left to fend pretty much for himself. He was pressured to grow up fast out of neglect.*

> *Despite his history and difficult living situation, Harry was doing reasonably well in school, was on the track team, and was seeing a girl from a well-to-do and happy family. A track meet was coming up and Harry asked his aunt for money to buy some new track shoes. She refused. Harry asked her several more times, always with the same result. The last time, he lost control and swore at her abusively. Unbeknownst to Harry, his girl friend's mother was in the next room. When she appeared and Harry realized that she had heard him, he was appalled, fled the house, and broke into the doctor's office for the drugs. He was not found until several days later.*

Adolescent suicide is but one possible consequence of the heightened power given to an imaginary audience when children are hurried to grow up fast.

Other hurried youngsters, those who from an early age have engaged in competitive sports or in the performing arts, and who have been exposed to real audiences as children, nonetheless still construct an imaginary audience when they become adolescents. Indeed, the audience they construct may even be more powerful than that constructed by young people with a less-exposed personal history. As a consequence, they may become supersensitive and extremely overconcerned with their appearance and performance to the point of refusing to engage in their professional activity. The opposite result can also occur, and the young person may become overly vain and conceited, relegating himself or herself to the level of superstar. Many child "prodigies" who have been pushed by their parents face a "mid-life crisis" in early adolescence when they have to deal with the imaginary as well as the real audience.

Closely tied to the imaginary audience is another construction which I have called the "personal fable." If everyone is watching you and is concerned with your behavior, then you must be something special, something unique upon this earth. The fable leads us to believe that other people will grow old and die but not us, other people may get sick but not us, and so on. Indeed, when personal tragedy strikes us, as it does everyone, one of our first reactions is "this could not be happening to me, these things happen to other people, they are not supposed to happen to me."

The concept of a personal fable helps to explain a great deal of adolescent risk-taking and also why hurried children are more likely to take risks than nonhurried children. The personal fable is, in effect, a belief in one's own invulnerability. "It will happen to somebody else, not me." This is a very adaptive concept because there is so much to fear in this world that if we did not operate on the assumption that we were relatively immune from danger, we would never step out of the house, ride in a car or airplane, or eat any packaged food. We would be immobilized. But there is also a danger in taking one's fable too seriously, and when this happens young people take unnecessary risks.

The examples of this phenomenon are well known: the young woman who fails to use contraceptives and who does not demand this precaution of her partner partly in the belief that it destroys the spontaneity but also under the conviction that "other girls get pregnant, not me." In the same way, the young man who experiments with stronger drugs after trying marijuana is convinced that "other kids get hooked, not me." And other young people cheat or steal at school because, to some extent, they believe that "other people will get caught, not me."

Why do some young people invoke the fable and take risks while others do not? While the answer is complex, I believe that hurried children are more seduced by the fable than nonhurried children. Basically (as discussed in more detail later), hurried children are stressed children. Under stress, people become more self-centered, more egocentric than when not highly stressed. Now the fable is an egocentric concept—it amplifies the individual's sense of uniqueness and invulnerability. A stressed young person thus has a heightened fable and is therefore more likely than a less-stressed person to act upon the fable, ignoring the factual knowledge of the risks involved. Although this personal fable is counter-intuitive, young people under stress are likely to be more risk-takers than more cautious ones.

In addition to these changes and events triggered by formal operations, other events are occurring in adolescence as well. The parents, who were once the primary attachment figures, now find themselves eclipsed as young people become attracted to members of the opposite sex. When this happens teenagers often feel guilty. It seems to them that when they "fall in love" they are, in a way, being disloyal to their parents. They behave as if love existed in a fixed quantity and that if you give some love to someone new, you have taken it from an old love.

Young people are not always aware of this dynamic, but they are aware of the guilt. They may get angry at their parents and find fault in all kinds of ways in order to assuage this guilt. Adolescents suddenly discover that their parents don't know how to walk or talk, how to dress or eat. Now that adolescents have developed formal operations they can construct ideal parents and compare them with their own, whom they usually find sadly wanting. When this happens they do not need to feel guilty about taking love away from parents who are not that great anyway.

In this regard, then, children are no different from adults. When an adult breaks off a relationship, he or she often demeans the other person in order to ease the guilt associated with the withdrawal of love. Children, of course, eventually discover that there is enough love to cover both parents and a friend or marriage partner. But this understanding comes in late adolescence and early adulthood. In early and middle adolescence, young people still have a need to find fault with and to be critical of their parents.

Among hurried children, who may harbor a lot of anger at their parents, the criticism and fault-finding may often be more cutting and exaggerated than it is among young people who do not harbor long-standing grudges against their parents. Freud called such anger that was out of proportion to its immediate object "overdetermined." The anger that hurried children express toward their parents is actually directed not at the parents' clothes or eating habits but at a long series of real and sometimes imagined abuses. The anger of hurried children sometimes goes beyond verbal criticism and, in extreme cases, can result in physical attack.

The final dimension of adolescence that needs to be covered is what Erik Erikson calls the "crisis of personal identity versus role diffusion." Formal operations make possible, among other things, the construction of theories. A theory is a second-order symbol system, and in this sense algebra could be said to be a theory of mathematics, and grammar a theory of language. Both are abstractions and operations upon the primary-symbol systems. What we call "personality," "personal identity," or "self" is a theory in this sense. A personality is a higher-order abstraction that encompasses lower-order abstractions seen as feelings, attitudes, traits, habits, and so on, some of which may be contradictory. Thus a personality is a theory about how the disparate facets of a given person mesh together and make sense.

It is not until adolescence that young people construct a sense of personal identity, of having a unique personality. Nor do young people attribute personal identity or personality to other people until adolescence. The construction of a sense of personal identity requires, in addition to formal operations, some consistent experiences of self. Young people who have a consistent sense of their sex role, their success as students, their work habits, and their relations to adults and to their peer group find that constructing a personal identity is a challenge and a rewarding task. The ingredients are all there, they just need to be put together once the requisite mental operations are attained.

On the other hand, if young people are unclear as to their sex role, unsure about their academic competence, and ambivalent in their relations to parents and peers, the construction of a sense of personal identity can be severely inhibited. In effect it is hard to construct an overriding theory of personal identity when the data are inconsistent and discrepant. When this happens young people experience a sense of "role diffusion," a lack of clear definition and cohesion that may lead to adopting a negative identity (such as a criminal or prostitute) in which the definition is clear or unambiguous. Other young people may choose a loss of identity in the subjugation to a cult or religious organization such as the "Moonies." The attraction of such groups is that they provide a preformed identity that the young person can assume without struggle and regardless of his or her personal history.

It is my sense that hurried children have problems with attaining a secure sense of personal identity. In the case of young people who have been immersed in athletics or the performing arts, identity formation comes too early. Such young people tend to define themselves quite narrowly, in terms of their accomplishment and not in terms of the many social and intellectual facets that we usually associate with personality. Likewise, children who are hurried into mature decision making and responsibility may have a distorted sense of their powers and capacities in this regard. Their sense of personal identity may appear more mature and secure than in fact may be the case. These ramifications of hurrying will be explored in more detail later.

For the moment it remains to reiterate the major argument of this chapter, namely, that growth into personhood in our contemporary society takes time and cannot be hurried. As we know it, growth occurs in a series of stages that are related to age. Each stage brings dramatic changes in intellectual capacity, in emotional attachments, and in social relations. The elaboration of these new capacities in all of their complexity and intricacy is a slow and deliberate process. When children are pressured to grow up fast, important achievements are skipped or bypassed, which can give rise to serious problems later.

7

Learning to Be Social

• • • • • • • • • •

Just as children have traditionally been seen as "plants" that "unfold from within" or as "raw material" that has to be "shaped from without," families have also been looked upon in metaphoric terms. One view of the family is that of a "haven in a heartless world," a sort of refuge from the trials and tribulations of the competitive world.[1] The notion of "a man's home is his castle" captures this "refuge" image of the family that has also been promoted by some American sociologists, namely, Talcott Parsons.[2]

A second, contrary image of the family is that it is not so much a refuge as a "prison" that promotes the worst rather than the best in its inmates. People imprisoned in family life become emotionally ill or socially disruptive. In socialist and authoritarian countries, the family is often seen as the enemy of the state, and communal childrearing is a way of lessening its debilitating effects. Even in democratic societies such as our own, the family has often been attacked by social scientists, such as psychiatrist R. D. Laing, as a breeding ground of neurosis and psychosis.[3] At one time or another, American families have been attacked for "momism," for "permissiveness," or for putting children into "double binds" (for example, the mother who says, "Come give me a kiss," but whose body language says that she finds the child offensive).

To some extent, of course, every family is both a haven and a prison. Both parents and children retreat to the security of the family at times of stress or catastrophe. When a parent or a child is seriously ill, for example, the family is the center of this person's support system. Nonetheless, each family member may at some time chafe at family responsibilities that interfere with personal plans or activities. With respect to children, however, the family is always more than just a haven or a prison, it is a school of human relations in which children learn how to live within a society. Discussed in this chapter is the family's human relations training function, how it socializes children, and how stress encourages parents to speed up the educational pace.

How does the family socialize children? At least four different answers to this question have been given by psychologists and sociologists. The "social-learning" theorists argue that children learn largely by "modeling" adult behavior. If parents are well socialized, law abiding, and respectful of authority, their children will be too. On the other hand, if parents take liberties with the law and are rebellious, their children will do the same. Social-learning theorists, such as Albert Bandura at Stanford University, have been particularly concerned with television violence because of its potential effect upon children who can be expected to "model" the aggression.[4]

A second approach to socialization is that of "behavior modification," which derives from the work of B. F. Skinner and his students. According to this point of view, socialization comes about as a matter of rewards and punishments. Parents who reward their children for learning and obeying rules and who withhold rewards when rules are broken will have children who can adapt to the larger social order. In contrast, parents who do not reward rule-regulated behavior, or who reward rule breaking, will have children who defy the social norms.[5]

Still another way in which socialization by parents has been explained is by "social cognition," a position stimulated by the work of Jean Piaget. According to this view, rules vary in their logical complexity and some rules are easier to understand than others.[6] Parents who gear their teaching to the child's level of understanding will have a much better chance of success than those who disregard rule difficulty. A variant of this approach, suggested by some investigators, is that mental development be accelerated by training so that children can learn difficult rules earlier.

The last position is that of Freud's psychoanalysis.[7] In psychoanalytic terms, a child becomes socialized by means of identification and internalization. The boy, for example, identifies with (sees himself as like) the father and progressively internalizes the father's values, beliefs, and prejudices. Likewise, the girl identifies with the mother and progressively internalizes the mother's values, beliefs, and prejudices. Freud did not discuss the processes of identification and internalization at great length, but he meant something more than simply modeling—it was an elaborate process of incorporation that came about as part of emotional identification.

Each of these theories of social learning contains a certain amount of truth. Human beings are complex, and in all probability we learn things in more than one way. Children sometimes do learn by modeling; one has only to hear a nursery-school child at play say with perfect adult inflection, "If you do that again, I'll break your arm!" to be aware of a child modeling adult verbalization. Likewise, rewards and punishments do work sometimes but always in more complex ways than we would like to suppose. And symbolic rewards, like a pat on the head or a loving word or look, are much more potent than objects in reinforcing behavior.

It is also true that children's learning of rules is limited by their level of cognitive understanding, as suggested in the last chapter. On the other hand, while some efforts to accelerate children's intellectual understanding have had limited success, the majority of studies give evidence that efforts at accelerating intellectual development have little if any lasting value. Finally, we know that children also learn by identification and internalization, because as adolescents and adults they may reveal values, beliefs, and prejudices that they never displayed as children but which can easily be traced to parental influences when they were young.

My own, "contract," model of socialization to some extent incorporates all of the positions presented above. This model argues that socialization always presupposes implicit, usually unverbalized, and unconscious reciprocal expectations on the part of children and their parents. The nature of the expectations varies with the age of the children and the sensitivity of the parents; hence, the "social cognitive" dimension of child-rearing is especially taken into account by the model.

Fulfillment of the contracts is often symbolized by specific rewards and punishments employed by the parents. When rewards and punishments work, it is not because of the immediate pleasure or pain they entail but, rather, because of what they symbolize about underlying contracts. For example, if children believe that what they have done (such as cleaned up their room) deserves a reward and the reward is not forthcoming, they will be upset. But they will be more upset by the fact that their good behavior went unrecognized—a contract was broken—than by the lack of a specific reward such as money or a special privilege. Thus rewards and punishments are important to children not only because of their intrinsic (immediate) value but also because of their contractual significance.

Modeling behavior is also part of this contract theory insofar as parents often contract with their children in the same way in which they have experienced contracts. All parents have at one time or another caught themselves saying something to a child in a tone and with words that echo tones and words that they themselves experienced as children. Modeling thus adds to the quality and content of contractual interactions between parents and their offspring.

Finally, the identification and internalization suggested by Freudians are probably the mechanisms by which children come to incorporate contracts and make them their own. In contemporary writing, however, identification can mean "attachment," a kind of emotional bonding between parent and child. Internalization can today be seen as a kind of "reflective abstracting" activity whereby the child abstracts the nature of the contracts from a series of parental acts. What the child acquires by this abstraction is not a set of specific behaviors but a general rule or sets of rules that govern classes of behaviors.

As discussed in the last chapter, children usually do not learn rules, such as those of games like checkers and dominoes, until they attain concrete operations. However, this does not mean that young children cannot learn rules but only that they cannot learn them by verbal instruction. Even young children can learn rules from adults by abstracting from adult behavior. It is likely that children learn language rules and many other rules that govern their behavior in everyday social situations through reflective abstraction; the children can acquire these rules because they are demonstrated rather than explained. Young children can also learn rules implicit in parental behavior even though they cannot learn comparable rules that are presented verbally.

Parent-Child Contracts

From a developmental position, reality is always relative in the sense that it is a joint product of the individual's intellectual activity and the materials provided by the environment. In the realm of physical reality, for example, the child's conception of the conservation of number—the notion that the number of elements remains the same despite their physical arrangement—requires both an experience with objects and reasoning activity. This is true because enumeration is more than a perceptual judgment. It is just about impossible, for example, to determine by sight how many jelly beans there are in a glass candy jar that is full to the brim.

The same premise holds true for social realities, although they are more complex because stimulus cues such as facial expression and voice intonation are much more subtle. Children must construct with their mental ability and from their social perceptions a social reality that will enable them to survive both within and outside of the family.

There is, however, a sense in which social reality is different from physical reality. At least initially, the child's discovery of physical reality is immediate—it is derived directly from contact with physical objects and events. The child's discovery of social reality, however, is always mediated by parents and caretakers. Mediation means simply that parents and caretakers act upon the child to mediate his or her construction of social reality. A child who smiles and is smiled upon acquires a different social reality from a child who receives a different reaction. The physical world, by and large, does not react differentially to the child, but the social world always does. (Children also condition parental reactions and realities, so that socialization is never one-sided.) Hence, from his or her first moments of life, the infant's social experiences are mediated by the particular caretakers in the environment.

The fact that social reality is mediated by particular caretakers does not mean that its construction is totally capricious. Constancies in the construction of social reality exist in the implicit expectancies that both parents and children carry with them; and these constancies result in "collective realities" that have some commonalities from family to family. Collective realities, constructed anew with each child, are what I call "parent-child contracts."

Contracting is a complex process and goes on at several psychic levels at the same time. For example, children who are excessively supported for a particular achievement may come to believe that all support is contingent upon that achievement or a particular level of success. I knew a girl who drew horses very well, for which she was much complimented, but then she was afraid to draw anything else. Sometimes, too, children may believe that parents expect more from them than they really do. One boy I saw as a client was terribly relieved to discover that his parents did not really expect him to get straight A's on his report card.

On the other hand, if parents fail to support children in a given achievement, the children may feel that they were not successful enough, that they did not do enough—in short, that they were at fault. An adolescent boy of my acquaintance joined a cult because he felt that he could "never do enough" to please his parents. The cult provided acceptance and support. Contracts, then, particularly interpersonal ones, can be misread and misunderstood by both the parent and the child. Violations of contracts, real or imagined, are stressful to children and adults. As discussed later, the pressure to grow up fast is often seen by children as a violation of a fundamental contract—the right to grow at one's own pace and time—and hence is experienced as stressful.

Freedom-Responsibility

The freedom-responsibility contract is fundamental in all parenting. Parents, recognizing the initial helplessness of infants, expect that as children grow they will progressively be able to take responsibility for their own behavior. But the parents must sensitively monitor the child's level of intellectual, social, and emotional development in order to provide the appropriate freedoms and opportunities for the exercise of responsibility. Consequently, as children mature, the freedom-responsibility contract is rewritten again and again. In effect, parents and children construct and reconstruct their collective realities. When this is not done, significant interpersonal damage can occur. But when there is a reasonably close match between parental expectations and child performance and between child expectations and parental performance, there is relatively little stress in family interactions. Contractual violations, hence stress, occur when parents do not reward responsibility with freedom or when children demand freedom without demonstrating responsibility.

The following examples illustrate how the freedom-responsibility contract operates. When children are infants, parents do not expect much in the way of responsibility, and they grant few freedoms. Infants are closely monitored. But parents do have some expectations that emerge as soon as infants want to do things for themselves. When, for example, an infant wants to feed himself or herself, the parent is likely to permit it as long as at least some of the food gets in the baby's mouth.

In early childhood, children become mobile and want to take liberties for which they may not be ready. A young child may, for example, want to lift a glass or plate that the parent feels sure will be dropped. It is critical for the parent to be able to assess adequately the child's competencies, which often involves a little trial and error and a few broken plates. (Substituting plastic for glass or ceramic dishes can make this trial and error less traumatic for parents.) As long as children understand that they will have more chances later, withholding freedoms after some exploratory failures can help children assess the limits of their own competencies.

During infancy, and to some extent during early childhood, the parent-child contract is generally communicated absolutely. The parent decides whether or not a particular freedom should be allowed, and the child has little recourse other than an emotional reaction to the parental dictate. In later childhood, however, because of the language facility and reasoning powers of school-age children, contractual arrangements become more relative. Children will often not accept a unilateral judgment by the parent and will argue their cases for particular freedoms, such as staying up late or eating junk food, with considerable vehemence.

It is at this juncture that parenting styles become evident. One can define the typical categories of parenting—democratic, authoritarian, or laissez-faire—with respect to their treatment of contracts. Democratic parents listen to the child's argument, give their own reasons, and make a judgment that takes the child's position into account. Authoritarian parents will not entertain the young person's arguments for a particular freedom and continue to make unilateral judgments. Laissez-faire parents, however, are persuaded by the child's argument and may grant freedom without demanding responsibility in return.

In adolescence, parent-child contracts reach new levels of complexity. Contracts become abstract or general and merge with moral and ethical principles as well as with the laws of the larger society. The use of the family car, for example, is controlled in part by the parents' understanding of the young person's responsibility but also by his or her age and the possession, or lack, of a driver's license. Smoking marijuana and drinking are also regulated, to some extent, by both parents and society. What seems to happen in adolescence is that the freedom-responsibility contract becomes one between the child and society, as well as one between parents and offspring. Thus the freedom-responsibility contract prepares the young person to become a responsible member of the larger community.

To illustrate, my middle son at age fifteen wanted to take a bicycle trip to Montreal with some of his friends. We sat down and went over the plans the group had made. I discovered that they had carefully planned their route and where they were to stay each night. They also had a plan for communicating regularly with parents. They had sufficient provisions, first-aid kits, and spare tubes for the trip. Finally, the young men who were planning the trip were high school seniors and in my judgment seemed like careful and responsible young men. It was at that point that I gave my son permission (and money!) to make the trip. The boys made the journey without incident and had a really great time.

The freedom-responsibility contract in adolescence becomes complex in still another way: parental power over adolescents' freedom is much more limited than it was over the freedom of children. Children can generally be controlled by parental words, but this is not the case for adolescents. Parents can tell their adolescents not to smoke, drink, or have sex, but this may often have little or no effect upon adolescent behavior, particularly if parental contracting during childhood was arbitrary or inconsistent. Young people who move into adolescence without a good sense of the freedom-responsibility contract are more likely to take freedoms that are unsecured (by appropriate demonstrations of responsibility) than children with a strong sense that freedom is earned by responsible behavior. In my experience, many young people arrested for drunken or reckless driving have not been well parented in the freedom-responsibility contract.

The freedom-responsibility contract is one that is often violated when children are encouraged to grow up fast, for example, by being given freedoms for which they may not be fully prepared, like staying home alone. What happens then is the children usually acquire the responsible behaviors required to adapt to the freedoms they were provided. But acquiring these responsible behaviors may be stressful and may be attained at the expense of other activities necessary to well-rounded growth, such as play and fantasy activities.

Achievement and Support

A second type of reality that is constructed between parents and children involves achievement and support. Parents generally have certain expectations about children's achievements that they support cognitively, affectively, and materially. Again, these contracts have to be rewritten as children mature and as the kinds of achievements of which they are capable begin to broaden. Parents, too, have to extend the types of support they provide for their offspring.

A few examples may help to make the evolution of this contract more concrete. During infancy, parents expect primarily sensori-motor achievements of their offspring, and their supports are largely affective. When infants begin to hold their heads up, stand up in the crib, or say a recognizable word, parents respond with hugs and cries and other affective signs of approval. In such ways, children quickly learn that achievement, or attempts at mastery, are rewarded by parents.

During the preschool years, sensorimotor achievements are coupled with symbolic achievements, and affective supports from parents are coupled with symbolic rewards. Young children not only begin to master their bodies but also their clothing, eating, and toileting. They also begin to master language, and parents who could not wait for the child to speak now cannot wait for him or her to be still. In addition to the affective supports of infancy, parents frequently add the symbolic supports of the preschool period—such phrases as "very good," "nicely done," and "look at that."

Childhood achievements become more differentiated as children enter school. Achievements are then evident in three domains: the academic, the interpersonal, and the extracurricular. Unlike the achievements of infancy and the preschool years, these achievements have a social dimension and involve interaction with teachers, peers, and other adults. At this stage, children are not as totally responsible for their achievements as in the years of infancy and early childhood. It is important that parents appreciate this interaction and recognize the children's success or failure in these domains is not entirely their doing.

Parents, in turn, expand the range and nature of the supports that they provide in this period. There is, for example, an increase in the amount of material support as children are provided with clothes and supplies for school and money and equipment for extracurricular activities. Middle-class parents show support by driving their children to friends' houses, to lessons, and so on. Parents also begin to show support by their presence at certain activities, particularly when the child is performing in a school or extracurricular event. As children's achievements become more social, they expect parental support to be more public.

The importance of parental presence as a support for children's achievements should not be underestimated. It is a clear sign that the parents care when they take the time to come see their children perform, particularly when the children know that the parents are not there for their own pleasure or enjoyment. This awareness of parental presence is even true among preschool children although in a somewhat muted form. I remember visiting my middle son's nursery school class, at the request of his teacher, so that I could observe a "problem child" in the class.

It so happened that as I was sitting and observing, a group of boys, including my son, sat in a circle nearby. The conversation went like this:

Child A: "My daddy is a doctor and he makes a lot of money and we have a swimming pool."

Child B: "My daddy is a lawyer and he flies to Washington and talks to the President."

Child C: "My daddy owns a company and we have our own airplane."

My son (with aplomb, of course): "My daddy is here!" with a proud look in my direction.

Children regard the public presence of their parents as a visible symbol of caring and connectedness that is far more significant than any material support could ever be. The most expensive gift will never replace the parent's presence at a child's birthday party.

In adolescence, academic, interpersonal, and extracurricular achievements are expected, and parents become more particular in their demands within these domains. They may expect adolescents to do well in certain courses, they may not be pleased with any of the adolescent's friendships, and some extracurricular activities may be frowned upon. In adolescence, for the first time, parents and their children may not agree on what sorts of achievements are most valuable and important.

In addition, particularly in middle-class families, young people often become enmeshed in "achievement overload." So much emphasis has been placed on achievement that young people overload their schedules: a child may be taking ballet and piano lessons, playing in the softball league, doing volunteer work in the hospital, and still carry a full course load in school. Many of these young people have to keep date books because their time is so tightly scheduled. Even committed and caring parents find it hard to support all of these activities, and parent-child conflicts often ensue over "cutting back."

Achievement overload often occurs because the child has misread the parent's support of achievement. When young people assume that parents are concerned only with how well they do, rather than with who they are, the need to achieve becomes addictive. True meaningful support should communicate to children that achievements are supported because they are *good for the children*. Then the children recognize that what they are doing is for their own good and not just for the parents. When children feel that achievement is for the parent, not for the self, they either eventually give up or go into achievement overload to assure continuation of parental support.

Adolescents continue to need the same sort of support they required when they were children. They still consider it support when a parent attends a play or concert in which they are participating. And adolescents still need affective support; despite their size and physical maturity, they still need a hug, a pat, a cuddle or two (in private, to be sure). We never grow too old or too big for this kind of support. Such affective support communicates that the parent is supporting the child as a person that the parent likes and loves, not just the attainments the young person has been able to achieve.

Loyalty and Commitment

A third collective reality constructed by parents and children involves implicit expectations regarding loyalty and commitment. In general, parents expect a certain amount of loyalty from their children in return for the time, energy, effort, and expense the parents expend in the children's upbringing. As in the other contracts, however, the realities have to be reconstructed as children and parents mature. Indeed, parents must come to expect new loyalties consistent with the child's expanding sense of self and world.

During infancy, as discussed previously, children progressively construct a world of permanent objects that are conceived as existing when they are no longer present to their senses. At the same time, infants also begin to construct a notion of self as existing in time and space. Parents intuitively come to expect that during infancy their offspring will be loyal to them as objects, showing attachment, fear of separation, and so on. Indeed, whereas much has been written about fear of separation as a sign of attachment, it is also an expression of loyalty for parents. The infant who refuses to respond to strangers gives the mother or father, or both, an important and gratifying sign of his or her loyalty to them.

A recent personal observation helps to amplify this point: A young faculty wife brought her infant son to our offices at the university. Everyone, the secretaries and other faculty members, made much of the baby, commenting upon his curly hair, his blue eyes, and so on. One of the secretaries asked if she could hold the baby, and the mother said yes. But as the other woman held out her arms to take him, the baby began to cry and cling to his mother. The mother was apologetic but at the same time held the baby a little closer, and there was a special, pleased look in her eyes—the satisfaction of knowing that her baby *knew* he was her baby. To the mother, I am sure, this was an expression of the child's loyalty to her.

As infants move into early childhood, they begin to construct a world of signs (conventional representations such as language) and symbols (personal representations such as dream images) to signify and extend their control over the object world. Consequently, the child also constructs a notion of the symbolic self associated with the words "I," "me," and "mine" with his or her name and with the family name. At this stage, parents begin to expect, in addition to loyalty to themselves as persons, a loyalty to the symbols that they represent. Parents, for their part, show commitment in the amount of time and concern they put into child-rearing. Children monitor very closely how much time parents spend with them and for them.

The birth of a sibling causes a crisis in the loyalty-commitment contract because, with pregnancy and the birth of a new sibling, the parents' commitment clearly becomes divided. Indeed, one way of looking at sibling rivalry and birth-order effects on personality is to consider the ramifications of siblings for the loyalty-commitment contract.

As children attain school age they construct a world of rules, and a "lawful" concept of self as a rule maker, follower, and breaker. The parental conception of loyalty must expand to include these new constructions, and children's loyalty is now measured in terms of the extent to which they abide by the rules. When school-age children lie and take things, parents become angry, in part, because they see these actions as disloyalty to them. Just as parents expect children to be loyal to the symbols they represent, they expect their children to be loyal to the rules (values, beliefs) that they espouse.

When young people reach adolescence, they become capable of higher-level modes of thought and new conceptions of the world and of the self. The new world that is constructed is ideological in the sense that young people become enamored with, and capable of, dealing with abstract ideas. But they also construct a concept of the reflective self that can think about itself, as well as about the thoughts of others. Not surprisingly, the kinds of loyalties parents expect change too. Parents want young people to be loyal to parental beliefs and values as well as to them as persons, to family symbols, and to moral rules. For example, parents may consider the dating of someone from an ethnic or religious group of whom the family disapproves as a sign of disloyalty.

The adolescent's new-found ability to construct ideals and con-trary-to-fact conditions sometimes produces a crisis in the loyalty-commitment contract in the following way: The adolescent con-structs an image of ideal parents who are perfect in every way. He or she then compares this ideal parent with the real parent and finds the real parent sadly wanting in appearance, manner of dress, personal habits, and so on. Such criticism is seen by parents as a lack of loyalty.

Young people who have been pressured to grow up fast often feel a lack of commitment by their parents and are more likely than those who have not been hurried to be critical of their parents. Hurried children may feel that parents are more committed to their own lives, careers, and friendships than they are to the child, who is hurried. When they reach adolescence, young people feel no need to be loyal to the parents as people nor to the values and beliefs they espouse. When young people feel that parents have vio-lated a contract, they feel no obligation to fulfill their part of the mutual obligation.

The peer group, a youth cult, adherence to a rigid discipline like vegetarianism, or joining a different church from the parents fills the vacuum left by giving up parental values and beliefs. The power these alternatives have over the young person is in direct propor-tion to the extent to which he or she feels a lack of commitment on the part of parents. One of the overall negative effects of hurrying children is the damage it does to the loyalty-commitment contract. Although the damage may be done in childhood, the conse-quences often only appear in adolescence.

This is a brief description of the kinds of realities that I believe par-ents and their offspring construct in the process of living and grow-ing with one another. It is just a framework for looking at how we go about teaching our children to be social. How does a child who has been on one side of the freedom-responsibility, achievement-support, and loyalty-commitment contracts come to be on the other side when he or she becomes a parent? Although a simple modeling of parental behaviors can provide part of the answer, it really does not tell the whole story, because contracts involve a whole series of implicit expectancies that may never be modeled directly and that are communicated in complex and subtle ways. Modeling is too sim-ple to account for the intricate transformations that take place.

It seems to me that one has to look at the interpersonal patterns that evolve in childhood and adolescence for the answer. Rela-tionships to parents tend to be unilateral in the sense that parents expect responsible behavior in return for which they grant free-doms. Children are not in the position to demand that parents act responsibly, and they cannot give freedoms. Thus it is unlikely that children learn the parental side of contracts by modeling their own parents' behaviors.

I believe that children learn the other side of contracts with other children and with siblings. Here the relationship is one of mutuality; it is not unilateral. In playing and working with other children, young people can begin to expect certain behaviors in return for certain favors. In childhood, the rewards for obeying contracts are most often personal acceptance. For example, a child that shows he or she is willing to abide by the rules of the game is permitted to play. It is with peers that children learn the reciprocal nature of contracts and how to be on the giving as well as on the receiving end.

This is perhaps most clear in adolescence when strong and abid-ing friendships are formed. In such friendships, one can discern contracts that have mutuality as their basis. In true friendships, for example, each friend supports the other's achievements. On a football or hockey team, everyone embraces the player who gets the winning point, but they would embrace any player who did it. This is a clear case of reciprocal achievement support.

In close friendships, loyalty and commitment are also apparent. Commitment is shown by working at the relationship, trying to be together; and loyalty is shown by defending it against those who would break it up. In the same way, good friends may advise one another about their actions, about the responsibilities inherent in certain freedoms. Thus friendships during childhood and adolescence are critical to the attainment of adult competencies, in particular to those dealing with the intimacy of marriage and parenting.

Contractual Violations and Hurrying

Thus far I have described what usually occurs in two-parent families in which one parent stays home for part or all of the time. In contemporary families, however, in which both parents work or in which there is only a single parent, the orderly progression of contractual learning is altered. In such families, children learn the reciprocal roles not through friendships in adolescence but largely by the demand of circumstances and parental pressure. Requiring children to play the reciprocal role in contracting is the most powerful mechanism by which parents can hurry children.

Some contractual violations that encourage hurrying occur in two-parent families when both parents work. In such families, children may be given certain freedoms—to make their own breakfast, to choose their own clothes—before they have demonstrated responsible behavior in these areas, such as choosing nutritious foods and putting on clothes appropriate to the temperature and time of year. It was clear to me that some children are not ready for these freedoms when I was asked to see a young girl of eight who brought empty ice cream cones in her lunch pail and wore a halter and shorts in the middle of a harsh northeastern winter.

Similarly, working parents sometimes expect achievements beyond what young children may be capable of; demands for achievements in the social domain may be among the most inappropriate. As suggested earlier, some children may be expected to adapt to three or four different social settings during the same day—to a nursery school, a day-care center, and a baby sitter. Such a child is being supported for achievements that require a level of social maturity and adaptability that few young children possess.

Finally, working parents may sometimes violate the loyalty-commitment contract by expecting children to be loyal in the adult sense of the term. I once witnessed the following event in a day-care center: A working mother had come to pick up her three-year-old daughter, Penny, at about 3:30 PM. It had been a difficult day at the day-care center with one emotional crisis after the other. Through it all, Penny went about her business despite the turmoil swirling around her. When Penny's mother arrived, Penny was sitting near a day-care worker. As soon as she saw her mother, she grabbed the day-care worker by the neck and clung on for dear life; she also began to sob, violently.

The mother was, of course, both appalled and embarrassed. She was appalled because, despite the commitment she felt she was showing by working so her daughter could have a better life, the daughter showed no loyalty. She was also embarrassed because her daughter seemed to prefer another adult to herself and because it seemed that she had provoked an emotional outburst in her child just by her very presence. In talking to the mother, I tried to explain that Penny could not really appreciate her working for the welfare of the family—the child only understood that her mother left her for long periods of time. As for Penny's emotional outburst, it was occasioned by the mother but not in the way the mother thought. Only when Penny saw her mother could she let go of her control and express the fear, anger, and anxiety she had been controlling all day. It was because she felt secure in her mother's presence—the true test of loyalty—that she allowed herself an emotional outburst.

Clearly, families in which both parents work are here to stay, at least for the near future. Nothing that has been said here should be taken as advocating that one parent stay home to take care of the children. However, the demands of two parents working should not blind us to children's built-in limitations of responsibility, achievement, and loyalty. So long as we arrange our lives and our children's lives so that they are not given inappropriate freedoms, not expected to achieve beyond their limits, and demands are not made for unconditional loyalty, parents can both work and still not rush their children into growing up fast.

Another contractual problem sometimes occurs in two-parent homes, most often with respect to girls but sometimes with respect to boys. The situation usually goes something like this: While the girl is growing up the parents may be quite democratic and give her freedoms to the extent that she shows responsibility. This may even involve wearing makeup and designer clothes at an early age, so the girl has a sense of growing up fast and of having her parents' support and encouragement for this process.

However, when the girl becomes adolescent, starts to menstruate, and shows breast development, some parents panic. These parents switch parenting styles and become authoritarian although they were once democratic. Now the girl is told that she cannot date, for example, until she is fifteen, regardless of how responsibly she has behaved. The girl feels that this is a contractual violation because up until this time freedom was granted on the basis of demonstrated responsibility. Now suddenly, and usually without discussion, a relative contract has become an absolute one.

Actually, the problem is more general than has been portrayed in the above example, and it provides one of the major stresses experienced by hurried children. Many young people who have been accustomed to dressing and talking like adults are often frustrated as adolescents because the maturity imposed upon them as children is thwarted. While adolescents today are more sexually active than in past generations, they are still restricted by law from smoking, drinking, driving, and working, at least until they are sixteen. Parents and other social institutions encourage children to grow up fast and to look and behave like adults, but when these same young people become adolescents, they are sometimes expected to forget all that they have been through and to talk and to behave as children. The real stress of being pressured to grow up fast as a child is that it leaves the young person unprepared for the never-never land of adolescence.

Single-Parent Families and Contracts

The late Erving Goffman, sociologist of the University of Pennsylvania, suggested that authority often exists as an "echelon" structure that has a natural hierarchy or chain of command. In two-parent families, the echelon structure is usually clear-cut: parents are in command and the children are subordinate. Parents decide which responsibilities warrant which freedoms, which achievements warrant which supports, and which loyalties warrant which commitments. In other words, much of the decision making is parental, even when the parents invite the participation of their offspring.[8]

In single-parent homes there is, of necessity, a breakdown in this echelon structure. This happens primarily because the effective exercise of authority requires some sort of support. In two-parent families, the parents usually support one another; they can discuss decisions, try out possible ideas, and so on. But in a single-parent family this is not possible; there is no one to work with who will provide support or encouragement.

It is not surprising, then, that many single parents turn to their children for support. In effect this means that contracts are rewritten so that children are full partners. This is a very common way in which children are hurried, and while it alone may not be overly stressful, combined with some of the other stresses young people are exposed to, it could be harmful.

The rewriting of a contract in single-parent homes is often in the freedom-responsibility domain. For example, children may become very involved in their parent's dating practices. If, say, the mother comes back very late and slightly high, the children may argue against her dating that particular man again. And if the parent brings a friend home to spend the night, children assess the responsibility with which that delicate situation is handled before giving their blessing for a repeat of the event.

Children also begin to participate on equal terms in the achievement-support contract. A mother who takes on a new job after years of being at home raising her children may get considerable support from her children, who listen to her stories about her boss and co-workers and help out at home by doing some of the cleaning, cooking, and yard work. Children may also support the mother in her decisions to take courses, give up smoking, diet, and so on. In all these instances children begin to play the supportive role that would ordinarily be played by a marital partner.

Finally, the children may also participate on equal terms in the loyalty-commitment contract. That is, the single parent may begin to go out with men or women who might pose a threat of loyalty to the children. In the two-parent family, the loyalty of parents is taken for granted because the adults are the biological parents and this imposes a sort of automatic loyalty. The affection of one parent for the other is not seen as a threat to loyalty, since both parents are biologically bound to the children. But when, for example, the mother dates a man who has no biological relation to her children, he can pose a loyalty threat that the biological father never did. Because the new man has no biological bond to the children, the mother's attachment to him could be seen as a withdrawal of loyalty, whereas her attachment to the biological father would have been seen as evidence of loyalty.

Accordingly, in single-parent homes, parental loyalty cannot be taken for granted, and the children are in the position of giving commitment in return for parental loyalty. Adolescent children, for example, may offer to stay home or go to a movie with their dad if he is dating a woman they do not like. In this instance the children are willing to show commitment, give of their time and energy to the father's happiness, in return for a demonstration of loyalty to them.

Thus the children of single-parent homes are encouraged to grow up fast because they are, of necessity, put into a reciprocal role with respect to contracts. Allocating freedoms in response to demonstrations of responsibility, offering support in reaction to achievement, and showing commitment in return for loyalty are adult functions. To operate in this way, the child has to try and behave like a knowledgeable adult. Children do not always succeed at this, but in this situation they have some pressure to behave as a parental partner, and this is pressure to grow up fast.

Reciprocal Contracting and Hurrying

The normal process of acquiring reciprocal contracting skills may also be impaired in children who have been hurried, for these children are often "out of phase" with their peers. Because hurried children are, consciously or unconsciously, expected to be "ahead" of their peers in intellectual or social skills, they are often competitive and egocentric in their peer relationships. These young people may adopt the adult unilateral approach to contracting to their peers. For example, an attractive adolescent girl I know had been groomed since childhood to be a physician. She met a young man she liked, but the relationship did not last long. She expected him to take her out regardless of whether he had to study or not, but if she had to study, she would refuse to go out and would rebuke him for asking her. This young woman, hurried since childhood, had no sense of the reciprocity of contracts; she treated her peer as a child.

Young people who have been hurried often have trouble knowing which type of contracting is appropriate. In college, for example, these young people may criticize a professor for such things as not grading exams immediately, although they never get their own work in on time. It is the professor's job to be responsible, not the students'. At work, such young people dislike being told what to do and how to behave as if the employer is dependent on their support for his or her achievement as much as the reverse. In marriage relationships, where reciprocity must be present, such young people will often behave unilaterally and demand achievement (do the dishes, clean the house) in return for support but without feeling that they have to reciprocate in any way (pay the bills, take out the garbage).

Hurrying children is thus not only a violation of contracts but can also impair the child's understanding of the appropriateness of unilateral and reciprocal contracting. Hurried children may adopt an authoritarian attitude with peers and friends where it is inappropriate, and a mutual attitude at school or at work, which is equally innapropriate. It is because they have difficulty knowing when to contract unilaterally or reciprocally that hurried young people often seem to be rude and ill-mannered. Understanding the structure of human relationships is essential to good manners. In French, the phrase *mal élevé* (badly brought up) is as bad an insult as can be leveled at a child. Unfortunately, many hurried children, because they seem to lack good manners, could be said to be *mal élevé*.

8
·········
Hurried Children: Stressed Children

·········
            Sigmund Freud gave us our first comprehensive understanding of emotional illness. Disturbed human behavior that had once been attributed to the work of the devil could now be understood in entirely human terms. Basically, Freud argued, disturbed behavior arises out of conflict; it is a symptom of conflict either within the individual or between the individual and others. The "hysterical" woman, for example, who dresses and behaves provocatively but insists that men are always bothering her is in conflict over her sexuality. Unconsciously, she wants to attract men; consciously, she does not. The treatment of such a problem, according to Freud, was to make the patient aware of her conflicted motives and in this way produce a resolution and a disappearance or diminution of the symptoms, namely, anxiety.[1]

Freud also suggested that the disturbed behavior of the neurotic or psychotic was an exaggeration of a normal reaction to conflict. We all have the potential to become neurotic or psychotic if we are faced with sufficient conflict. Indeed, animals have been made "neurotic" experimentally by presenting them with a situation where pain was the price of a reward. In one experiment, rats were trained to find food in a certain place, then the path to the food was electrified so the animals would be shocked en route. Animals in this situation, desiring to get the food but afraid to do so, showed many disturbed behaviors—they urinated, defecated, went around in circles, and moved toward the food and away from it again and again.

It is clear, then, that conflict is a major cause of emotional distress. And to the extent that hurrying causes conflict, which it often does, it is also a cause of distress. But some years ago Hans Selye, a neurophysiologist at McGill University in Montreal, identified a type of distress reaction that is common to everyone and which, while it may not produce neurotic or psychotic behavior, can have negative effects for the individual's psychic and physical well-being.[2]

Selye demonstrated that our bodies react in a stereotyped and specific way to any special or extra demand (physical, emotional, intellectual) made upon it. Selye wrote of situations, events, or people who produce the stress reaction as "stressors." Stressors are not bad or good, they are just special demands. A passionate kiss, a large raise, a surprise victory, the success of a child, are all stressors in the sense that they call for an extra effort of adaptation. In some ways our bodies are like machines—the more we use them, the sooner they wear out. Whether the machine is used for good or evil, to make guns or tractors, is not relevant. It is the *amount* of use to which the machine is put, not the purpose, that determines how quickly it will start to break down.

In effect, then, stress is the wear and tear on our bodies that is produced by the very process of living. When we say of someone, like the President, "How he has aged in the job," we are talking about a stress reaction. The special demands made upon a President are enormous and the effects are not neuroses or psychoses but, rather, premature aging. Clearly there are individual differences and some people don't wear out as quickly as others, but undue stress always hurries the aging process.

What Selye has done, therefore, is to make us look beyond conflict to understand human distress. The theory of conflict suggests that in the absence of conflict, life is smooth and harmonious. Emotional and physical health are predicated on the avoidance of debilitating intrapsychic or intrapersonal conflict. But we know that living itself is stressful and that a life without conflict is not a life without stress. Indeed conflict is just one, albeit a powerful, stressor.

It is my contention that the practice of hurrying children, in any of the ways described in the earlier chapters, is a stressor. Whether we are hurrying children from baby sitter to nursery school, or to do well on tests, or to deal with issues such as adult problems of sexuality, we are putting children under stress. While no one of these demands may overstress a child, the more hurrying demands are made on a child, the more likely it will be that the child will be overstressed.

Stress and the Stress Response

According to Selye, each of us has a certain amount of "adaptation energy" that allows us to deal with the contingencies of everyday life. Adaptation energy enables children to learn at school and adults to perform their duties at work. Ordinarily this energy reservoir is replenished each day by the ingestion of food and by sleep.[3]

There are wide individual differences in the energy reservoirs we are blessed with at birth. Research by Alexander Thomas and Stella Chess of New York University, for example, shows that even shortly after birth, infants with different temperament types can be distinguished. Some infants are very active and some are very phlegmatic. These individual differences persist throughout life. We all know people who never seem able to sit still, who make us edgy because of the restless energy they communicate. Other people always seem tired and need a lot of sleep.

We tend to organize our lives in keeping with our relative energy levels. Most jobs are geared to what is probably the average energy level that allows us to work for eight hours, to sleep for eight hours, and to eat, relax, and play for eight hours. Individuals with higher energy levels often take on additional work and seem to need less time for rest, food intake, and relaxation. Other people, with low adaptation-energy levels, find even the average workday too long.

Most of the time we organize our lives so that we do not totally exhaust our daily supply of adaptation energy by the time we go to sleep; we keep a certain amount in reserve just in case of emergencies. If the car breaks down on the way to work, or if the furnace goes out, or the boiler bursts, or a relative gets ill or dies suddenly, we need to call on our energy reserves to meet such situations, which go beyond our usual energy requirements.

It is our energy reserves that enable us to deal with acute situations that demand enormous energy output. The mother who lifts a car that has fallen off a jack and onto her child is a case in point, but there are many less dramatic examples. After a busy day we rush our child to the emergency room when he or she has stepped on a dirty nail. We wait for a doctor and an examination, suffer with our child through the pain of the antiseptic and the bandaging, then rush home to finish the day's chores of making dinner, cleaning house, and so on. In the course of everyday life we call upon our energy reserves a great deal.

Ordinarily, there is time in between emergencies to replenish our energy reservoirs. We may sleep for a few extra hours after stressful occasions and neglect some routine chores, or we may decide not to go to a movie or out to dinner but to stay home, which is less energy-consuming. Usually we are vaguely conscious of what we are doing. After a long and difficult day we are aware that we are near the end of our reserve energy and that we badly need to replenish our energy sources. Fatigue is our cue to low energy levels.

Stress, then, is any *unusual* demand for adaptation that forces us to call upon our energy reserves over and above that which we ordinarily expend and replenish in the course of a twenty-four-hour period. Although stress, or extraordinary demands for adaptation, can be of all kinds—accidents, breakdowns, being late, major decisions, major failures, successes, and so on—the response to stress is fairly specific and well documented. In other words, our bodies have a very specific way of calling upon and utilizing our energy reserves. Selye calls this the "stress response."

The stress response dates back to the earliest stages of human evolution, to our animal heritage. We in fact have two brains: an old brain, which regulates most of our bodily functions—heart rate, respiration, adrenaline levels in the blood, and so on—and a new brain, which permits memory, perception, reasoning, and the like. The old brain, was essential when humans were still hunter-gatherers and were dependent upon the immediate physical environment for sustenance. Early man was constantly engaged in fighting off predators and in protecting himself and his family from severe weather and disasters.

Humans used, on such occasions, what they inherited from their animal ancestors—the old brain. Walter Cannon, an American physiologist, first described the stress response initiated by the old brain. He suggested that when the old brain was activated beyond normal levels, it prepared the individual for "fight or flight": "If fear always paralyzed, it would result in injury or death. But fear and aggressive feelings, as anticipatory responses to critical situations, make us ready for action and have great survival value."[4]

The stress response, as described by Cannon and later by Selye, has four steps. The first is a rapid mobilization of energy reserves. Messages are sent from the old brain to the nervous system and a general alarm is sounded. Adrenaline is pumped into the blood, heart rate quickens, breathing becomes more rapid, the stomach and intestines stop digesting, blood pressure rises dramatically, and the senses become more acute and more attuned to every sight and sound. Hormonal activity of many different kinds is at work to increase our energy reserves.

Often we may not be aware of this mobilization until after the stress is gone. For example, I do a good deal of public speaking in the United States, Canada, and abroad. Usually I don't feel self-conscious or anxious before a talk to a large group of people. After the talk, however, I feel tired and emotionally drained. I always prefer to eat after a lecture rather than before because I sense that my digestive processes work better after the stress of public speaking is over. Giving a talk before a large group of people is an extraordinary event and calls forth the stress response. The same is true in many situations. When we have barely escaped a serious accident in a car, we experience the emotional surge only after we have taken the preventive action.

Once the alarm system has sounded, the next step is a rapid increase in energy consumption. At such times, we draw up our energy reserves of which, according to Selye, there is only a finite amount. The burning up of new energy as a response to stress helps to explain why some people lose weight when they are anxious or under pressure, even though they may be eating and drinking more than usual. Anxiety and worry burn up energy. Of course, some people overcompensate for the energy depletion caused by stress, and overeat. Paradoxically, both underweight and obesity can be direct or indirect responses to the body's rapid utilization of energy under stress.

The next step, for which the mobilization and energy consumption were preparatory, is vigorous physical activity of the sort that was essential to our ancestors' survival. They either had to run away quickly or engage in combat. In either case, our sensorimotor system is ready for quick action. This preparation is still useful in some situations today. If you have ever had to rush someone to the hospital, run away from a vicious dog, or swim a long distance to assist someone in trouble in the water, you can really appreciate the mobilization for action provided by the stress response.

The last and final step in the stress reaction is a return to equilibrium. After a stressful situation, the usual reaction is to find peace and quiet. After a lecture to a large audience and a challenging question-and-answer period, I just want to sit quietly. In the same way, someone who has had to work an extra shift, console grieved relatives, or deal with an angry customer needs some time to restore equilibrium and replenish energy reserves.

Although the stress response is clearly adaptive in many situations today, in many others it is not. For example, the motor action that we need to employ in steering to avoid an oncoming car in the wrong lane is far less than what we are prepared for by the stress response. Indeed, the stress response may often be maladaptive in today's world. Consider a young man who had been told in front of the whole class, "Can't you do anything right?" His face flushed, his body tensed, his palms began to sweat, and he wanted in the worst way to run from the room. But he couldn't, because that would only compound the felony. He continued to sit in his chair beneath the snickering stares of his classmates. He didn't run, but his head began to ache and his stomach felt distended; he was swallowing air in huge gulps. I know the reaction well because the young man was myself.

What happens if the stress response is elicited but the mobilization for action is prevented from running its course? The whole pattern of the stress response is interrupted, and equilibrium is restored not by the expenditure of energy through the musculature but rather by its dissipation in other body systems. Headaches, for example, are produced by constriction of blood vessels in the head. When we are stressed and our bodies are ready to take physical action, even the tiny muscles of the blood vessels contract so as to use up some of the mobilized energy. Selye describes the response to unrelieved stress reactions as "stress diseases." These diseases include hypertension, peptic ulcers, headaches, and heart disease.

When the stress diseases were first identified, it was assumed that they were simply a direct reaction to unrelieved stress. But in recent years it has become clear that the relationship between stress and stress diseases is a fairly complicated one and that some intuitive assumptions need to be seriously examined. Consider a study of air traffic controllers, who track incoming and outgoing planes and must make instant decisions involving hundreds of lives:

> Air traffic controllers, according to a classic study, track planes with their blood pressure; as the skies grow crowded, their arteries constrict and their blood pressure shoots up as much as 50 points. Their glands also squirt more of the nerve-stimulating chemical epinephrine, presenting a textbook picture of psychological stress. It goes without saying that the controllers develop a range of stress-related diseases and die of strokes by the age of 50 . . . except that they don't. On the contrary, the study found, by some measures the controllers are actually healthier than the rest of the population.[5]

Research is just beginning to indicate that objective stress, such as that faced by air controllers, is only one of many factors that determine how individuals respond to stress. Just as important as the objective stress that air controllers face is their attitude toward stress and their strategies for dealing with it. In one study it was found that air controllers who were dissatisfied with their jobs were more at risk for stress-related diseases than were air controllers who were happy at their jobs. How we perceive stressful situations is apparently as important to our well-being as the objective stress situation itself.

Another example of incorrect inferences about the relation of stress to disease is the case of women at work. Conventional wisdom says that as women increasingly take on what were once considered male jobs, they become increasingly susceptible to the diseases of stress usually experienced by males. Women's magazines are replete with articles about the negative effects of "trying to have it all." Even Hans Selye has written that "the more women assume male jobs, the more women are subject to so-called male diseases, such as cardiac infarction, gastric ulcers and hypertension. They get the same satisfactions too, of course, but at a price."[6]

But reporter Barbara Ehrenreich began looking for the data that indicated an increase in women's death rates from heart disease and other stress-related diseases. Although many professionals quoted such statistics, Ehrenreich could not track down any reference for them. When she asked a physician who had written a book on women's stress about his sources, he said: "I don't believe in statistics. Women have more love problems than men and now they have more work problems too. That is why they are dying."[7]

In fact, death rates for coronary heart disease, for example, are declining for both males and females, but the rate for females is declining faster than the rate for males. In 1960, males were 1.62 times as likely to die of coronary heart disease as females. In 1976, males were 2.1 times more likely to die of heart disease than women. Ehrenreich concluded:

> *The story on gender and longevity has not changed since the 1920s. Despite women's continuing influx into the work force, despite the "lifestyle" upheaval of the sixties and seventies (and it should be said— despite all the unnecessary surgery performed on women, the reckless prescribing of estrogens and other hazardous drugs and devices) women live longer than men and the gap continues to widen.*[8]

What does seem to matter is the attitude of women toward their work or home. An eight-year study of 900 women in Framingham, Massachusetts, found that women who worked outside the home for more than half their adult lives were not significantly more likely to have developed heart disease than women who had remained at home. What seems to be stressful is not working or staying at home but rather the person's attitude toward these choices. A woman who has to work but would prefer to stay home is under more stress than a woman who prefers to work. In the same way, a woman who stays home when she would prefer to work is under more stress than the woman who prefers not to work and doesn't have to. Thus both work *and* staying home can be stressful if the woman is unhappy.

We cannot determine just from the objective amount of stress a person is under what his or her reaction to that stress may be. We need to know something about the person and about the stress situation before we can predict how the stress will affect the individual. The same is true for children, and we will now look at some of the basic types of stress that have been identified as affecting children and suggest how hurrying can promote or exacerbate these forms of stress.

Stressed Children

Janet is ten years old but has many adult responsibilities. In addition to taking care of her clothes and room, she must prepare breakfast for herself and her younger sister and make sure that they get off to school on time. (Her mother leaves for work an hour before Janet needs to get to school.) When she gets home, she has to do some housecleaning, defrost some meat for dinner, and make sure her sister is all right. When her mother gets home, Janet listens patiently to her mother's description of the "creeps" at work who never leave her alone and who are always making cracks or passes. After Janet helps prepare dinner, her mother says, "Honey, will you do the dishes? I'm just too tired," and Janet barely has time to do some homework.

Children like Janet (and there are many of them) are stressed by *responsibility* overload. It is not just that Janet has a lot of work to do, for most children today could probably do more than they are required to do. In previous generations, the children of immigrants worked long, hard hours and nevertheless became competent, productive, and sound adults. What is really stressful in Janet's case is not the work but the responsibility the work entails. Janet feels responsible for her little sister, for her mother, for the house. This is really what distinguishes the hard-working children today from the immigrant children of previous generations. In the newly arrived families there was usually a mother and a father so that children did not have *parental* responsibilities. But in the one-parent home of today, children have to assume parental responsibilities. Such responsibilities are a lot for young people to carry and forces them to call again and again upon adaptation energy reserves.

Now consider Peter, a boy four years old. Both his mother and father work and they have enrolled him in a full-day private nursery. In addition, because both parents have to leave home early, they have arranged to leave Peter with a neighbor, who will prepare him for the car pool person, who will take him to school before nine o'clock. After school, the car pool person drops him off at the neighbor's house again until his parents come to pick him up after work. By the time he gets home, Peter has been out of the house for almost twelve hours and has adapted to a number of different places (neighbor's house, car, school) and a number of different people (neighbor, car pool person, teachers).

This is a lot of adaptation for a four-year-old, and he has had to call upon his energy reserves in order to cope. Is it really surprising that his teachers complain that he is whining and fussy, that he does not seem interested in playing with the other children, and that he sometimes sits quietly staring into space while touching two blocks together, back and forth, back and forth? Peter is clearly at the limit of his energy reserves. He suffers from *change* overload.

Emotional overload can occur as well as responsibility and change overload. When, for example, children overhear parents quarreling, they are not only upset by the negative emotions but also by what is being said. Threats made in anger to a spouse are often branded upon the child's psyche even when the child cannot really understand their full import. As one four-year-old said to his father some months after overhearing a particularly violent quarrel, "Are you really going to take a job out West and find a woman who appreciates a man who brings home a steady pay check?" The child knew the threat by heart, adult words and all—he carried it with him as a continual source of stress.

Of course, parents have always quarreled and children have heard such quarrels. But it is much more common today since parents are encouraged to "let it all hang out" and even to learn how to fight in a productive way. In his book *Intimate Enemies,* George Bach provides rules for couples doing battle with one another.[9] In addition, because more and more workers are engaged in service or white-collar activities, there are more people who lack physical avenues for "letting off the steam" (the old-fashioned term for the stress response) generated at work. Unlike the laborer, the white-collar worker has no physical outlet for stress and often brings it home. Quarreling, complaining, and bickering between husband

and wife stresses children by overloading them with fears and anxieties for which they may have no outlet.

In addition, emotional overload is produced by separation of any kind—being left with a baby sitter, going to nursery or public school, going away to a camp for a couple of weeks, business travel of a parent, parental divorce or death—and is stressful. Separation is a normal and healthy part of growth, and no child can, or should be, spared the pain of separation. But too much separation can overstress a child and lead to symptoms of stress disease. It is not separation per se but too much separation too soon that is stressful and harmful to children.

Children today experience separation most frequently in connection with the divorce of parents. Divorce hurries children because it forces them to deal with separations that, in the usual course of events, they would not have to deal with until adolescence or young adulthood. Divorce and separation are painful even when parents take care to prepare children for the rupture and if they cooperate in the child care and do not use the children as weapons against one another. Although children under such circumstances usually cope quite well, there is always some pain and confusion about what is happening and why it is happening.

When separation is not handled well, the stress for children is considerable. Separation may entail a move to a new house or apartment, new friends, or a new school. In addition, the family's economic situation can be dramatically different, with much less money to spend; children may have to take on new responsibilities for self and home care. And the child may be torn between mother and father, each of whom is trying to win the child away from the other. This is the real loss of innocence: losing the implicit belief that the world is a good and stable place in which to live—that the family, the child's basic source of security, will always be there.

The stress on a child of separation from the father (more often the parent to leave in a divorce) has only come to be appreciated fully in the last fifteen years. Outrageous as it may seem, it was once thought that a father's absence was not stressful to children, that fathers were really not important in a child's upbringing. In an official report issued by the World Health Organization in 1951, child psychiatrist John Bowlby—the first to highlight the stress of separation from a loved one as a serious health risk—wrote that the father is "of no direct importance to the young child, but is of indirect value as economic support and in his emotional support of the mother."[10] Even the late Margaret Mead expressed the same attitude when she quipped that "a father is a biological necessity but a social accident."

This attitude toward fathers was reflected in comic strips such as "Blondie," where Dagwood Bumstead's adventures involved his bathtub, his boss, his neighbor, or some traveling salesman. He was rarely seen interacting with his own children. Usually Blondie intervened. And the one child who did interact with him, a paperboy, often won out in the confrontation.

In the past decade or so, however, we have come to understand how much even young children are attached to their fathers and how important this attachment is for healthy growth and development. In part this may be because contemporary fathers are likely to be more involved in child care than in the past and to feel more comfortable in the nurturant role. But fathers were probably always more important to children than was thought in the past. Separation from the father as a result of divorce is an emotional overload and is a powerful stressor to children.

The potency of separation as a stressor is evidenced by the fact that today—because divorce is so common—children from two-parent families are stressed by the very possibility of divorce. The following conversation gives evidence of this concern.

"Daddy, when are you and Mommy getting divorced?" My five-year-old son asked this question nonchalantly as I drove him to school on a Tuesday morning not long ago. I was stunned and a little panicked by the question, and I tried desperately to recall if Ann and I had been bickering lately.

"What do you mean?" I asked, in a tone of syrupy solicitousness that grown-ups often inflict upon kids. "Mommy and Daddy haven't been fighting, have we?"

"No," he allowed, cheerful. "But everybody gets divorced."

"No, no, not everybody," I said. "Lots of Mommies and Daddies stay married all their lives."

"Oh yeah, what about Jason? and Tommy? and Lisa?" He rattled off the names of a dozen or so of his playmates and classmates, all of them children of divorced parents. "And what about Grandpa and Grandma. They were divorced, weren't they?"

"Well, yes." I was caught in the withering cross fire that kids often inflict upon grown-ups. "But your Mommy and Daddy are never going to get divorced. So don't worry about it, okay?"

"Okay." He was satisfied and moved on to more urgent concerns. "Can we go to McDonald's for dinner tonight?"[11]

Divorce and the threat of divorce are not the only separation fears children have to deal with. Modern jet travel has created a new breed of traveling business men and women who spend as much time on the road as they do at home. The following anecdote illustrates the kind of stress this separation can produce.

It is Mark's seventh birthday. His school friends are gathered at the house for Sunday lunch and it's time to blow out the candles, cut the cake and open the presents. The room is filled with noise and laughter. The parents of some of Mark's friends line the room, their faces beaming with delight. One figure, however, is glaringly absent, Mark's father. He is 1,500 miles away on a business trip.

Mark's father, vice president of an industrial consulting firm, spends nearly a third of his life "on the road." When family togetherness is natural and precious—on holidays, the days of school performances, birthdays, the little league championship game—Dad is likely to be elsewhere: in a hotel room, conference hall or taxi.[12]

Separation from parents as a result of divorce or travel—or imagined separation—can overload children emotionally with distress, fears (that the parent will never return), and anxieties (maybe the child caused the parent to leave). Parents are the most important people in the world to their children and separation is a very powerful stressor.

Stresses of Schooling

Schools today stress children in a variety of ways quite beyond the familiar stress of competition for grades and honors. For example, schools are much more a host to theft and violence than ever before. Likewise, schools tend to stereotype children and impose false expectancies upon them. Finally, students are increasingly taught in environments that impede effective learning. These features of schooling force children to deal with adult issues and ineptitudes at an early age and hence are stressful pressures to grow up fast.

Not long ago a sixth grader who lives in the affluent suburb of Lexington, Massachusetts, and I were talking about his going to junior high school the next year. I was curious about his feelings—whether or not he was looking forward to it. Although he was a good student and well liked by his peers, he seemed unenthusiastic about junior high. I wondered whether this was because he would no longer be with his friends, or because he would be in the youngest (least powerful) group rather than the oldest. But his lack of enthusiasm was eventually expressed in a rather unexpected way: "I don't want to get beat up," he said.

What this young man, and many of his friends, feared about junior high were the "druggies" he had heard hang out there. Stories of getting held up or getting beat up are rife among young people and constitute an ironic fear of growing up too fast just when many societal pressures are pushing children in that direction. Unfortunately, young people's fears are not unfounded and too many teenagers have discovered the hazards of leaving a bike unlocked or a watch or clothing unattended.

The following comment was made to David Owen, a writer posing as a student in Bingham High School, serving working- and middle-class families. It was made by a male student about the "hoods" in his school.

"They're *tough* mothers," Bill said. "Those guys don't think twice about stomping on you if you get in their way."

Reporter Owen commented: "Bill's anxiety about hoods is the main reason it's taking us so long to get to our lunch. The food line is generally known as the Hood Line, and Bill doesn't want to take chances. Most of the guys in the Hood Line are about six feet tall and 180 pounds. They're all wearing leather jackets and seven-pound motorcycle boots. In their back pockets are oversized black leather wallets that hook onto their belts with metal chains. Not exactly the kind of guys who would lend you a dime for chocolate milk."[13]

Although there are no reliable statistics about the incidence of violence or theft among young people, the statistics with respect to teachers are revealing. If young people are not afraid of attacking or stealing from teachers, they certainly not going to be afraid of attacking or stealing from peers. According to the National Education Association (NEA), assaults against teachers are increasing. And the same is true for acts of theft and vandalism with teachers as targets.

According to a 1979 NEA survey, some 110,000 teachers—one out of every twenty—were physically attacked by students on school property during the 1978–79 school year. Another 10,000 were attacked by students off school property. The 110,000 victims represent an increase of 57 percent over the estimated 70,000 teachers who were attacked during 1977–78. Of the teachers who were attacked, an estimated 11,500 required medical attention for physical injuries and an estimated 9,000 required medical attention for emotional trauma.

A 1996 national poll of American students commissioned by the Children's Institute International revealed that nearly half of all teens, 47 percent, believe that their schools are becoming more violent, and one in every ten reported a fear of being shot or hurt by classmates who carry weapons to school. More than 20 percent reported being afraid of going to rest rooms because these are unsupervised areas where student are frequently victimized.[14] The rate of victimization is quite high. In 1991, more than half (56%) of juvenile victimizations occurred at school or on school grounds. Few of the victims (only 20%) reported their victimization to the police and fewer than half reported them to either the police or school officials. Most of this victimization is in the form of theft, vandalism or threats of violence without a weapon. The peak time for victimization is 3:00 PM, usually the end of the school day for most children and teenagers. For older teenagers the risk of violent victimization remains quite high from 3:00 to 11:00 PM and drops dramatically after midnight.[15]

What all this means is that young people today are hurried by their schools into attitudes of wariness and fear, which have no place in schools where children's major energies need to be directed toward learning. Indeed, one of the issues not addressed by the educational reform movement is the level of violence and crime that of necessity touches all pupils. Could it be that at least some school failure is attributable to the fear of personal injury engendered by the educational experience?

Schools also hurry and stress children when the teachers and administrators operate on the basis of *stereotypes* and *false expectancies,* which place children in fixed compartments of behavior and thought that are often alien to the child's own inclinations. Stereotyping and false expectancies are particularly common with respect to children of separation and divorce, a growing segment of all school populations.

Teachers and administrators, for example, frequently expect that a child from a divorced family is going to have problems. Likewise, any difficulty the child does encounter is immediately attributed to the family problem without any consideration of possible other problems such as, say, poor vision.

As John Orth, principal of Oak Terrace High School in Highwood, Illinois, writes:

> When families face a crisis there is a great deal the school can do to help without usurping traditional parental prerogatives. . . . The most important one, in my belief, is also the most basic and that is to re-examine our own attitudes and how they come across to the children in our care. Do we, in our own minds, attach a stigma to separation and divorce? Do we automatically expect the worst when we learn that a child's parents have separated? Are we sensitive to the signs, many of them subtle, that signal real confusion and stress in a child? Do we recognize and openly acknowledge the strength and independence many children develop when they learn to cope with that confusion and stress?[16]

Schools also hurry children by labeling children too quickly and too early for management rather than pedagogical reasons. Sometimes such labeling and its consequences for the children involved come close to being criminal. Many young children, for example, are diagnosed as learning disabled or retarded when in fact they may have limited vision or hearing or come from a bilingual home and have limited command of English. It is much easier for teachers and administrators to label such children and to relegate them to some special program than to deal with their special needs.

Our language is really of little help in this regard because it reverses the true order of things and puts the adjective before the noun—retarded child rather than a child who is retarded. Branded and put into special classes early, many children decide, "If you have the name, you might as well play the game," and become what they are expected to be: retarded, learning disabled, or whatever.

Schools stress children in other ways that have recently been enumerated by writer Leslie A. Hart:

- *The classroom size is the wrong size for all activities except rote— too small for films, lectures, and visitors; too large for discussions, projects and the like. . . .*
- *The classroom day involves thousands of events and interactions. Rarely is a teacher activity continuous for as long as two minutes. Disciplinary remarks and actions may take more time than instruction. Seldom can teachers have a one-on-one talk with a student that exceeds thirty seconds. In actuality none of the individualizing that gets talked about happens: simply putting a child into a different group may be called individualizing.*
- *Little time is given to actual instruction in classrooms. Management, busywork, waiting, leaving and arriving, and other diversions reduce gross instructional time to around ninety minutes a day. . . . In class, attention to single students may average, per student, only six hours per year.*
- *To "cover the material," teachers need response from students able and willing to give it, and so they pay attention to about a third of the class, largely ignoring those who need instruction most, who may be written off as "failures" in the early weeks of the semester. A high percentage of failure is expected and accepted.*[17]

Such practices hurry children both in a clock and in a calendar sense. They hurry children by rushing them from one subject or activity to another. Children thus never have a sense of completion, and this is stressful. Children who learn at school often do so despite, rather than because of, educational practice. This practice hurries children in the calendar sense by pushing them into adult attitudes of resignation about the inadequacies, rigidities, and unchangeability of "the system."

School can also stress children because it is so tedious. One of the stresses that contributes to job burnout among adults is work that is repetitious and meaningless. Boredom can sometimes be much more stressful than excitement. A bored person often feels unhappy and trapped, and this brings on the stress reaction. But workers in repetitious, meaningless jobs have no safety valves for their stress reaction and so they become fatigued, inattentive, and careless. The result is that they often lose, or quit, their jobs.

For many young people school represents a boring, meaningless activity. In this respect schools hurry children by pushing them into the dull routines of much adult work. A sensitive portrayal of this sort of academic boredom and stress was provided by a young man interviewed by Thomas Cottle. The young man is "Bobby" Hardwicke, who attends a private school in the suburbs of Hartford, Connecticut, and has parents who are professionals. Bobby says:

> No one likes to recognize what people like me have to go through.
> I'm sure if you asked most people, they'd say the life of a teenager is
> a dream. Everyone I talk to seems to want to be young again, which
> is one of the sicknesses of the culture. We've discussed this in school
> many times. But no one sees us for what we are. First off, teenagers
> or whatever you want to call us, are people. Real, live people. I
> know that sounds strange, but you can't believe how many times
> I'm treated like a thing. In stores, or the post offices, I'm this one's
> son, that one's classmate, that one's student.
>
> I'll go to college, although I think now the best thing for me would
> be to take a year out and work somewhere. I've never really
> worked—at something real, I mean. Something that would make
> the slightest difference to somebody. I've studied Latin for two years,

all right. I get A's. I get A's in History, European History. Okay, so I've done well, although I think anybody could do well at this place if they were half-way verbal. All the classes are small and we don't have that many exams, so all you have to do, like we always kid each other, is talk good. "I talk good, Mrs. Arnold, so can I get a good grade now?"

So with all the studying and talking good, you know what I'd really like to do? Carpentry. I'd like to build a house, or fix someone's stairs or porch. Something real.

You know what it is? You go to a school like this, it costs a lot of money, a whole lot in fact, and all you think about is doing well so you can get into a good college, and because just going to college doesn't mean a thing, you ask yourself, "What am I doing? What does any of this matter!" And the answer is, it doesn't matter at all. One course is only meant to get you to the next one and then the one after that and not one of it makes the slightest bit of difference until you are all done. So you can look back and say, "Well, I did it, I passed; so now what?" All school is, you know, is the great time passer. It's a big invention to keep kids from becoming anything.[18]

School can stress children by hurrying them into dealing with threats of violence and crime; into stereotyped roles and attitudes; and into boring, no-end, meaningless activities. Schools thus often add to rather than subtract from the stress experienced by children in contemporary society.

Media and Stress

As we have seen, contemporary media hurry children in one of two different ways; they may give children too much information too fast, or they may give young people information that is too complex or abstract for children to understand. The first kind of hurrying produces the stress of *information overload;* the second produces the stress of *emotional overload.*

Ordinarily, children have ways of resisting information overload. Once, for example, I took my three sons, who were four, six, and nine years old at the time, to a three-ring circus. I bought good seats in anticipation of my sons' delight at what I remembered with such good feelings. But once the show began, I was dismayed that the boys were not watching. "Look at that lady in the pink dress on the elephant," I said, or "Look at that man on the bike on the tightrope." But the boys were paying attention to only one thing, namely, the vendors selling hot dogs, cold drinks, peanuts, and cotton candy. My boys seemed more excited about eating than about watching the show. I told myself that I had learned a lesson—never again.

Some weeks later, however, much to my surprise, the boys spontaneously began to discuss the circus at the dinner table. "Boy, did you see the lady in the pink dress on the elephant!" exclaimed Ricky. "How did she manage to stay on with just one foot?" Then Bobby piped in, "Yeah, and that guy on the bike on the tightrope was pretty neat too, I'd like to try that." And so it went; the boys had enjoyed the circus, but there had been just too much information to deal with all at once, and they needed time to digest it.

Television, in particular, does not permit time for digestion of information overload. Because children watch television every day, there is little time for reflection. And because television is in the home and is a shared experience, it is more a natural experience than the contrived experience of the circus. Children handle the overload by tuning in and out or by using television as a backdrop for playing, doing homework, or practicing the guitar.

Accordingly, it is probably the form of television, its omnipresence as an information conveyer, that may be as stressful or more stressful than the content per se. Television forces children to accommodate a great deal and inhibits the assimilation of material. Consequently, the television child knows a great deal more than he or she can ever understand. This discrepancy between how much information children have and what they can process is the major stress of television.

Perhaps this is why Marshall McLuhan writes: "The television generation is a grim bunch. It is much more serious than children of any other period—when they were frivolous, more whimsical. The television child is more earnest, dedicated."[19]

In a sense, because children constantly have to accommodate to the information provided by television, they work more and play less. And play, as we shall see, is an important stress valve. Ironically, one way television hurries children is by depriving them of time for play and hence for relieving stress.

The media also stress children by presenting them with material that is too complex or abstract for them to deal with. Sometimes when children are confronted with difficult concepts and ideas, as in programs such as *Nova*, the struggle to understand can be intellectually stimulating. But there is much on television, and in some books and movies, that is puzzling to children but that is not intellectually stimulating. Indeed, much of the sexual and violent material can have a disturbing and stressful effect.

Children are not fully secure in who they are, what their roles are. Even teenagers are not yet fully comfortable with their sexuality, or with their angers and hostilities. When children see angry outbursts, rape, or violent physical attacks on television, it is stressful because it portrays adults who have no control over the very same impulses the young person is struggling to master.

This, by the way, is quite a different issue from a child's modeling of the violence he or she sees on television. Modeling is not in question here; emotional maturity is. Adults who have considerable experience with their emotions and impulses can usually view those who have lost control with some degree of distance. But loss of control can be threatening even to adults. With children, in whom controls are just developing, the observation of adults who have lost control or who are viciously deviant can be a powerful stressor, as it suggests that they may not gain control either.

Thus the media stress children by giving them too much information too fast or by giving them information for which they are not intellectually or emotionally ready.

A Stress Test for Children

Children, then, are stressed by a wide variety of incidents—some positive, others benign, many negative. Like the many adult stress tests given today, we can chart a child's stress level by assessing the stressors he or she has undergone recently. The following scale gives an estimate of the impact of various changes in a child's life that hurry and stress them. Add up the total points for all of the items your child has experienced in the last year. If your child scored below 150, he or she is about average with respect to stress load. If your child's score was between 150 and 300, he or she has a better than average chance of showing some symptoms of stress. If your child's score was above 300, there is a strong likelihood he or she will experience a serious change in health and/or behavior.[20]

Stress	Points	Child's Score
Parent dies	100	
Parents divorce	73	
Parents separate	65	
Parent travels as part of job	63	
Close family member dies	63	
Personal illness or injury	53	
Parent remarries	50	
Parent fired from job	47	
Parents reconcile	45	
Mother goes to work	45	
Change in health of a family member	44	
Mother becomes pregnant	40	
School difficulties	39	
Birth of a sibling	39	
School readjustment (new teacher or class)	39	
Change in family's financial condition	38	
Injury or illness of a close friend	37	
Starts a new (or changes) an extra-curricular activity (music lessons, Brownies, and so forth)	36	
Change in number of fights with siblings	35	
Threat of violence at school	31	
Theft of personal possessions	30	
Change in responsibilities at home	29	
Older brother or sister leaves home	29	
Trouble with grandparents	29	
Outstanding personal achievement	28	
Move to another city	26	
Move to another part of town	26	

Stress	Points	Child's Score
Receiving or losing a pet	25	
Change in personal habits	24	
Trouble with teacher	24	
Change in hours with baby sitter or at day-care center	20	
Move to a new house	20	
Change to a new school	20	
Change in play habits	19	
Vacations with family	19	
Change in friends	18	
Attend a summer camp	17	
Change in sleeping habits	16	
Change in number of family get-togethers	15	
Change in eating habits	15	
Change in amount of TV viewing	13	
Birthday party	12	
Punished for not "telling the truth"	11	

9

How Children React to Stress

How children respond to chronic stress depends upon several different factors, including the child's perception of the stress situation, the amount of stress he or she is under, and the availability of effective coping mechanisms. Thus, how children respond to chronic stress is in part an individual matter. "The boiling water that hardens the egg softens the carrot" is but one of many proverbs that speaks to the fact that the stress that will cause one person to fall apart will strengthen another person's resolve—"when the going gets tough, the touch get going."

It is not always easy to predict how a particular child will respond to stress. Sometimes children surprise you. I have seen a rather clingy, dependent boy become quite independent and self-sufficient when this was demanded of him. And I have seen another young man do well at school and at home, despite a mother who had deserted and a father who was alcoholic. But when some boys threatened this young man while he was doing his paper route and took the money he had collected, he went into hysterics and had to be hospitalized.

Free-Floating Anxiety

For some children, chronic stress is translated into what Freud called "free-floating anxiety," in the sense that it is not attached to a specific fear or apprehension. The child feels restless and irritable and is unable to concentrate but is not really sure what the trouble is. One often sees such free-floating anxiety in children whose parents have just separated. Children at such times really don't know what to expect, and it is simply not knowing what to be afraid of that produces free-floating anxiety. Here are a couple of examples:

For most of an hour, Saul angrily protested the excessive demands being made upon him by his sixth grade teacher. "How can he expect me to do all this work when I'm so busy thinking of the divorce? It's not fair." Normally a good student, Saul was unable to finish assignments or prepare for tests. When he was admonished for incomplete work, he sullenly fled the classroom. Had he explained his distress to his teacher? "No," said Saul, "my teacher wouldn't understand, he doesn't even care, he just wants my work." Saul's distressed and angry preoccupation with his parents' divorce had interfered with his ability to concentrate and now everything seemed to be falling apart.

Carol's second grade teacher reported that the girl seemed relieved, "lighter, more carefree" after her parents' separation. Then, two months later, Carol began to whine and cry often begging for her classmates' possessions. "She eats her lunch at 10:00 in the morning," said the teacher, "then she pleads for more food at lunchtime because she has nothing left." Carol told her teacher she no longer cared about her school work and didn't want to help anymore in the classroom. In fact, she said fearfully, "I don't want to do anything."[1]

These examples were taken from a five-year study of 131 children, of ages three to eighteen, who had experienced separation and divorce. As suggested in the examples above, more than 90 percent of the children experienced the divorce as extraordinarily stressful. Two concerns seemed to dominate their thinking: Who will take care of me (protect me, feed me, love me)? Will my relationship with my mother and father last? At all age levels, youngsters felt that they now

faced a world that was suddenly less reliable, less likely to be concerned with future hopes and needs. Their preoccupation with the newly felt unpredictability of life invaded much of their thinking and attention. Many of the children displayed a sadness and yearning for the family as it was and were unhappy with the amount of time they were spending with the noncustodial parent. Most of the children also harbored the wish that their parents would be reconciled. Such wishes persisted alongside a clear intellectual understanding that the divorce was final. Another characteristic revealed by the study was an increase in aggressive behavior. The children were more irritable, more given to losing their temper, and more aggressive (pushing and shoving) toward peers and siblings than they had been before.[2]

Other studies also give evidence that the free-floating anxiety associated with the stress of separation and divorce affects children's school behavior. A recent large-scale study of almost twenty thousand children, both elementary and secondary pupils, from all over the country determined that certain general trends distinguished children from one-parent homes and those from two-parent homes.[3] For example, children from one-parent homes were lower in school achievement and had more tardies and absences than did children from two-parent homes. Likewise, children from one-parent homes visited the health clinic more, had more referrals for discipline, and were suspended more often than children from two-parent homes. These findings suggest the many different ways that the free-floating anxiety, associated with the stress of separation and divorce, appears in children's school behavior. However, remember that these are averages and do not hold for every child who has experienced separation and divorce.

Separation is perhaps the major factor in the free-floating anxiety of children of divorce, but it is not the only one. Other events related to divorce can unduly stress children and leave them anxious and unsettled. For instance, an increasing number of children are kidnapped and retained by the noncustodial parent. It has been estimated that some 100,000 children are snatched by mothers and fathers each year, and about one-fifth are found. The stress on a kidnapped child is enormous. Constantly on the move, with a parent anxious about being found out, children are without consistent schooling and peer friendships. Such children are forced to grow up fast, and those who are eventually returned show many stress symptoms, usually free-floating anxiety. The following case is illustrative:

In January 1979, James Kennedy was kidnapped by his father. In March 1981, an alert schoolteacher, responding to a picture of James that was published in the Ladies Home Journal, *reported to the authorities. When James was returned to his mother, he was quiet and fearful whereas before he had been outgoing. The two and a half years he spent with his father are still a mystery. Pat Kennedy, James's mother, knows that "James lived in Florida, Massachusetts, Tennessee, Connecticut and Pennsylvania, and stayed for short times in Vermont and New Hampshire. He was enrolled in five or six schools at least and at one point was left for several months with one of his father's acquaintances."*

"He was obviously a very lonely little boy, very forlorn," says the teacher who called Pat from Pennsylvania. "Once I saw his father carrying him through a crowded hallway at school by the back of his collar and belt, and he just flung Jimmy into the classroom so that he landed on the floor. The boy was crying pretty hard, and I just knew there was something wrong with the way things were at home."

Once back with his mother, James has settled into a more routine existence, but evidence of free-floating anxiety persists.

"He seems a normal, endearing little boy—except that even now his life is far from normal. You can tell from the way he jumps when he hears a noise outside that the fear is still there. . . . The fear of being snatched again."[4]

In addition to the stresses associated with divorce, contemporary children may be stressed into free-floating anxiety by films or television programs that the children are not emotionally prepared to handle. Free-floating anxiety is also common among young children who are hurried from baby sitter to day-care center to baby sitter. Free-floating anxiety in the form of restlessness, irritability, inability to concentrate, and low mood is perhaps the most pervasive immediate response children exhibit to the stress of hurrying.

And all the signs point to a large increase in this syndrome. Pediatricians are reporting an increase in children with stomachaches and headaches that appear to be stress related. In adolescents, free-floating anxiety can take the form of depression and contribute to suicide. In Toronto, as in many large cities, the increases in stress reactions among young people have been so great that special child and adolescent services have been set up to care for these youngsters. Clinical psychologist Diane Syer, on the staff of the crisis intervention unit at Toronto East General Hospital, says this trend can be blamed on the fragmentation of the family and the erosion of social institutions such as religion, the mobility of people in our society, and a pervasive sense that the future will be grim.[5]

Type A Behavior

It has long been known that some adults cope with stress with a characteristic personality pattern. This pattern, Type A, includes competitive achievement, striving, impatience, and aggression, both verbal and physical. Such personalities can be identified either by clinical interview or by a questionnaire. Another type of personality, Type B, is defined by the absence of Type A characteristics. The significance of the Type A personality is that persons who manifest it are twice as likely to develop coronary heart disease as Type B persons.

In the last few years investigators have been able to identify children with Type A and Type B personalities. In one investigation, for example, it was found that Type A children responded to stress in a manner comparable to Type A adults. That is, when Type A children and adults feel they are losing control of a situation that really matters to them, they make vigorous efforts to maintain control. Type A adults and children do not differ, however, from Type B adults and children when they perceive that they are in complete control of the situation. Type A characteristics are brought out in response to a perceived loss of control over a significant situation.[6]

The significance of these findings was made clear by Dr. Gerald Berenson and his colleagues at Louisiana State University, who examined 378 children of ages two to seventeen in Franklinton, Louisiana. This is but part of a larger sample of a long-term study of some 6,000 to 7,000 Louisiana youngsters. The aim of the study was to determine whether Type A behavior in children had the same physiological correlates that seem to predispose Type A adults to coronary heart disease. The results were as expected—Type A children had more cholesterol in their bloodstreams than did Type B children. The investigators concluded: "It is highly probable that certain personality and behavior traits (competitiveness, overeating, restlessness) that occur in children influence the early development of coronary artery disease and essential hypertension." Responding to the results of the Louisiana study, Dr. W. B. Kannel, a noted investigator of Type A behavior in adults, said, "The Louisiana study may show that patterns of heart disease formed in childhood by diet, behavior and other factors become self sustaining in adults even when the childhood causes seem to disappear."[7]

Of particular interest in relation to Type A behavior in children is some research relating the child-rearing practices of Type A and Type B mothers with their Type A and Type B sons. Psychologist Karen Matthews of the University of Pittsburgh writes:

> *The results revealed that Type A boys were treated differently from Type B boys. Specifically, Type A and Type B mothers gave fewer positive evaluations of task performance to Type A boys than to Type B boys, and Type A boys were pushed harder than were Type B boys, particularly by Type B mothers. An example of the latter is, "you're doing fine, but next time let's try for 5" (a higher score on the test the boy had taken).*[8]

It is not always clear just what is cause and what is effect in such studies, but the indicators are that parental hurrying can be related to Type A behavior in children.

Perhaps the most serious implication of this research is that patterns of reaction to stress established in childhood can be carried over into adulthood and become autonomous. Hurried children, for example, may not show serious symptoms in childhood but may carry with them patterns of emotional response that can lead to serious illness as adults. The child who gets tension headaches will, in all likelihood, be the adult who experiences migraine headaches. Excessive stress in childhood can have life-long effects by producing patterns of stress reaction that stay with the young person throughout life.

School Burnout

When a person's job places him or her in a situation of chronic unrelieved stress, the end result is what has come to be called "job burnout." Usually what happens is that the person loses all enthusiasm for the job, hates to go to work, and is either lethargic and constantly tired or always tense with nervous energy. Physical symptoms like tension headaches and high blood pressure or behavioral symptoms like drug and alcohol abuse are common. The end result is that the person either quits or gets fired from the job.

Going to school is the job or occupation of children and adolescents. As we have seen, schools are academically oriented; children have to learn the tool skills and basic knowledge about science, social studies, and literature. But not all young people are academically oriented, and even those who are may not learn best under the competitive, test-regulated school program. For young people who may be interested in farming, animal husbandry, forestry, carpentry, plumbing, automotive mechanics, and so on, the academic thrust of schools, particularly high schools, is frustrating. And it is also frustrating for students who cannot keep up with the unrelenting academic pressure.

For such young people, school is like a bad job. It imposes chronic stress on them, and the symptoms of school burnout begin to appear. Often these young people hate to go to school and stay home because of sickness whenever they can. They are frequently tardy and often cut class. Many begin to use and abuse alcohol and drugs; occasionally they vandalize the school or deface it with crude graffiti. Eventually, they drop out of school as soon as it is legally possible. Some may become so-called "in-house" truants, who hang out at school but do not attend classes.

Students who burn out at school rarely go back to complete their high school diploma. One study of high school dropouts showed that about 75 percent of the males had had some form of military training and the rest either held nonskilled jobs or had received training on the job. Of the young women who had dropped out, 40 percent became housewives, 30 percent were employed in nonskilled jobs, and 30 percent were secretaries or clerks.

In their study of job burnout Robert L. Veninga and James P. Spradley identified what they said were five stages in job burnout: 1) the honeymoon, 2) fuel shortage, 3) chronic symptoms, 4) crises, and 5) hitting the wall.[9] Roughly the same stages seem to occur with young people who have undergone school burnout. A child begins school eagerly and happily with high expectations (the honeymoon). But soon the endless demands for learning in a nonsupportive environment and the competition force the young person to call upon energy reserves that are not always replenished. The result (fuel shortage) is exemplified in the child's dissatisfaction with school, fatigue, poor work habits, and sleep disturbances.

When children have to drag themselves to school day after day to face repeated failure, they sometimes develop chronic symptoms, which can be physical or psychological. Allergies, for example, are exacerbated by chronic, unrelieved stress. Proneness to accident and illness can be byproducts of unrelieved school stress. Headaches, ulcers, and colitis can also be symptoms. Some children show behavioral symptoms like aggressive bullying or quiet withdrawal. Still others become "Alibi Ikes," who invent elaborate excuses and justifications for their repeated school failures.

Excessive drug and alcohol use are also symptoms of school burnout. Consider the following account which appeared in the *Hartford Courant:*

> *The four students crouching behind a car in a visitors' parking lot of Hall High School in West Hartford were getting ready to take a test.*
>
> *But no textbooks were open and none of the students was studying notes, they were passing around a marijuana cigarette.*
>
> *"We're mellowing out," said one student.*
>
> *"Relaxing so we can do well on the test," said another. "We have to get a good grade."[10]*

Another symptom of incipient school burnout is chronic cheating. Again, an account from the *Hartford Courant:*

At Westport's Staples High School five young men were taking a calculus quiz. They squirmed in their chairs as their teacher walked around the room surveying the students' progress. The five students' heads bobbed up and down as they glanced from the test to the teacher waiting for him to turn his back. He did and they cheated by exchanging papers. They, too, had to get good grades.[11]

In the first stages of school burnout, the initial challenge and excitement are replaced by dissatisfaction and unhappiness, which are dealt with in a variety of symptoms, or stress valves. If these stress valves don't work, or if they come to be overused, a *crisis* can result. What happens then is that the symptoms become so severe that the young person has to remain home from school or manages to get himself or herself expelled from school. The stresses of school become unbearable, and the safety valves used before no longer work.

Consider the case of Timothy K (not his real name):

Timothy looked forward to going to school because his older brothers and sisters talked about all the interesting things they did there and teased him because he did not know the alphabet and couldn't count. So Timothy began kindergarten eager to learn. But somehow he couldn't quite get the hang of those marks on the paper. He would confuse b's and d's and would read "saw" as "was." Sometimes the other children laughed and the teacher did not say anything to them. Timothy felt as if she was laughing at him too.

School wasn't as much fun as Timothy thought it was going to be. It wasn't fun at all. Timothy began being tired, and it was hard for his mother to get him up in the morning. He became draggy and had to be hurried through his washing, dressing and eating. If his mother was not after him every minute he would stop what he was doing and seem to be lost in a trance or a daydream. Often his mother had to drive him to school because he was so late. Then he was reluctant to get out of the car and seemed to have to drag himself up the walk to the school steps. This pattern continued as Timothy showed the signs of fuel shortage and chronic symptoms.

Then one day Timothy's mother was called to come to the school immediately. She went to the principal's office where a defiant Timothy sat rigidly in his chair, black eyes ablaze, fingers clenched, lower lip clenched tightly by his upper teeth. "We have a problem," the principal said. "Timothy was openly rude to his teacher, he not only talked back, he swore at her and now he refuses to apologize." His mother was distraught and insisted that Timothy apologize that minute to his teacher who was standing there. But Timothy remained mute, his eyes still spitting defiance. The principal told his mother to take Timothy home and not to bring him back until he was ready to tell his teacher he was sorry and to behave like a responsible student.

Timothy had reached the crisis stage of school burnout; his symptoms had become critical. It was at this point that Timothy was brought to see me. What I had to do, first of all, was to defuse the crisis atmosphere. Timothy's mother was sure the world had come to an end, and Timothy would have been glad if it had. I talked a little about the fact that Timothy was far from unique, that many other children had hard times at school, said something nasty, and refused to retract it. Timothy and his mother needed to know that he was not off the continuum of the human race. What Timothy needed was to feel good about himself again and to get a sense that he could succeed at school. He needed to be able to forgive himself before he was able to forgive his teacher and say he was sorry.

The fifth stage of school burnout is less common than the others because most children are taken out of the situation before "hitting the wall" occurs. The phrase "hitting the wall" is taken from the experience in long-distance running when the runner feels that every last ounce of reserve has been exhausted and that he or she cannot run another step. The experience is like trying to run against a cement wall. Physically, all the blood sugar (glycogen) stored in the muscles is used up, the body becomes dehydrated, and there is a loss of blood volume. The person experiences dizziness, fainting, muscle paralysis, and sometimes complete collapse.

Although "hitting the wall" is infrequent, one still sees it in the high school student who has studied so hard for college entrance exams that he or she is too physically spent to take the exams. Often the response is not to the particular set of exams but rather to the accumulated stress of a long history of exam-taking that has taken its toll of the young person's reserve energy.

Obviously the majority of young people who go to school and compete for grades, scholarships, and so on do not experience school burnout. Many young people seem to thrive on the stress of school and academic pressure. It is not just the stress of schooling but how the stress is perceived and responded to that will determine whether or not the young person experiences school burnout.

Learned Helplessness

One stress reaction in children that has been extensively studied is "learned helplessness." In general, helplessness is what we experience when events around us are beyond our control. I recall, for example, when I was a young man going into the hospital for minor surgery—the removal of a benign cyst. As I was being rolled into the operating room and as the anesthesia began to take effect, I heard the nurse say, "It's all right, young man, your appendix will be out in no time." I remember trying to protest but was unable to speak or move. Before going out completely, I experienced a profound sense of helplessness and lack of control as to what was being done to me. Fortunately it was the cyst and not my appendix that was removed.

In the situation described above, I felt helpless because 1) something bad was about to happen to me, and 2) there was nothing I could do to avoid it even though I knew it was coming. Helplessness always involves the sense of impending danger to oneself or one's loved ones and also the awareness that there is nothing one can do personally to help the situation. Every parent who has ever taken his or her child to an emergency room, and seen the child whisked away by strangers in white, knows the stress of helplessness, the knowledge of danger, the inability or impossibility of taking appropriate action. Helplessness is a kind of second-order stress; it is the stress of not being able to respond to stress.

We now know, thanks to the work of Martin Seligman and his students and associates, that the helplessness response, the feeling that we cannot help ourselves or others, can be learned.[12] Children, for example, can learn to feel helpless, to feel threatened and unable to take action, even when this is not the case. Such children become withdrawn, listless, and apathetic and seem to lose all motivation for learning and for relating to other children.

Much research has now been done to show that when some people experience situations over which they have no control, they tend to give up and not perform well. In one study, for example, college students were exposed to escapable, nonescapable, or no loud noise. Afterward, they were asked to solve anagram problems like IATOP (PATIO). Students who had been exposed to inescapable noise were much less successful than students who were exposed to escapable noise or no noise. Apparently, students who have been put in a helpless position carry that attitude over to other situations.

Consider the following case reported by Seligman:

In the early hours of a February morning in 1971, a powerful earthquake struck Los Angeles. Marshall's experience was typical for an eight year old in the San Fernando Valley, the epicenter of the quake: He awakened at 5:45 to find himself in what sounded like a railroad tunnel, with a train bearing down upon him. The floor undulated; he screamed and from the next room heard the frightened screams of his mother and father. Although it was only thirty seconds, it seemed like an eternity of terror while the very ground shook beneath him.

Three years later, Marshall still showed psychological aftereffects of that morning. He was timid and jumpy; slight unexpected sounds terrified him. He had trouble getting to sleep, and once he had, his sleep was very light and restless; he occasionally woke up screaming.[13]

Many children acquire learned helplessness at school when they are confronted with learning tasks that are too difficult for their level of ability. Some children, for example, fail to learn to read because the way in which it is taught confronts them with a task they cannot comprehend or control. Under these circumstances the learned helplessness response is produced and the child retreats from any experience having to do with reading:

*Victor was a slow starter when reading instruction began in kinder-
garten and first grade. He was eager, but just wasn't ready to make
the connection between words on paper and speech. He tried hard at
first, but made no progress; his answers, readily volunteered, were
consistently wrong. The more he failed, the more reluctant to try he
became; he said less and less in class. By second grade, although he
participated eagerly in music and art, when reading came around
he became sullen. His teacher gave him special drilling for awhile
but they both soon gave up. By this time he might have been ready to
read, but simply seeing a word card or a spelling book would set off
a tantrum of sullenness or of defiant aggression. This attitude
began to spread to the rest of his school day. He vacillated between
being dependent and being a hellion.[14]*

In a sense, the learned helplessness described by Seligman is the
obverse of the Type A personality described earlier. Both are exaggerations of the fight or flight reaction, and both are rigid and
inflexible. Faced with an important situation over which he or she
has no control, the Type A child goes all out while the learned-help-
lessness child totally retreats and gives up. In neither case is there
a realistic assessment of the situation or a consideration of alternatives. As a result of the stress of hurrying, children may be conditioned to patterns of response that are stereotyped and maladaptive and that stay with them and become their adult patterns
of reaction to stress.

Premature Structuring

Freud was once asked what became of the clever shoe-shine boys
so common on the streets of Vienna around the turn of the century. These boys, street wise and witty, were able to charm their customers into giving them big tips. Freud reflected a moment and
then replied, "They become cobblers." In a sense these children
had grown up too fast and as a consequence were not able to go
further. Their characters had become structured so early, there was
little room for further growth and differentiation of personality.

Premature structuring is most often seen in children who have
trained from an early age in one or another sport or performing

art. What often happens is that the child becomes so specialized so early that other parts of his or her personality are somewhat undeveloped. Some tennis stars, who have been trained since childhood to be champions, can talk about little else than tennis off the courts. Other adults who were overspecialized as children show rather strange behavior as adults: consider Michael Jackson, his plastic surgery, and his chimpanzee confidant.

Hurrying children into a sport or a performing art need not result in premature structuring and personality constriction. Yehudi Menuhin, who played difficult concerts with leading symphony orchestras at the age of seven, is an example. He was blessed not only with talent but also with parents who put his career and needs before their own but without the exploitative motive of realizing themselves through their son. He was also blessed with gifted and extraordinarily devoted teachers. These teachers were major performing artists of the period, who would even stop by his house to tune his violin for him.

But many other child prodigies are not that lucky. The child prodigy is as likely to fade as to become a superstar. "One such example in recent years is Lilit Gampel. At age twelve Lilit's nationally televised performance of Mendelssohn's concerto with the Boston Pops won her a contract with Columbia Artists Management and a score of engagements with symphony orchestras in Europe and the United States. But for the California wunderkind, all the travelling, including regular visits to a new teacher in New York, the late Ivan Galamian, proved too much. Her playing slipped, she could manage fewer and fewer concerts, relations with her too ambitious parents grew strained and even early admission to Julliard on a full scholarship failed to pull her out of the slump. Colleagues from her performing days say that except for a stint with a small New Jersey orchestra Lilit simply dropped out of sight."[15]

An even more tragic case is that of Christian Kriens. "A celebrated Dutch prodigy, Kriens excelled at conducting and composing as well as at the violin and piano, but he ended up as a disc jockey in Hartford, where in his early twenties, he committed suicide."[16]

Some of the stresses encountered by children who achieve early include conflicts between school and practice time and the incessant interviews with the media. According to Howard Gardner of Harvard, every prodigy goes through what he calls the "midlife crisis of the prodigy." As children, prodigies perform out of curiosity, out of the challenge of learning, and for the approval of parents. But when they become adolescents, they begin to raise questions like: "Why am I doing this, who am I doing it for? Some may decide they just don't want the pressure and that is their right. Others will decide to continue, but in their own way."[17]

Premature structuring has always been common in low-income families, who were more likely than middle-class families to be single-parent homes, to have both parents working, and not to be school oriented. Children in low-income homes often work early, attain independence early, marry and have families early. But it makes sense to low-income young people because they can see the need for their independence, working, and so on.

But now middle-income parents are often single parents, and many middle-income families have both parents working. So middle-income children are now being hurried to grow up fast, are being prematurely structured, for the same reasons low-income children are—namely, parental need. But the parental needs of middle-income parents are different from those of low-income parents; they don't need children to do chores or to earn money. The middle-income child is supported materially but hurried socially and intellectually to serve parental emotional need, not parental material need.

Like the prodigy, the hurried child takes stock in adolescence and asks, "What am I doing?" and "Why am I doing it?" If the answer is that it is for parents and not for the self, the young person may revolt in any number of different ways, such as by running away, getting into drugs, dropping out of school, becoming delinquent, or simply refusing to perform. In every case young people are giving evidence that premature structuring, growing up fast to satisfy parental ego needs without concern for their own needs, is not acceptable.

The Invulnerables

When I worked for the family court in Denver, Colorado, and later in Rochester, New York, I dealt primarily with delinquent children and youth. Occasionally I was able to see the whole family, and that was sometimes a surprise. For example, I once saw a fourteen-year-old girl who, with a friend had been "tricking it" in a trailer parked near an air force base. The mother was obese, on welfare, and was frequented by many men. The father was long since gone. But the younger sister, ten years old, was doing fine; she was a straight A student and was well liked by her teachers and peers.

Such children have often been ignored in psychological and psychiatric research, which has focused upon pathology rather than health. As Lois Murphy wrote in 1962:

> *It is something of a paradox that a nation which has exulted in its rapid expansion and its scientific, technological achievements should have developed in its studies of childhood so vast a problem literature. . . . The language of problems, difficulties, inadequacies, of antisocial or delinquent conduct, or of ambivalence and anxiety, is familiar. We know there are devices for correcting, bypassing, or overcoming threats, but for the most part these have not been directly studied.[18]*

In effect, the helping professions too have hurried children into categories of pathology and disturbance that were once reserved for adults.

But in the last two decades there has been increasing interest in those young people who respond positively to stress. Foremost in this work are psychiatrist E. J. Anthony of St. Louis University and psychologist Norman Garmezy of the University of Minnesota. Both were at first interested in "children at risk"—children of schizophrenic parents who were more likely than the offspring of non-schizophrenic parents to develop symptoms of mental illness. Both investigators noticed that some young people who, by all that is sacred in clinical psychiatry and psychology, should be ill, were not. They then began to study these children to glean some understanding of effective ways of coping with overwhelming stress.

The following case described by Dr. Garmezy provides an example:

> *In the slums of Minneapolis, there is a 10-year-old boy who lives in a dilapidated apartment with his father, an ex-convict now dying of cancer, his illiterate mother, and seven brothers and sisters, two of*

whom are mentally retarded. Yet, his teachers describe him as an unusually competent child who does well in his studies and is loved by almost everyone in his school.[19]

And Dr. Anthony reports on the different reactions of three children whose schizophrenic mother believed that someone was poisoning the food at home. The oldest girl, a twelve-year-old, shared her mother's fears and refused to eat except in a restaurant. The middle child, who was about ten years old, also refused to eat at home—except when her father was there. But the seven-year-old son ate at home every day. When Anthony asked him how he could do so, the boy shrugged and said, "Well I'm not dead yet." He was an invulnerable. Yet his older sister eventually became as psychotic as her mother. The middle child remained sane and did moderately well, although she had occasional symptoms of maladjustment. The boy, however, went on to a brilliant career. "His mother's illness gave him a tremendous need to overcome obstacles, to cope with problems," says Anthony. "He seemed to see the environment as a sort of challenge."

What enables these young people to cope so well with stress? Researchers suggest that at least five different qualities are involved:

1. *Social competence.* Invulnerables seem at ease with peers and adults and make others at ease with them. It is almost as if they have taken a Dale Carnegie course in "How to Make Friends and Influence People."
2. *Impression management.* Invulnerables are able to present themselves as appealing and charming. They seem to really like adults, not in a dependent way but rather in a way that suggests that they have much to learn and are willing to do so. It is a subservience with pride that is most attractive and wins adults over to them as mentors.
3. *Self-confidence.* Such children have a sense of their own competence and ability to master stress situations. Accordingly, they see problems as a challenge rather than as evidence of their incompetence. Garmezy tells of one child who made "bread sandwiches" so that she would give the appearance of

having a lunch like her friends even if there was no filling. "Bread sandwiches" became a metaphor for her whenever she had to cope with a difficult problem. "I guess I will just have to make a bread sandwich."

4. *Independence.* Invulnerables are independent and are not swayed by suggestion. In effect, they think for themselves and are not dissuaded by persons in authority or power. They often find a place for themselves where they can find privacy, peace, and a chance to create an environment suitable to their needs and interests.

5. *Achievement.* Invulnerables are producers. They get good grades, have hobbies, write poetry, sculpt, paint, do carpentry, and so on. Many are exceptionally original and creative. Many develop intense interests at an early age. Perhaps, had they been born to a different family, they would have been prodigies. But born into stressful home situations, some of their strengths and talents seem to be directed to the most important task—survival.

We are just beginning to learn what factors lead some children to become case hardened in the crucible of stress. Some of what we know can be used in suggesting ways of combating stress in all children. But it is also true that invulnerables may be gifted children who in other circumstances would have outstanding careers. Such children are a good example of nature-nurture interaction. In a favorable environment a bright, creative child is gifted; in an unfavorable, stressful environment he or she is an invulnerable.

These are but some of the ways in which children react to the stress of hurrying. Emotional distress and behavioral disturbance can no longer be traced to conflict alone. Today, disturbed children have to be seen, evaluated, and helped within the context of an over-whelmingly stressful environment. If anything, the children we see in the clinic today are more like the shell-shock victims (the war neuroses) of battle than the neurotic children of the past. In a sense, war is to adults what hurrying is to children—an enormous stress that brings much harm and some good.

10
•••••••••
Helping
Hurried Children

•••••••••
Ours is a hurried and hurrying society. We are always on the lookout for ways of doing things faster and more expeditiously. We have the supermarket to speed up shopping and fast-food restaurants to speed up eating. We build superhighways to speed up transportation and household gadgets to speed up housework. And the current revolution in information processing will dramatically speed up the work done in offices. We even hurry our recreation with automated pinsetters, golf carts, and ball tossers. And designers work hard to increase speed for leisure craft, whether driven by motor or sail. We are a time-oriented and time-regulated society, and we impart these values to our children. What is the first expensive utilitarian gift we usually give our children? A watch. We hurry our children because we hurry ourselves.

Although the pressure to get things done more quickly and efficiently has positive benefits—it has made us the most innovative society on earth—it has its drawbacks, such as producing impatience. For all our technological finesse and sophisticated facade, we are a people who cannot—will not—wait. Compulsive about punctuality and using our time most efficiently, we become surly when forced to relax and wait our turn. We switch lines in a bank or grocery store if we think another cashier is faster; we leave waiters less of a tip if service is slow; and when traveling we are willing to pay a high premium to arrive at our destination as quickly as possible—whether we are going abroad, to another city, or to visit friends across town. Only in the context of a society that is hell-bent on doing jobs more quickly and better and is impatient with waiting and inefficiency can we really understand the phenomenon of hurried children and hope to help them.

What can we do to help children who are being pressured to grow up fast and who experience this as inordinate stress? First of all, it is important to recognize what we cannot do. We cannot change the basic thrust of American society, for which hurrying is the accepted and valued way of life. Nor can we eliminate the abiding impatience that goes along with hurrying. When hurrying reflects cultural values like being punctual, then urging children to be on time has social justification. But the *abuse of hurrying* harms children. When hurrying serves parental or institutional needs at the expense of children without imbuing them with redeeming social values, the result on the child is negative.

The abuse of hurrying is a contractual violation. Contractual violations are experienced as exploitative and stressful by children because the implicit contracts between parents and children are the fundament of the children's sense of basic trust, a kind of standard against which the children's social interactions are measured. If something happens to a child's sense of basic trust, the sense that the world is a safe and benevolent place and the sense that people are well meaning and caring are damaged, so too is the child's sense of self and his or her trust in interpersonal relations.

Two different types of contractual violation and exploitation can be identified. One is qualitative and might be called *calendar hurrying*. It occurs whenever we ask children to understand beyond their limits of understanding, to decide beyond their capacity to make decisions, or to act willfully before they have the will to act. But children can also be hurried quantitatively, and this might be called *clock hurrying*. We engage in clock hurrying whenever, through our excessive demands over a short time, we force children to call upon their energy reserves.

All of us have engaged in calendar or clock hurrying at times. Firstborn children, for example, are often subject to calendar hurrying because new parents are unfamiliar with children; thus, not surprisingly, many firstborns are hurried children—hard working, competitive, driving. Likewise, we all engage in clock hurrying when we take young children on long trips. Children can accommodate to such contractual violations because they are not experienced as evidence of rejection or lack of caring.

However, when calendar or clock hurrying occurs because the parent or parents habitually place their own needs ahead of the child's, hurrying can produce real damage. Contracting is based upon mutuality, with the needs of parent and child more or less in rough balance. When parental need routinely takes precedence over child need, calendar and clock hurrying are perceived as stressful to children, even though sometimes putting our needs ahead of children's is inadvertent rather than deliberate. One way we can help keep track of whether or not we are unreasonably hurrying our children is to periodically review our contractual relationships by making some lists, like the one below, of our current contractual arrangements.

Contract Evaluation Form

Child
Age
Sex

Contract 1

Achievements expected   Supports provided

Contract 2

Responsibilities expected   Freedoms provided

Contract 3

Loyalties expected   Commitments provided

In filling out these forms there should be a reasonable balance between achievements and supports, responsibilities and freedoms, and loyalties and commitments. If it is easy to specify what you expect in terms of achievement, responsibility, and loyalty but difficult to itemize what you provide in the way of support, freedom, and commitment, you may be committing some contractual violations and may want to add to your side of the contractual arrangement. With respect to calendar hurrying, it is useful to compare your list of expectations with the kinds of capacities children have (as outlined in Chapter 6). If the expectations are unreasonable for children at that stage, some developmental hurrying may be going on, and you may want to revise your expectations. Looking at the balance sheet, you can decide whether or not there is any abuse of hurrying.

The Child's Perception of Hurrying

If we are asking too much and are engaged in calendar or clock hurrying, we can either cut back on our demands or increase our supports. This is an objective way of helping children deal with hurrying in the sense that it deals with the actual, often unverbalized expectancies that we have of our children and with the amount and variety of supports we are willing to offer.

But hurrying, like any stressor, has a subjective dimension. How children perceive hurrying determines its effects as much as the fact of hurrying itself. We know, for example, that children of about eight years and younger tend to engage in "magical thinking"— they often believe that their wishes, feelings, or acts bear a causal relationship to parental acts. To illustrate, many young people feel that something they did (teased Daddy about his beard) or felt (anger at Daddy for not buying a toy gun) caused Daddy to go away. They may also deprive themselves of some treat (not eat candy) or sacrifice a favored toy (by giving it away or breaking it) in hopes that these magical acts will bring Daddy back.

How children perceive hurrying, then, will depend in part on their level of mental development; it will also depend on their temperament, past experience, intelligence, and so on. We as parents or teachers need to look a little more closely at how children in the four major stages of development view hurrying and what we can do to make those perceptions less stressful. It is important, however, to step back from our adult perspective and recognize that there is more than one way to perceive reality.

Young children (two to eight years) tend to perceive hurrying as a rejection, as evidence that their parents do not really care about them. Children are very emotionally astute in this regard and tune in to what is a partial truth. To a certain extent, hurrying children from one caretaker to another each day, or into academic achievement, or into making decisions they are not really able to make *is* a rejection. It is a rejection of the children as they see themselves, of what they are capable of coping with and doing. Children find such rejection very threatening and often develop stress symptoms as a result.

Children at this stage take the part for the whole. They sense a little rejection in the parent and take it for the whole of the parental attitude. Young children are not relativistic but, rather, think in absolute terms. (Literature for young children is replete with one-dimensional characters such as witches, ogres, fairy godmothers, and prince charmings.) So, even when we engage in some necessary hurrying, our young children may misperceive a part of our attitude for the whole and miss our very real love and concern for them in their global and undifferentiated perception of a bit of rejection.

The situation with young children is compounded by what I have found to be an almost universal assumption on the part of adults regarding young children: we tend to assume that children are much more like us in their thoughts than they are in their feelings. But in fact, just the reverse is true: *children are most like us in their feelings and least like us in their thoughts.* Below is an example of the response of a two-year-old to his father's devastating cerebral hemorrhage, which left the man retarded and helpless. The outburst occurred when the mother and son went for counseling. The mother reported:

> *Will stopped playing and stared. Then all at once, he started picking up toys and throwing them around the room viciously, as hard as he could. I thought "Oh God, what am I doing here?" I had had a perfectly happy little boy. Then my little Will ran over and started hitting me. I was mortified. I was furious at the counselor, but before I could speak, she had calmly knelt next to Will and was quietly explaining that it was okay to throw toys because they were only toys; and while he certainly didn't have a right to hit his mother, he certainly had a right to be mad at her.*

"Mom didn't take care of everything, did she, Will?" the counselor asked.

"No," said Will with feeling, "she didn't. She let my daddy get sick and I hate her." Carefully and at length the counselor explained that even doctors had no way to keep Daddy from getting sick and neither did Mommy . . . then Will climbed into his mother's lap, clung to her and sobbed. "I was astonished," Will's mother concluded, "I never dreamed that two-year-olds have such deep feelings."[1]

Accordingly, when we have to hurry young children, when they have to be at a day-care center or with a baby sitter, we need to appreciate children's feelings about the matter. Giving children a rational explanation, "I have to work so we can eat, buy clothes, and so on," helps, but it isn't enough to deal with the child's implicit thought—"If they really loved me, they wouldn't go off and leave me." We need to respond to a child's feeling more than to his or her intellect. One might say, for instance: "I'm really going to miss you today and wish you could be with me." The exact words are less important than the message that the separation is painful for you too but necessary. And it is equally important, when you pick your child up at the end of the day, to say something about how happy you are to see him or her. By responding to the young child's feelings, we lessen some of the stress of hurrying.

Sometimes our tendency to think of children as not sharing our feelings leads us to compound the stress of hurrying in a different way. When we are in a hurry, we are sometimes impolite and thoughtless to young children because we assume they are not as concerned about such things as we are. But children are very sensitive to signs of parental caring. If we need to break a promise about taking a child to a movie, the park, or the zoo, it is very important that we apologize and make it clear that we really are sorry. In the same way, when we ask children to do something for us, to save us time, or to help us out, it is really important to say "please" and "thank you." Being polite to children speaks to their feelings of self-worth (as it does to adults), which are always threatened when we hurry them. Being polite to children helps them to perceive hurrying in a less stressful way.

Being polite to children is very important and may do as much for improving parent-child relations as many of the more elaborate parental strategies that are currently being proposed. The essence of good manners is not the ability to say the right words at the right time but, rather, thoughtfulness and consideration of others. When we are polite to children, we show in the most simple and direct way possible that we value them as people and care about their feelings. Thus, politeness is one of the most simple and effective ways of easing stress in children and of helping them to become thoughtful and sensitive people themselves.

Once children attain school age and the concrete operations described by Piaget (see Chapter 6), they begin to view hurrying in more complex ways. At the deepest emotional level, they still experience hurrying as a kind of rejection. But instead of blaming themselves or their parents, they use their new mental abilities to rationalize parental behavior and to find acceptable, rather than real, reasons for hurrying. This is why, for example, prodigies do not question parental hurrying during childhood. At this stage, children either accept the rationale offered by their parents or construct their own.

School-age children are more independent and more self-reliant than young children. Consequently, they often seem to welcome hurrying in the sense that they are eager to take on adult chores and responsibilities, particularly in single-parent homes, where they may try intuitively to fill the role of the absent parent. The danger with this age group is for parents to accept this display of maturity for true maturity rather than for what it is—a kind of game. The image to keep in mind for this age group is Peter Pan, who wanted to assume some adult responsibilities (leadership, protection, etc.) but did not really want to grow up and take on some of the negative qualities that children perceive as characteristic of adults. Children want to play at being grown up but they really don't want adults to take them too seriously.

For this age group, it is important that we communicate our appreciation for all that they do for us—helping around the house, baby sitting, and so on—but also that we know they are still children and that there are some things they should not be burdened with. To illustrate, when the oldest child feels that he or she is old enough to baby sit the younger ones but we do not, it is important to say that we feel good about their wanting to help and that we will be happy to let them baby sit when the young ones are a little bigger and easier to manage. By setting limits and by suggesting that the limits are as much a function of the younger children's immaturity as of their own, we can communicate our awareness of their willing-ness to be grown up but also of their desire to retain the prerogatives of children.

As young people move into adolescence and attain new, more complex mental abilities, hurrying is again seen in a new way. Although adolescents also perceive hurrying as a rejection at a deep young-child level, they begin to see it in more abstract, complex terms. First of all, adolescents construct concepts of ideal parents who are all-knowing, all-good, and all-generous and then compare their real parents with this ideal and find them sadly wanting. This is one reason why young adolescents criticize their parents for the way they dress, eat, talk, look, act, and so on. And when adolescents feel hurried by parents, the criticism often reaches a frenzy. If we summarize the way in which the three age groups react to hurrying, we might say that young children tend to blame themselves, children tend to blame the world, and adolescents tend to blame their parents.

Secondly, adolescents blame their parents not only for hurrying them as adolescents but also for hurrying them as children. While school-age children rationalize parental hurrying, they don't forget it. In effect, *adolescents pay us back in the teen years for all the sins, real or imagined, that we committed against them when they were children.* As parents, we really need to begin preparing for our children's adolescence when they are in the cradle. By the time they are fully grown, it is often too late to be thoughtful of their feelings.

Dealing with adolescents is complicated, to say the least. Their new-found intellectual abilities make them formidable opponents in any argument, and their size, strength, and physical maturity wipe out any previous physical inequalities. What needs to be kept in mind is that adolescents still care about their parents and want to be cared about. Now they resist hurrying directly because they feel that it is a violation of parental contracting, that it is a kind of exploitation. But it is because they want to be cared about that they react so strongly to contractual violations. Perhaps they really do not want to admit how much they care and want to be cared about. Accordingly, contractual violations are painful, at least in part because such violations force the adolescent to acknowledge how much she or he is still dependent upon parental love. In any case, in my experience with delinquent young people, the most common feeling expressed was one of exploitation, of being used by parents who put their own needs ahead of their children's.

In dealing with this perception of hurrying, we must recognize that this is the young person's reality. Although parents may have perfectly good reasons for doing what they are doing, young people do not see it in the same way. And arguing with an adolescent usually has just the opposite of the intended effect. When adolescents say that they should not have the responsibility of cleaning up their rooms, doing the dishes, or caring for younger siblings, there is little point to arguing the issue. Adolescents see such demands as their being pushed into responsibilities that are, to their way of thinking, not really theirs but someone else's. They are exempt, by virtue of being adolescents, from doing mundane chores. Arguing with adolescents merely entrenches them in their position.

What is a parent to do? Well, as the old saying goes, "If you can't beat them, join them." Sometimes it helps to accept the young person's premise or perception of the situation and to proceed from there. In working with delinquents, for example, I used to argue with them about their negative perceptions of their parents. They would tell me how bad their parents were and I would try and point out the efforts the parents had made to help the situation, but to no avail. The more I defended the parents, the more the adolescents attacked them. Then I decided to try another approach. I accepted their perception but also noted that it did not agree with my own. "You may be right, but they don't seem that way to me. I wonder why we see them so differently."

So one strategy in dealing with adolescents' perception of hurrying as exploitation is to accept their perception as correct at least for them. The middle ground between totally accepting their reality and totally rejecting it is the acceptance of the fact that while we can recognize that their reality is valid for them, it is not necessarily valid for us. So when a teenager argues about a request, we might say, "Okay, I know that you feel what I am asking you to do is unreasonable. I don't think so, but I can appreciate that you might see it that way. What do you think are reasonable responsibilities for a person your age in our circumstances?" Often, when this question is asked, young people list a set of responsibilities much more stringent than the ones the parents have laid down. Unfortunately, this is usually not enough to get young people to do what we ask. It does, however, help them perceive our position more realistically and to acknowledge that it is laziness, procrastination, or some other reason, rather than parental exploitation, that is at issue. This diffuses the emotional impact and lessens the stress, which is probably as much as can be hoped for.

Thus, children perceive hurrying differently from the way we do. If we want to reduce some of the stress of the inevitable hurrying that all children in our society experience, it is important to appreciate the particular way in which they perceive the hurrying. To do this, we have to decenter from our own adult perspective. Since we are committed to our realities as much as children are to theirs, this is not always an easy thing to do. It is even more difficult when we are under stress; when we are stressed we become egocentric and have trouble seeing the world from another person's perspective.

In these transitional and stressful times, it is particularly important that we try and look at the world the way in which hurried children do. Only when we start from their view of the world can we really hope to help them acknowledge our reality that hurrying is not rejection and that contractual violation is really not exploitation.

Play: An Antidote to Hurrying

So far we have talked mainly about what parents might do to help hurried children, but as we have seen, schools and media hurry children too. While it is not always possible to change schools and media, concerted efforts have been effective. Parent groups, for example, have encouraged a number of school systems to offer alternative educational programs so that parents can choose between, say, a curriculum-centered or a child-centered program. Likewise, Action for Children's Television (ACT) has been very effective in getting programmers to cut down on violence, on advertisements for sugared foods, and so on. Parent groups can succeed in getting schools and media to decenter and to take the children's point of view. This is particularly important in the domain of children's play.

Unfortunately, both the value and the meaning of play are poorly understood in our hurried society. Indeed, what happened to adults in our society has now happened to children—play has been transformed into work. What was once recreational—sports, summer camp, musical training—is now professionalized and competitive. In schools, when budgets are tight, the first subjects to be cut are art, music, and drama. And the media, suffused with the new escapism, offer little in the way of truly imaginative fantasy. Perhaps the best evidence of the extent to which our children are hurried is the lack of opportunities for genuine play available to them.

What is play, and why is it so important to growing children? Over the years, there have been many theories of play, each of which has contained some aspect of truth. Philosopher Herbert Spencer regarded play as a means of reducing "surplus energy."[2] According to Spencer, we have more energy than we need to adapt to modern society, and the surplus is "burned off" in play that has no productive purpose. Around the turn of the century, biologist Karl Groos wrote a two-volume work on the play of animals and humans in which he argued that play was a "preparation for life."[3] He noted that young animals play at stalking games (such as a young kitten pouncing upon a ball of twine) that prepare them as adults to pursue their prey. In a like manner, when children play house, they are engaging in preparatory activity for assuming adult roles. Groos also pointed out, however, that play is a preparation for aesthetic appreciation.

Groos's theory that play is a preparation for life was very influential in educational circles. Italian educator Maria Montessori made it a tenet of her educational program. Her approach to education, which has undergone a renaissance and become very popular in the contemporary United States, transformed Groos's theory into a simple formula that has become a kind of motto for contemporary early childhood education: "play is the child's work." Montessori, who worked first with retarded and then with slum children in Italy, had little use for play or fantasy as ends in themselves. She wrote:

> *Imagination has always been given a predominant place in the psychology of childhood and all over the world, people tell their children fairy stories which are enjoyed immensely, as if children wanted to exercise this great gift, as imagination undoubtedly is. Yet when all are agreed that a child loves to imagine, why do we give him only fairy tales and toys on which to practice this gift? If a child can imagine a fairy and a fairyland, it will not be difficult for him to imagine America. Instead of hearing it vaguely in conversation, he can help to clarify his own ideas of it by looking at the globe on which it is shown.[4]*

This attitude toward play as subordinate to social adaptation and as preparation for life had a brief vogue in this country, as did Montessori education just before the First World War. But Montessori's ideas came under attack by American educators at the time when Freud's work was becoming better known and went into decline between the two world wars as the Freudian influence on education was waxing strong. For Freud, play was important in its own right as a kind of safety valve for dealing with societal repressions. Dreams, jokes, and drama were all forms of play in the broad sense. They were all socially acceptable ways of discharging unacceptable feelings, wishes, and desires. This view of play became distorted in some variants of progressive education. In some "progressive" schools it was felt that any control of the child's impulses would lead to repression and neurosis. The attitude of "anything goes" dominated these schools. In one such school I visited, a troubled boy was allowed to sit crunched up in his cubby the whole morning.

But Freud never meant that play was to be the major preoccupation of children nor that repression was "bad." It was *too much* repression, rather than repression per se, that could result in neuroses. In contrast to Montessori, who regarded all adaptation as social adaptation, Freud distinguished two modes, or poles, of adaptation.[5] One of these involves satisfying the individual's basic needs for food, water, sex, self-esteem, and so on. These needs, at least initially, are expressed in a special mode of thinking that Freud called the "primary process." Primary-process thinking involves non-logical processes like substitution, displacement, and condensation. These processes in turn give rise to dreams, jokes, slips of the tongue, fantasy, and play. All of these activities enable the individual to express troublesome needs and desires in a socially acceptable way.

The second mode of adaptation has to do with the outside world of physical laws and social interactions. Inasmuch as we are biological beings, we have to adapt to our physical environment, and as social beings, we must adapt to our social environment. For this adaptation we have a different mode of thinking that Freud called the "secondary process." In contrast to the primary process, which operates by means of imaginative substitutions, transformations, and condensations, the secondary process is essentially rational—it is geared to deal with environments that are essentially rule regulated.

Accordingly, from a Freudian point of view, healthy adaptation requires a kind of equilibrium between the needs of the individual and the needs of society. Healthy people need to be able to look after themselves before they can look after others. In a sense, play is an expression of self-love because by means of it the individual looks after his or her own needs. But play is healthy self-love in that it enables the individual to work and thus serve others.

Freud's distinction between the two modes of adaptation and between work and play as representing two somewhat opposed modes of adaptation were seconded by Jean Piaget.[6] Like Freud, Piaget distinguished two different modes of adaptation, which he called "assimilation" and "accommodation" respectively. In some ways, Piaget's assimilation was like Freud's primary process in that it can transform reality in nonrational ways and is concerned with the satisfaction of personal needs. Likewise, Piaget's notion of accommodation in some ways parallels Freud's notion of the secondary process in that it too is concerned with the individual's adaptation to the external world. For Piaget, as for Freud, play involves a transformation of reality in the service of satisfying personal needs. Both play and work, the primary and secondary processes, and accommodation and assimilation are necessary for healthy adaptation.

Over the last several decades, the Montessori idea that play is the child's work has replaced the Freud/Piaget view that play and work are separate but complementary activities. Indeed, one might define the abuse of hurrying as the pressure on children to make social accommodations at the expense of personal assimilations. From this point of view, hurried children work much more than they play, and this is the reason that they are so stressed. One evidence of this new negative attitude toward children's play is the rapid growth of Montessori schools in the past two decades—there are now thousands of Montessori classrooms and schools all around the country, and the number keeps growing. By and large this is a healthy development because Montessori teachers are often better trained in the art of teaching than most young people who graduate from teachers' colleges. But the prejudice against play still exists and may be one reason parents are attracted to Montessori schools over the more conventional "play" preschools.

The following example illustrates how the dictum "play is the child's work" gets translated into teaching practice: While observing in one of my favorite nursery schools, I watched a group of four- and five-year-olds playing with some plastic dinosaurs. "I am going to eat you up," said one boy, moving his menacing-looking beast close to his neighbor's. "You will have to catch me first, I'm faster than you," said the other boy as he ducked his smaller animal behind a wall of blocks. At this moment a student teacher came over and decided to capitalize upon the children's interest (the so-called teaching moment) and to instruct them in some size concepts with the aid of the dinosaurs. "Which one is larger?" she asked. But the boys, clearly sniffing a teaching situation, quickly ended their dinosaur play and went on to other projects.

For young children, dinosaurs have a great deal of symbolic significance—they are big and powerful. Yet reduced in size and power by being rendered in plastic, they are quite manageable. They are also remote and safe because there is little danger of encountering one in the street. Dinosaurs, then, provide children with a symbolic and safe way of dealing with the giants in their world—namely, adults. Young children are constantly being told "no" or "don't do that" or "leave that alone" or "get away from there." Adults frustrate them at every turn but are too big to combat directly. So children fight back indirectly, and dinosaurs are stand-ins for controlling the world of giants. When the student teacher interfered and tried to transform personal adaptation into social adaptation—play into work—the children gave up the game because their interest in dinosaurs was personal, not social.

Certainly, children need to learn size comparisons, and their spontaneous interests can be a cue to teaching topics. And children need to do more than play. At every turn they are learning social rules—how to behave in a restaurant, on a plane, at a friend's house, how to put clothes on, how to take them off, how to eat with utensils, how to wash behind the ears, how to wipe oneself with a towel. Children are also learning basic concepts about space, time, number, color, and so on.

All of this and much more social learning—such as described in Chapter Seven—is the real work of childhood. But children need to be given an opportunity for pure play as well as for work. If adults feel that each spontaneous interest of a child is an opportunity for a lesson, the child's opportunities for pure play are foreclosed. At all levels of development, whether at home or at school, children need the opportunity to play for play's sake. Whether that play is the symbolic play of young children, the games with rules and collections of the school-age child, or the more complicated intellectual games of adolescence (like *Clue*) children should be given the time and encouragement to engage in them.

Basically, play is nature's way of dealing with stress for children as well as adults. As parents, we can help by investing in toys and playthings that give the greatest scope to the child's imagination. Windup and battery-operated toys are amusing because they behave in unexpected ways, but they leave little possibility for personal expression. Money spent on such toys could well be saved and put toward a good set of blocks that give children leeway to create and that can be used for years. Other materials such as crayons, paints, clay, and chalk are all creative playthings because they allow for the child's personal expression. It is not necessary to ask children what they have created, for they probably have no conscious idea. Asking about the meaning of a child's production is like the teacher trying to turn children's play with dinosaurs into an adult-oriented lesson plan.

As concerned citizens, we need to assert the value of the arts in the schools. The overemphasis on the basics in contemporary education without a corresponding emphasis on personal expression through the arts hurries children by destroying the necessary balance between work and play. The need for workers to have modes of personal expression at work is just beginning to be realized and appreciated by American industry. Schools need to recognize that children also work better, learn better, and yes, grow better, if time spent in social adaptation—learning the basics—is alternated with time periods given over to avenues for self-expression. Far from being a luxury, time and money spent on the arts enhances learning and development by reducing the stress of hurrying and by giving children an aesthetic perspective to balance the workday one.

Finally, as media consumers, we need to reassert the value of true play and fantasy. The real need is for creative writers who can produce quality material for children that challenges the imagination as well as entertains. It would be a mistake to dismiss the value of fantasy because of the poor quality of material on most children's television programs and in many children's books. Imaginative fantasy has redeeming personal value and may have important social learning fringe benefits as well. The media need to provide better fantasy, fantasy such as fairy tales, that help children to deal with the stress of life. The success of the Harry Potter books speaks to the abiding power of this need.

How to Live on Twenty-Four Hours a Day

The title of this section is borrowed from a book by Arnold Bennett—novelist, playwright, and self-help specialist.[7] In the title he incorporated a time-honored strategy for dealing with stress that has been passed down by philosophers such as Epictetus and warriors such as Marcus Aurelius. Basically, their message is that much of human stress and misery comes from dwelling in the past, on what might have been, or in the future, on what will be. In fact, there is nothing to do about the past, and the future is problematic. We have control only over the present, and this is where we need to direct our energies.

Unfortunately, this approach is sometimes misunderstood as an argument for hedonism: "Enjoy today, for tomorrow you may die." But this was not the intent of the philosophers. They saw life as a whole, guided by moral purpose and principle. While each day was to be lived on its own terms, those terms had to be in accord with the abiding laws of society and ethics.

> *Every moment think steadily as a Roman and a man to do what thou hast in hand with perfect and simple dignity, and feeling of affection, and freedom and justice and to give thyself relief from all other thoughts. And thou wilt give thyself relief if thou doest every act of thy life as if it were thy last, laying aside all carelessness and passionate aversion from the commands of reason, and all hypocrisy and self love, and discontent with the portion which has been given to thee.*[8]

Although children are too young to appreciate these thoughts, they can learn from parental action. If we concentrate on the here and now, without worrying about yesterday or tomorrow, our children will do likewise. If you are a working mother, enjoy the time you spend with your child and don't spoil it for him or her by worrying about the time you were not around or about the times you will be separated in the future. Children live in the present, and they know when we are with them physically but not mentally. By worrying about the past and future, we lose the present and our children don't have us, even when we are around.

Over the years, I have made it a practice to take a little time for myself each day, to enjoy a sunset, watch a sparrow, admire a snowflake. Such moments can and should be shared with children. I also take a moment to review the events of the day, to evaluate, without regret, how well I lived up to the goals of devoting full energies to the task at hand. My sense is that such practices are communicated to the children we live with and that the more we incorporate stress relief valves into our daily routines, the more children can learn similar strategies.

I have outlined above one of many different philosophies or

styles for the art of living. Hans Selye, for example, argues for "altruistic egotism"—in effect, that we serve ourselves by serving others. And Albert Schweitzer had a philosophy he called "Reverence for Life," according to which all living things were to be valued. No one philosophy of life will satisfy everyone, but everyone needs a philosophy of life, a way of seeing it whole and in perspective. The art of living is the most difficult task children have to learn, and they do this best if their parents or caretakers have a way of looking at life as a whole.

No matter what philosophy of life we espouse, it is important to see childhood as a stage of life, not just as the anteroom to life. Hurrying children into adulthood violates the sanctity of life by giving one period priority over another. But if we really value human life, we will value each period equally and give unto each stage of life what is appropriate to that stage.

A philosophy of life, an art of living, is essentially a way of decentering, a way of looking at our lives in perspective and of recognizing the needs and rights of others. If we can overcome some of the stresses of our adult lives and decenter, we can begin to appreciate the value of childhood with his own special joys, sorrows, worries, and rewards. Valuing childhood does not mean seeing it as a happy innocent period but, rather, as an important period of life to which children are entitled. It is children's right to be children, to enjoy the pleasures, and to suffer the pains of a childhood that is infringed by hurrying. In the end, a childhood is the most basic human right of children.

NOTES

Preface to the Twenty-fifth Anniversary Edition

1. McCluhan, M. [1964] 1994. *Understanding Media*. Corte Madera, CA: Gingko Press.
2. BabyPlus. 2006. www.babyplus.com.
3. athleticBaby. 2006. www.athleticbaby.com.
4. Khermouch, G. "Brainier Babies? Maybe. Big Sales? Definitely." *Business Week*, 2004, 34.
5. Cohen, A. J. 1996. "A Brief History of Federal Financing of Child Care in the United States." *The Future of Children*, 6, 26–34.
6. U.S. Census Bureau. 2002–2005. "Child Care Arrangements." In *Who's Minding the Kids?* Washington, DC: U.S. Census Bureau, 70–101.
7. Alexander A. 1997. "Children and Television." In *Encyclopedia of Television*, 1st ed., edited by Horace Newcomb. Chicago: The Museum of Broadcast Communications, 1997.
8. Toppo, G. 2006. "School Recess Isn't Exactly on the Run." *USA Today*, May 16.
9. Ibid.
10. Loveless, T. 2003. *Homework: An Easy Load*. Washington, DC: Brown Center for Educational Policy, The Brookings Institution, 2.
11. Hofferth, S. L. 1999. *Changes in American Children's Time, 1981–1997*. Ann Arbor: University of Michigan.
12. Gibboney. R. A. 1994. *The Stone Trumpet*. Albany, NY: State University of New York Press, 1994.

Chapter 1

1. J. J. Rousseau, *Emile*. New York: Dutton, 1957.
2. A. Toffler, *The Third Wave*. New York: Bantam, 1980.
3. Ibid.
4. A. B. Alcott, *Observations on the Principles and Methods of Infant Instruction*. Boston: Carter & Hendee, 1830.
5. M. W. Shinn, *The Biography of a Baby*. Boston: Houghton Mifflin; J. Piaget, *The Origins of Intelligence in the Child*. New York: International Universities Press, 195 2.

6. E. L. Holt, *The Care and Feeding of Children*. New York: Appleton, 1903.
7. Arnold L. Gesell, *The Mental Growth of the Pre-School Child*. New York: Macmillan, 1968; Benjamin M. Spock, *Baby and Child Care*. New York: Dutton, 1976.
8. J. Bruner, *The Process ofEducation*. Cambridge, Massachusetts: Harvard University Press, r g6o.
9. J. C. Holt, *How Children Fail*. New York: Pitman, 1964.
10. J. Kozol, *Death at an Early Age*. Boston: Houghton Mifflin, 1967.
11. H. R. Kohl, *36 Children*. New York: New American Library, 1967.
12. Arnold L. Gesell, Louise B. Ames, and Frances L. Ilg, *Infant and Child in the Culture of Today*. New York: Harper & Row, 1943.
13. Tim Appelo, "Bringing Up Baby," *Savvy*, March 1988.
14. C. Emerson, "Summer Camp, It's Not the Same Anymore," *Sky*, March, 198 r , pp. 2g-34.
15. Barbara Kantrowitz et al., "The Youngest Jet Setters," *Newsweek*, June 29, 1987.
16. Peggy Mann, "Drugs? Not My Child!" Family Circle, September 24, 1 985.
17. E. M. Hetherington, M. Cos, and R. Cox, "The Aftermath of Divorce." In J. H. Stevens, Jr. & M. Mathews (Ed.s) *Mother-Child, Father-Child Relations*. Washington, DC: NAEYC, 1978.
18. President's Council on Physical Fitness and Sports; National Center for Health Statistics.
19. CDC, *Youth Risk Behavior Surveillance: United States* 1993, in *Morbidity and Mortality Weekly Report*, 1995). 1995: Washington DC. p. 5-34.
20. Lowry, R., et al., *Adolescents at risk for Violence*. Educational Pscyhology Review, 1995. 7: p. 7-39.
21. Kingery, P.M., B.E. Pruitt, and G. Heuberger, *A profile of rural Texas youth who carry handguns to school. Journal of School Health*, 1996. 66: p. 18-22.
22. Harris, L. and Associates, *Violence in America's Public Schools: A Survey of the American teacher*. 1993, Metropolitan Life Insurance Company: New York.
23. Elliot, S., B. Hamburg, and K.R. Williams, *Violence in American Public Schools: an overview, in Violence in American Public Schools*, S. Elliot, B. Hamburg, and K.R. Williams, Editors. 1998, Cambridge University Press: Cambridge England.
24. Author, National Television Violence Study: Executive Summary 1994-1995. 1996: Studio City, CA.
25 Services, U.S.D.o.H.a.H., *Youth Risk Behavior Surveillance*. 1997: Washington, D.C.
26. "Suicide Belt," *Time*. September i, 198o.
27. Ibid.

Chapter 2

1. W. Whitman, *Leaves of Grass*. New York: New American Library, 1980.

2. J. Piaget, *The Psychology of Intelligence*. London: Routledge & Kegan Paul, 1950.
3. J. Locke, *An Essay Concerning Human Understanding*. New York: E.P. Dutton, 1961.
4. John Watson, *Psychological Care of Infant and Child*. New York: Norton, 1928.
5. B. F. Skinner, *Walden Two*. New York: Macmillan, 1948.
6. Tom Wolfe, "The 'Me Decade' and the Third Great Awakening," *New York,* 23 August, 1976, pp 26–40.
7. C. Lasch, *The Culture of Narcissism*. New York: Norton, 1979.
8. J. Underwood, "A Game Plan for America," *Sports Illustrated,* February 23, 1981.
9. Ibid.
10. Ibid.
11. Ibid.
12. Colette Dowling, "The Cinderella Syndrome," *New York Times Magazine,* March 22, 1981.
13. K. M. Pierce, "Big Crunch for Kindergartens," *Time Magazine.* September 29, 1980.
14. Ibid.

Chapter 3

1. A. Binet and H. Simon, "Methodes Nouvelles pour le Diagnostic du Nouveau Intellectual des Anormaux," *L'Année Psychologique* 1905, *11,* 245–236.
2. Ibid.
3. D. P. Gardner and Y. W. Larsen, "A Nation at Risk," National Commission on Excellence in Education, U.S. Department of Education, 1983.
4 A. Bloom, *The Closing of the American Mind*. New York: Simon & Schuster, 1987.
5. E. D. Hirsch, *Cultural Literacy*. New York: Houghton Mifflin, 1987.
6. H. Gardner, *Frames of Mind*. New York: Basic Books, 1983.
7. R. Sternberg, *The Triarchic Mind*. New York: Viking, 1988.
8. Edward B. Fiske, "America's Test Mania," *New York Times Education Life,* April 10, 1988.
9. Laurie Denton, "Real Life Wobegon No Joke," *Psychological Monitor,* August 1988, pp 8–9.
10. K. Keniston, "The 11-Year Olds of Today Are the Computer Terminals of Tomorrow," *New York Times,* February 19, 1976.
11. Irwin Hyman, "Japanese vs. American Schools," *Children,* February 1988, pp 33–36.
12. Carol Simons, "They Get by with a Lot of Help from Their Kyoiku Mamas," *Smithsonian Magazine,* 1987, pp 44–52.

13. "Japanese Education Today," Report of the U.S. Department of Education.
14. Hideo Kojima, "The Role of Belief-Value Systems Related to Child Rearing and Education: The Case of Early Modern to Modern Japan." Paper read at the Workshop on Social Values and Development of Third World Countries, Hong Kong, April 27–29, 1987.
15. Stanley G. Hall, *Adolescence: Its Psychology and Its Relations to Pedagogy, Anthropology, Sociology, Sex, Crime, Religion and Education*. 2 vols. New York: D. Appleton, 1904.
16. *Time Magazine*. November 24, 1986.
17. Ibid.
18. Ibid.
19. Ibid.
20. B. Bettelheim, "Our Children Are Treated Like Idiots," *Psychology Today*, July 1981, pp 28–44.
21. Ibid.
22. R. E. Slavin, "Grouping for Instruction in the Elementary School," *Educational Psychologist, 22*, pp 109–127.

Chapter 4

1. M. McLuhan, *Understanding Media* (New York: Mentor, 1964).
2. E. Kaye, *The ACT Guide to Children's Television* (Boston: Beacon Press, 1979).
3. L. Kronenberger, "Uncivilized and Uncivilizing," *TV Guide* (February 1966).
4. Ibid.
5. G. Cowan, *See No Evil* (New York: Touchstone, t 1980).
6. P. Charren and M. W. Sandler, *Changing Channels* (Reading, Mass.: Addison-Wesley, 1983).
7. D. Ephron, "TV Families: Clinging to the Tried and Untrue," *New York Times* (June 26, 1988).
8. L. Loevinger, "There Need Be No Apology, No Lament," *TV Guide* (April 1968).
9. G. Weinberg, "What Is Television's World of the Single Parent Doing to Your Family?" *TV Guide* (August 1970).
10. M. Mayer, "Out of Shape," *TV Guide* (July 1962).
11. Ibid.
12. M. Winn, "What Became of Childhood Innocence?" *New York Times Magazine* (January 25, 1981).
13. R. Lipsyte, "For Teenager's Mediocrity," *Horn Book* (1987).
14. W. D. Myers, "I Actually Thought We Would Revolutionize the Industry," *New York Times Book Review* (November 9, 1986).
15. F. Prose, *Boy's Books: Let Spot Live, Horn Book* (1987).
16. C. Epstein, "Young Adult Books," *Horn Book* (1987).

17. P. Gray, *Time* (September 20, 1999).

18. A. Bloom, *The Closing of the American Mind* (New York: Simon and Schuster, 1987).

19. J. Pereles, "Heavy Metal, Weighty Words," *New York Times Sunday Magazine* (July 10,1988).

Chapter 5

1. M. Galley, "Computer Companies Give Birth to 'Lapware' for Babies," *Education Week* (2000).

2. J. G. Auerbach, "Tots + Computers = Controversy," *Wall Street Journal* (1998).

3. D. L. Marcus, A. Mulrine, and M. Wong, "Babies Are Quick Studes and Parents Are Cramming Them with Mozart and French Lessons," *US News and World Report* (September 13, 1999).

4. J. T. Breur, *The Myth of the First Three Years* (New York: Free Press, 1999).

5. S. Kuchinskas, *Techno Toddlers* (1996).

6. M. Bornstein. "Infants Are Trichromats," *Experimental Child Psychology* 21 (1976): 425–445.

7. D. Y. Teller and M. Bornstein, "Infant Color Vision and Perception," in P. Salapetek and L. B. Cohen, eds.,*Handbook of Infant Perception*. New York: Academic Press, 1987.

8. N. Baron, *Growing Up with Language* (Reading, Mass.: Addison-Wesley, 1992).

9. P. Bishop, "Toddler Tested: Little Tykes Stake a Claim for Their Place at the PC," *Family PC* (January 1998).

10. J. Healy, Failure to Connect: How Computers Affect Our Children's Minds. 1999.

11. L. Dunn and S. Kontos, "What Have We Learned About Developmentally Appropriate Practice?" *Young Children* (July 1997): 73–81.

12. J. T. Breur, "Education and the Brain: A Bridge Too Far," *Educational Research* 26 (1997): 4–16.

13. S. leVay, T. Wiesel, and D. Hubel, "The Development of Ocular Dominance in Normally and Visually Deprived Monkeys," *Journal of Comparative Neurology* 191 (1980): 1–51.

14. W. T. Greenough, J. E. Black, and C. S. Wallace, "Experience and Brain Development," *Child Development* 58 (1997): 539–559.

15. W. T. Greenough, "We Can't Just Focus on the Ages Zero to Three," *APA Monitor* 28 (1997): 19.

16. M. Diamond and J. Hopson, *Magic Trees of the Mind* (New York: Dutton, 1998).

17. E. Jensen, *Teaching with the Brain in Mind* (Alexandria, Va.: SRCD, 1998).

18. S. Greenspan, *The Growth of the Mind* (Reading, Mass.: Addison-Wesley, 1997).

19. M. Nash, "Fertile Minds," *Time* (February 3, 1997): 48–56.

20. S. Bagley, "How to Build a Baby's Brain," *Newsweek* (1997): 28–32.
21. R. Shore, Rethinking the Brain. 1998, Family and Work Institute: New York. p. 1–92.
22. S. Fitzpatrick, "Smart Brains: Neuroscientists Explain the Mystery of What Makes Us Human," *American School Board Journal* (1995).
23. P. Goldman-Rakic, J. P. Bourgeios, and P. Rakic, "Synaptic Substrate of Cognitive Development in the Prefrontal Cortex of the Non-Human Primate," in *Development of the Prefrontal Cortex: Evolution, Biology and Behavior,* ed. N. A. Krasegnor, G. R. Lyon, and P. S. Goldman-Rakic. Baltimore: Paul H. Brooks, 1997.
24. "Pedophiles Surfing the Internet to Find Victims," *Orlando Sentinel* (1997).
25. National School Boards Council, T.C.s.T.W.a.t.M.C., Survey on Children's Internet Use. 2000, Office of International Information Programs U.S. Department of State.
26. Surveilance, C.f.D.C.a., Youth Risk Behavior Surveilance. Atlanta: Centers for Disease Control, 1997.

Chapter 6

1. J. Piaget, *The Psychology of Intelligence.* London: Routledge & Kegan Paul, 1950.
2. E. H. Erikson, *Childhood and Society.* New York: Norton, 1950.
3. J. Piaget, *The Construction of Reality in the Child.* New York: Basic Books, 1954.
4. J. Bowlby, *Attachment and Loss:* Vol. *1 Attachment.* London: Hogarth, 1971.
5. E. Gosse, *Father and Son: A Study of Two Temperaments.* London: Heinemann, 1909.
6. H. S. Sullivan, *The Interpersonal Theory of Psychiatry.* New York: Norton, 1953.
7. M. E. Seligman, *Helplessness.* San Francisco: W,H, Freeman, 1975.
8. B. Inhelder and J. Piaget, *The Growth of Logical Thinking from Childhood to Adolescence.* New York: Basic Books, 1958.
9. Piaget, ibid.
10. M. Twain, *The Adventures of Tom Sawyer.* New York: Dodd, 1979.

Chapter 7

1. C. Lasch, *Haven in a Heartless World.* New York: Basic Books, 1977.
2. Talcott Parsons, *Social Structure and Personality.* New York: Free Press of Glencoe, 1964.
3. R. D. Laing, *The Politics of the Family and Other Essays.* New York: Pantheon Books, 1971.
4. A. Bandura, *Social Learning Theory.* Englewood Cliffs, New Jersey: Prentice Hall, 1977.

5. B. F. Skinner, *Science and Human Behavior.* New York: Macmillan, 1953.
6. J. Piaget, *The Moral Judgment of the Child.* Glencoe, Illinois: The Free Press, 1960.
7. S. Freud, *A General Introduction to Psychoanalysis.* New York: Liveright, 1935.
8. E. Goffman, *Asylums.* Garden City, New York: Anchor Books, 1961.

Chapter 8

1. S. Freud, *A General Introduction to Psychoanalysis.* New York: Liveright, 1935.
2. H. Selye, *The Stress of Life.* New York: McGraw Hill, 1978.
3. Ibid.
4. W. B. Cannon, *The Wisdom of the Body.* New York: W. W. Norton, 1932.
5. S. Adler and M. Gosnell, "Stress, How It Can Hurt," *Time Magazine,* April 21, 1980.
6. B. Ehrenreich, "Is Success Dangerous to Your Health?" *Ms.,* May 1979.
7. . Ibid.
8. Ibid.
9. G. Bach and P. Wyden, *The Intimate Enemy.* New York: Morrow, 1969.
10. J. Bowlby, *Maternal Care and Mental Health.* Geneva: World Health Organization, 1951.
11. J. Kirsch, "California Kids," *New West.* July 1981, pp 66–73.
12. J. Segal, "When Business Travel Makes You an Absent Parent," *Frequent Flyer,* January 1981, pp 42–46.
13. David Owen, "I Spied on the Twelfth Grade," *Esquire,* March 1981.
14. International, C.s.I., *Armed and Ready for School.* Pacific Visions Communication: Los Angeles, California, 1996.
15. J. Richters, *The NIMH Community Violence Project I: Children as Witnesses and Victims of Crime. Psychiatry,* 1993. 56: p. 7-21.
16. J. Ourth, "The School Factor," *The Principal.* September 1980, p. 40.
17. T. J. Cottle, "Adolescent Voices," *Psychology Today,* February 1979, p 43.
18. M. McLuhan, *Understanding Media.* New York: Mentor, 1964.
19. Toronto *Star,* September 3, 1980.

Chapter 9

1. J. B. Kelly and J. S. Wallenstein, "Children of Divorce," *The Principal,* October 1979, pp 51–58.
2. Ibid.
3. A. Evans and J. Neel, "School Behaviors of Children from One Parent and Two Parent Homes," *The Principal,* September 1980, p 38–39.
4. K. Barrett, "I Always Knew You'd Find Me, Mom," *Ladies Home Journal,* August 1981, pp 86, 77, 151, 152. with Type A Coronary-Prone Behavior Pattern," *Child Development,* 1979, 50, pp 842–847.

5. P. Hluchy, "Depressed Can Find Help at Metro Centers," *Toronto Star,* March 7, 1981.
6. K. A. Matthews, "Efforts at Control by Children and Adults with Type A Coronary-Prone Behavior Pattern," *Child Development,* 1979, 50, pp 842–847.
7. "Study Says Heart Ills Can Begin in Childhood," *New York Times,* March 19, 1981.
8. Karen A. Matthews, "Antecedents of the Type A Coronary-Prone Behavior Pattern." In S. S. Brehn, S. M. Kassen, F. X. Gibbons (Ed.s), *Developmental Social Psychology.* New York: Oxford, 1981, pp 235–248.
9. R. L. Veniga and J. P. Spradley, *The Work Stress Connection.* Boston: Little, Brown, 1981.
10. Stephanie Sevick, "Students Driven to Succeed," *Hartford Courant,* July 13, 1981.
11. Ibid.
12. M. E. R. Seligman, *Helplessness.* San Francisco: W. H. Freeman, 1975.
13. Ibid.
14. Ibid.
15. Megan Marshall, "Musical Wonder Kids," *Boston Globe Magazine,* July 25, 1981.
16. Ibid.
17. Ibid.
18. Lois B. Murphy, *Widening World of Childhood.* New York: Basic Books, 1962.
19. M. Pinas, "Superkids," *Psychology Today,* January 1979, pp 52–63.

Chapter 10

1. Janet Marks, "Crises Intervention for Children: A Psychological Stitch in Time," *Town & Country,* October 1980.
2. Herbert Spencer, *Education: Intellectual, Moral, and Physical.* New York: A.L. Fowle, 1860.
3. K. Groos, *The Play of Man.* New York: Appleton, 1901.
4. M. Montessori, *The Absorbent Mind.* New York: Delta, 1967.
5. S. Freud, "Formulations Regarding the Two Principles of Mental Functioning," 1911. In *Standard Edition of Complete Works,* Vol. 7. London: Hogarth, 1958.
6. J. Piaget, *Play, Dreams and Imitation in Childhood.* New York: Norton, 1962.
7. A. Bennett, *How to Live on Twenty-Four Hours a Day.* New York: William H. Wise, 1905.
8. M. Aurelius, *Meditations.* Chicago: Henry Regency, 1949.

most like adults in emotions and least in thoughts, 208
as partners, 41–43
as "raw material," 23
and self-blame for failures, 57
statistics of increasing difficulties relative to, xxvii
as status symbols, 39–41
as surrogate self for parents, 28–31
as therapists, 44–47
used as symbols, 27–28
See also Adolescence and adolescents; Preschoolers; School age children
"Child Study Movement," 5
Cinderella Syndrome, The (Dowling), 40
Civil rights movement, 7
Closing of the American Mind, The (Bloom), 54
"Colors" infantware program, 105–106
Comic books, 87–88
Commitment. *See* Loyalty and commitment contracts
Competence conception of children, xxvii-xxviii
and acceptance of stress for children as "normal," xxix
alive in the present, xxix
as business opportunity, xxix
difficulty with changing model of, xxviii
as justification for lack of time to nurture, xxvii, xxix, 3
Competition, 31, 34–35
Computer programs for infants and young children, 101–108
BABYROM, 103
BABYWOW, 102 103
and "Colors" infantware, 105–106
criticisms against, 103–106

harmful side effects of lapware, 106–107
and idea that younger is better, 102
Jumpstart Baby, 102
and preschoolers, 107–108
support for, 104
and writers of program do not understand child development, 106
Computers and demands on children, xxii, 102
Conflict and disturbed behavior, 163–164
Contracts
evaluation form for, 206–207
See also Achievement and support contracts; freedom and responsibility contracts; Loyalty and commitment contracts; Socialization
Contractual violations, 205–207
and adolescents, 212
and calendar hurrying, 205
and clock hurrying, 205–206
Cowan, Jeffrey, 82
Crime
and increase of possession of weapons, 16
in schools, 15–17
violent and youth, 16–17
Crisis intervention services for children, 190
Cultural Literacy (Hirsch), 54

Daly, Maureen, 92
Dangers to children's playing, 33–34
Dawson's Creek (television program), 82, 85
Decision making and children as partners in, 44
Dinosaurs, 217–218
Displacement, xxxi-xxxii

Divorce
  as a middle-class status symbol,
    20–21
  of children from parents, 11
  and free-floating anxiety,
    187–189
  and greater sexual behavior of
    children of families with, 14
  high rate of, xxxi
  and loneliness and stress, 25
  and requirement of women to
    work, 39
  and separation, statistics of, 44
  and single women, 44–46
  and stress, 173–175
Dollars & Cents Camp, 9–10
Doman, Glen, xxviii
Dowling, Colette, 40
Dress and pressure to grow up fast,
    8–9
  and adult costumes available to
    children, 8–9
  and media promotion of, 11
Drugs
  and school burnout, 193
  and use by children, 12

Education system
  and comparison with Japan,
    59–62
  and pressure to develop quickly
    in 1950s and 1960s, 7, 71
  and reform movement of 1980s,
    54
  universal, and its development
    with Industrial Revolution, 4
  See also Academic skills; Schools;
    Testing
Ehrenreich, Barbara, 170
Electric Company (television
    program), and reading, 38–39
Elkind, Bob, 148, 182–183
Elkind, Bruno, 91, 182–183
Elkind, Rick, 36–37, 182–183

Emile (Rousseau), 4
Emotions
  of children always reflective of
    problems in family, xxx
  impossibility to hurry child's
    development of capacity for,
    11–12
  of children and the family, xxx
  See also Feelings
Employment
  changes in and the family, 23–24
  of children and Industrial
    Revolution, 4
  and loss of joy and team spirit in
    United States, 28–29
  loss of meaningfulness of,
    29
Energy reservoirs, 165–166
Ephron, Nora, 83–84
Epictetus, 219
Equality, national movement
    towards, 20–21
Erikson, Eric, 74, 124, 139

Family
  as a "prison," 141–142
  as a "refuge," 141–142
  and changes in employment,
    23–24
  changing styles of, xxvi
  and children's' emotions, xxxii
  and creation of smaller units of
    in Industrial Revolution, 4
  and the Internet, 141–142
  and socialization, 141–142
  and therapy, xxxii
  See also Parents; Socialization
Fantasy, 219
Father, separation from, 173–175
Father, single
  and failure to support or visit
    children, 47
  and starting new relationship
    too quickly, 46

and contractual violations, 156, 158–160

and loyalty-commitment contract, 159–160

and poorer school achievement, 188

and rewriting of freedom-responsibility contracts, 159

Parents, working

and contractual violations and hurrying, 156–157

and stress of time constraints, 42

Parents groups and actions taken as antidotes for hurrying, 214

Partners, children as, 41–43

Piaget, Jean

and conception of child as a growing plant, 22

and dual modes of adaptation of assimilation and accommodation, 216–217

and observation of his own children, 4–5

and social cognition, 142, 210

theory of child development, 119–140

Pinkwater, Daniel, 91

Plato, 97

Play

and adaptation to both play and work, 216

as antidote to hurrying, 213–219

and current ascendancy of negative view towards, 217

and Freudian point of view as safety valve, 215

and less and less opportunity for real, 214

and Montessori program's motto, "play is a child's work," 214–215, 217

and necessity for pure, 218

Piaget's view of as necessary for healthy adaptation to life, 217

as stress valve, 183–184

and theory that it is preparation for life, 214

and trend to use of play for instructional purposes, 217–218

Politeness, 209–210

Potter, Harry, books, xxii, 93, 219

Poussant, Alan, 104

Poverty, increase of children living in, xi

Poythress, Darla, 40–41

Pregnancy, teenage

increased rates of, xxvii

statistics of, 13

Pregnaphone, xxviii-xxix

Premature structuring, 198–200

and Japanese school system, 61

Prenatal instruction of children, xxiii-xxix

Preschoolers

achievement and support contracts, 149–150

and computer programs, 107–108

and limited power of adaptation, 42–43

perception of hurrying, 43

Prodigies, 199–200, 210

Projection, xxx, xxxii-xxxiii

"Readiness" concept of education, demise of, 7–8

Reading

and difficulties of introduction to too early, 37–38, 39

and early starting on learning, 35–39

motivation for is social, 38

not a spontaneous or simple skill, 36

and programs for infants and toddlers, 35